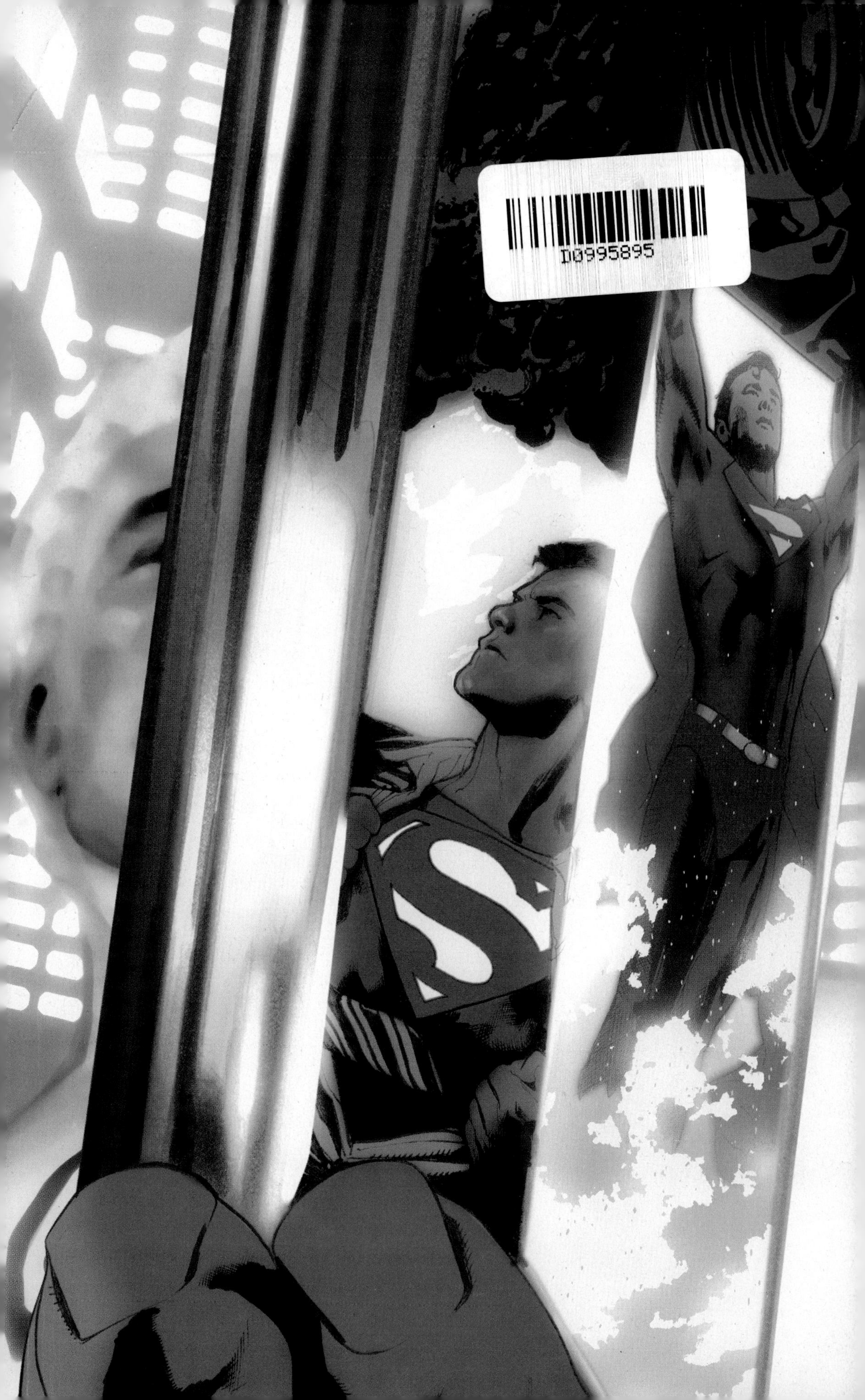

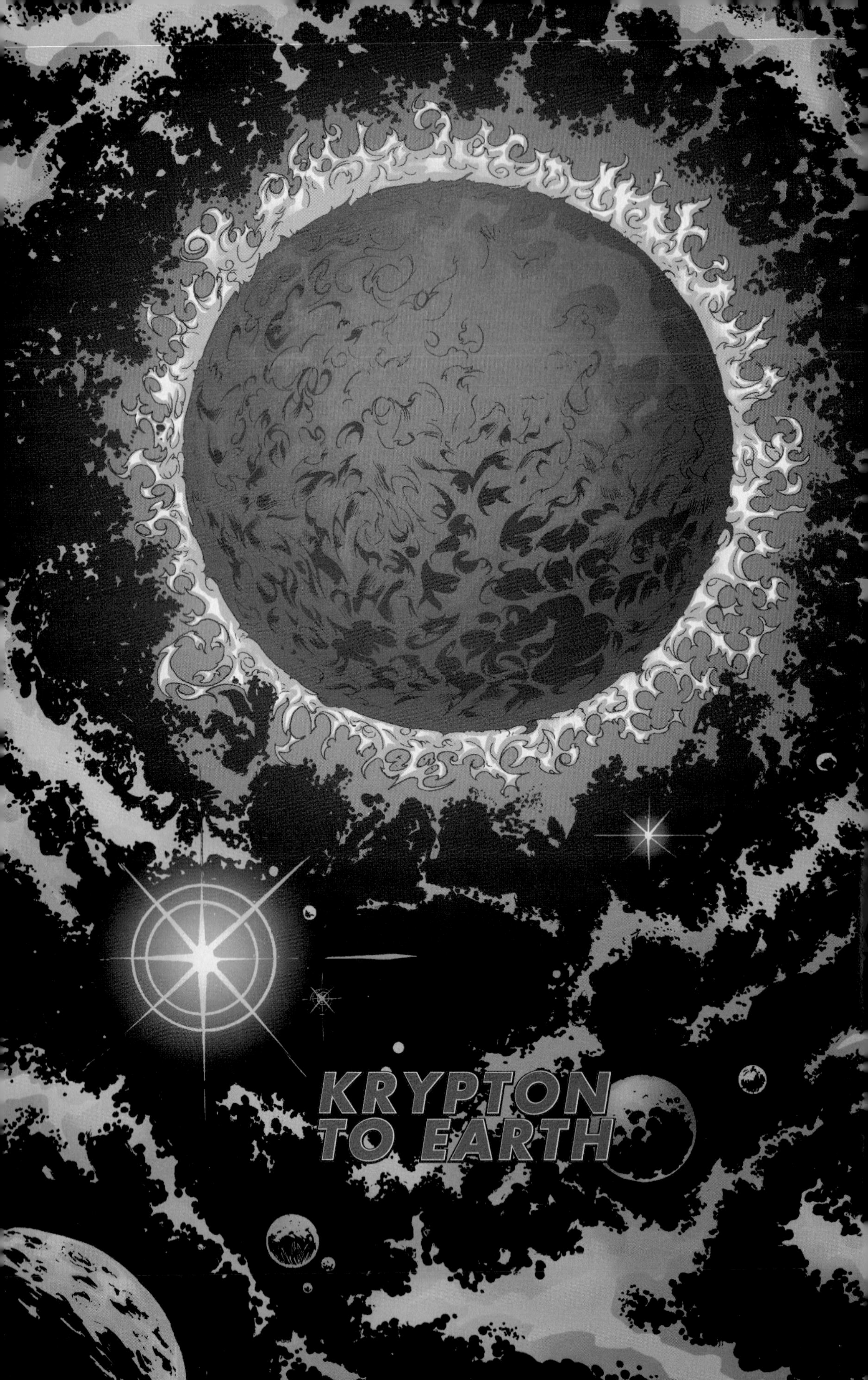
KRYPTON
TO EARTH

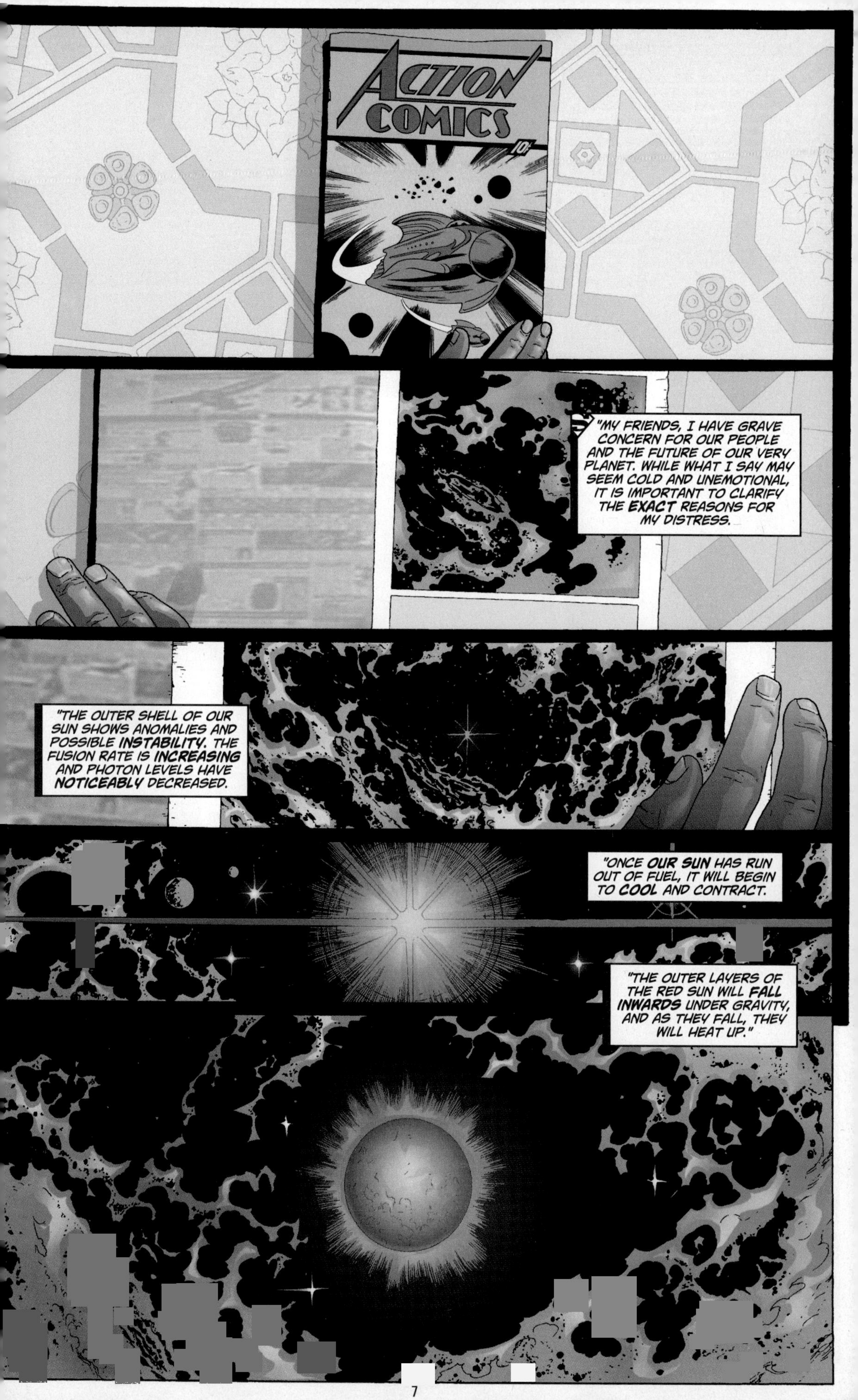
ACTION COMICS
10¢
"MY FRIENDS, I HAVE GRAVE CONCERN FOR OUR PEOPLE AND THE FUTURE OF OUR VERY PLANET. WHILE WHAT I SAY MAY SEEM COLD AND UNEMOTIONAL, IT IS IMPORTANT TO CLARIFY THE EXACT REASONS FOR MY DISTRESS.
"THE OUTER SHELL OF OUR SUN SHOWS ANOMALIES AND POSSIBLE INSTABILITY. THE FUSION RATE IS INCREASING AND PHOTON LEVELS HAVE NOTICEABLY DECREASED.
"ONCE OUR SUN HAS RUN OUT OF FUEL, IT WILL BEGIN TO COOL AND CONTRACT.
"THE OUTER LAYERS OF THE RED SUN WILL FALL INWARDS UNDER GRAVITY, AND AS THEY FALL, THEY WILL HEAT UP."

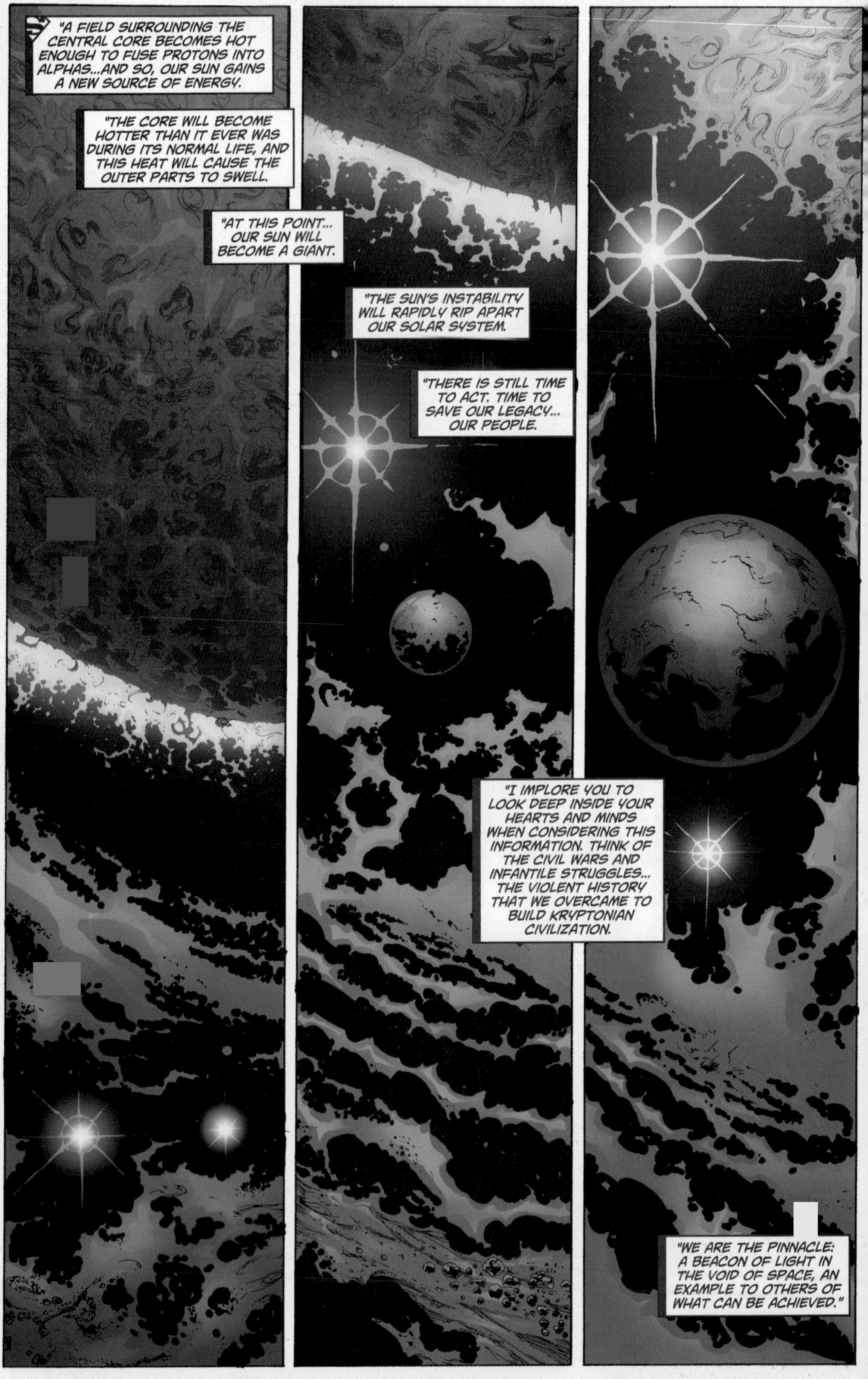
"A FIELD SURROUNDING THE CENTRAL CORE BECOMES HOT ENOUGH TO FUSE PROTONS INTO ALPHAS...AND SO, OUR SUN GAINS A NEW SOURCE OF ENERGY.
"THE CORE WILL BECOME HOTTER THAN IT EVER WAS DURING ITS NORMAL LIFE, AND THIS HEAT WILL CAUSE THE OUTER PARTS TO SWELL.
"AT THIS POINT... OUR SUN WILL BECOME A GIANT.
"THE SUN'S INSTABILITY WILL RAPIDLY RIP APART OUR SOLAR SYSTEM.
"THERE IS STILL TIME TO ACT. TIME TO SAVE OUR LEGACY... OUR PEOPLE.
"I IMPLORE YOU TO LOOK DEEP INSIDE YOUR HEARTS AND MINDS WHEN CONSIDERING THIS INFORMATION. THINK OF THE CIVIL WARS AND INFANTILE STRUGGLES... THE VIOLENT HISTORY THAT WE OVERCAME TO BUILD KRYPTONIAN CIVILIZATION.
"WE ARE THE PINNACLE: A BEACON OF LIGHT IN THE VOID OF SPACE, AN EXAMPLE TO OTHERS OF WHAT CAN BE ACHIEVED."

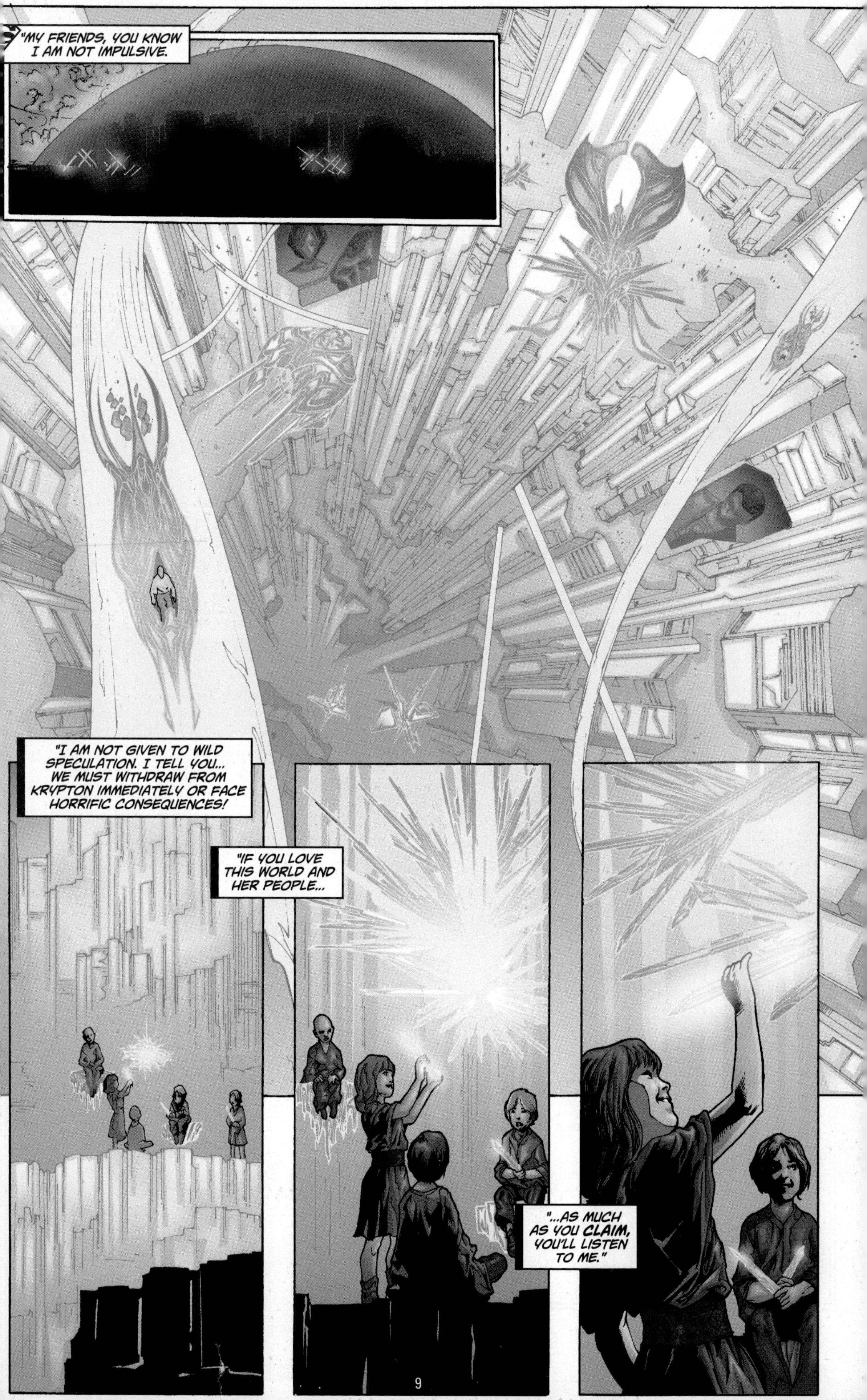
"MY FRIENDS, YOU KNOW I AM NOT IMPULSIVE.
"I AM NOT GIVEN TO WILD SPECULATION. I TELL YOU... WE MUST WITHDRAW FROM KRYPTON IMMEDIATELY OR FACE HORRIFIC CONSEQUENCES!
"IF YOU LOVE THIS WORLD AND HER PEOPLE...
"...AS MUCH AS YOU CLAIM, YOU'LL LISTEN TO ME."

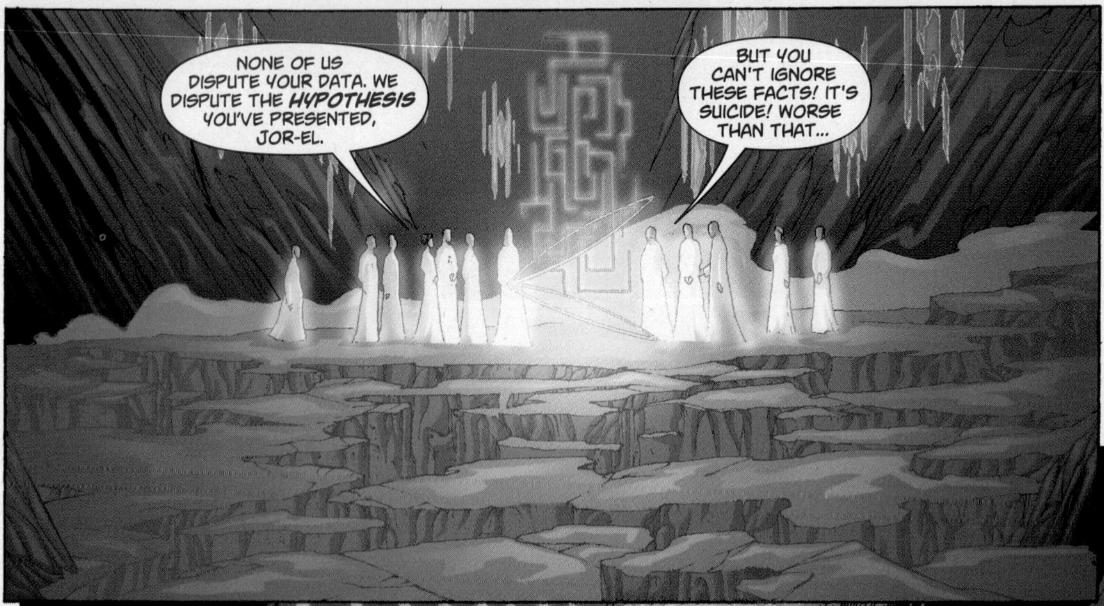
NONE OF US DISPUTE YOUR DATA. WE DISPUTE THE *HYPOTHESIS* YOU'VE PRESENTED, JOR-EL.
BUT YOU CAN'T IGNORE THESE FACTS! IT'S SUICIDE! WORSE THAN THAT...

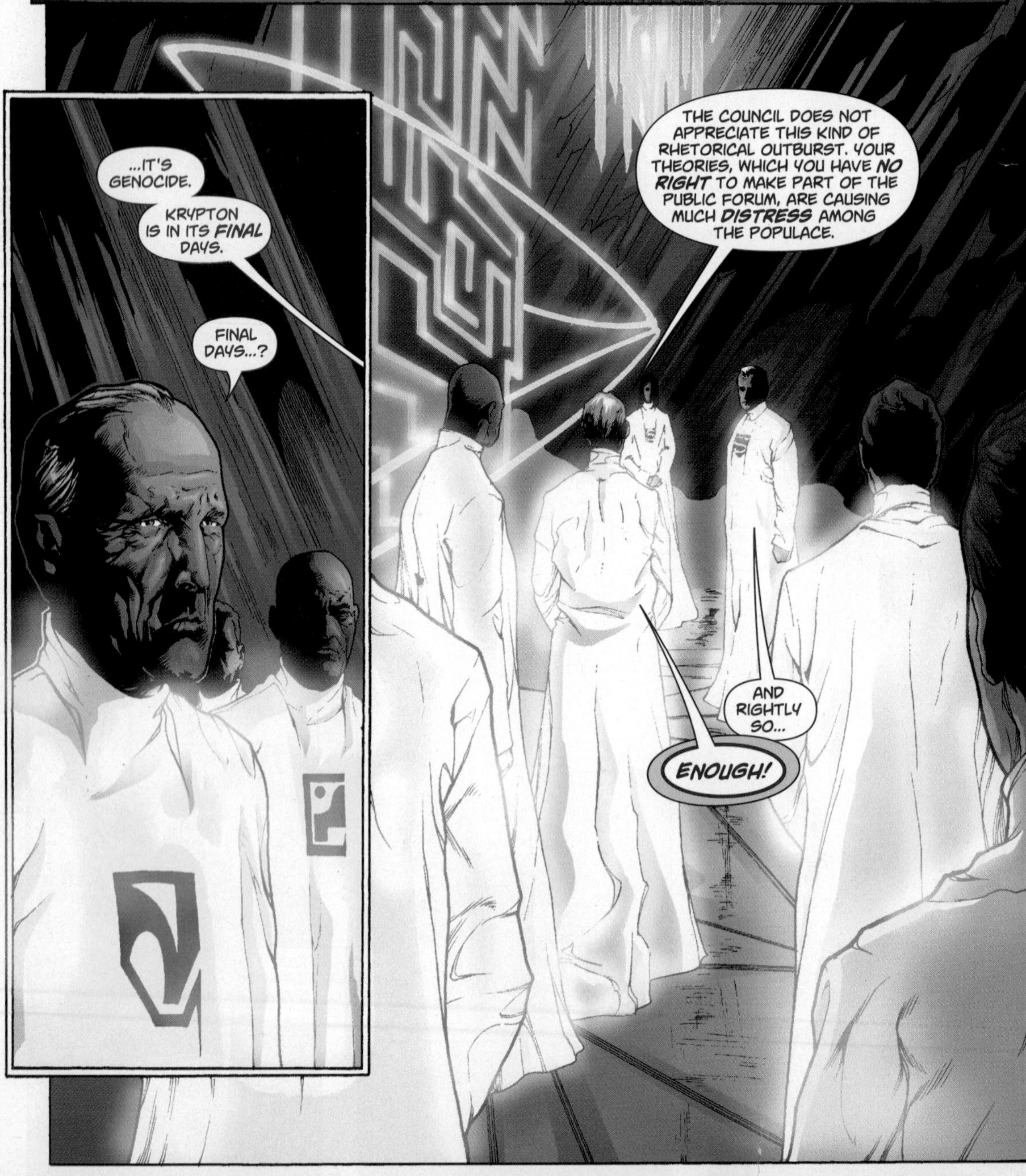
...IT'S GENOCIDE.
KRYPTON IS IN ITS *FINAL* DAYS.
FINAL DAYS...?
THE COUNCIL DOES NOT APPRECIATE THIS KIND OF RHETORICAL OUTBURST. YOUR THEORIES, WHICH YOU HAVE *NO RIGHT* TO MAKE PART OF THE PUBLIC FORUM, ARE CAUSING MUCH *DISTRESS* AMONG THE POPULACE.
AND RIGHTLY SO...
ENOUGH!

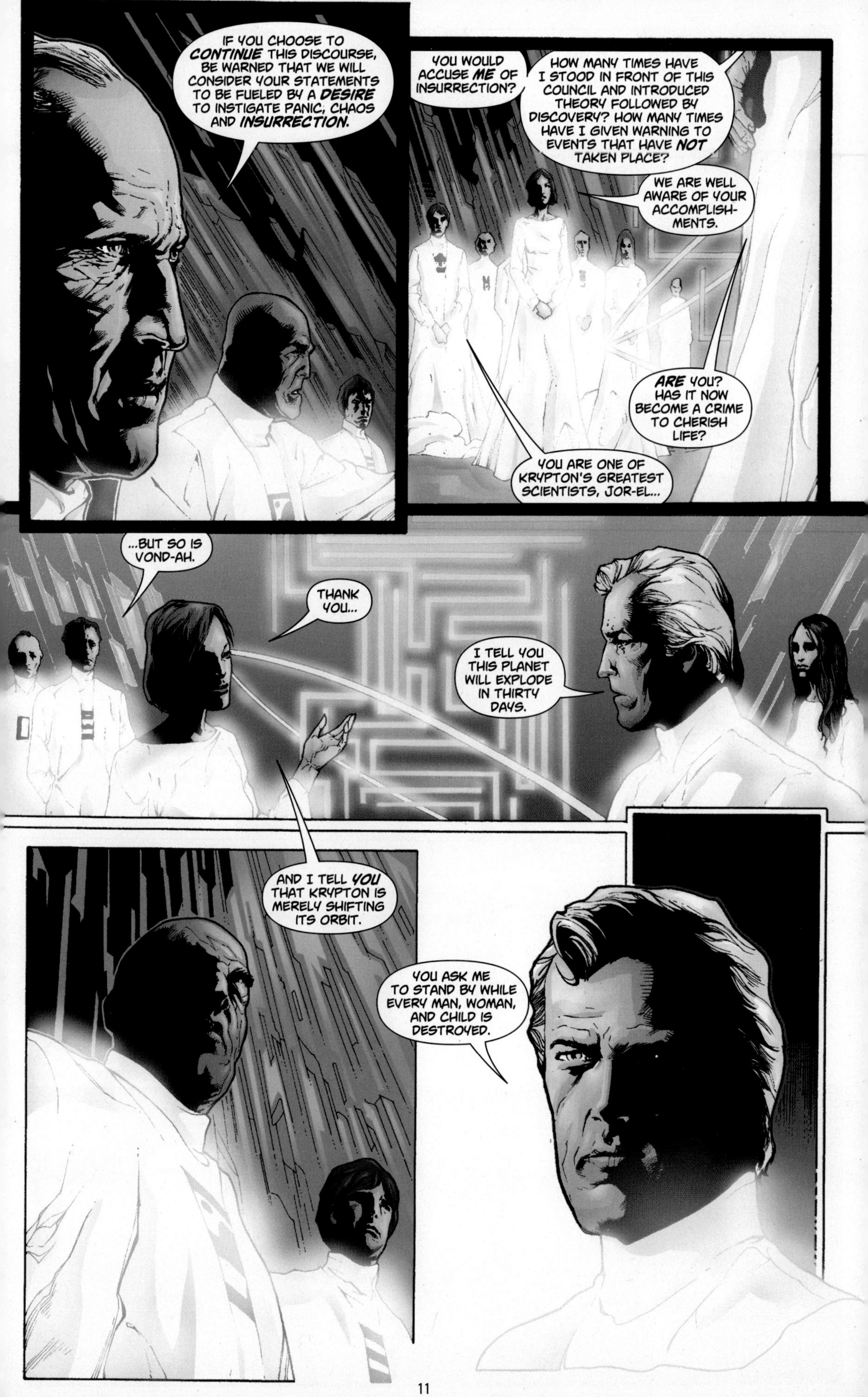

IF YOU CHOOSE TO CONTINUE THIS DISCOURSE, BE WARNED THAT WE WILL CONSIDER YOUR STATEMENTS TO BE FUELED BY A DESIRE TO INSTIGATE PANIC, CHAOS AND INSURRECTION.
YOU WOULD ACCUSE ME OF INSURRECTION?
HOW MANY TIMES HAVE I STOOD IN FRONT OF THIS COUNCIL AND INTRODUCED THEORY FOLLOWED BY DISCOVERY? HOW MANY TIMES HAVE I GIVEN WARNING TO EVENTS THAT HAVE NOT TAKEN PLACE?
WE ARE WELL AWARE OF YOUR ACCOMPLISH-MENTS.
ARE YOU? HAS IT NOW BECOME A CRIME TO CHERISH LIFE?
YOU ARE ONE OF KRYPTON'S GREATEST SCIENTISTS, JOR-EL...
...BUT SO IS VOND-AH.
THANK YOU...
I TELL YOU THIS PLANET WILL EXPLODE IN THIRTY DAYS.
AND I TELL YOU THAT KRYPTON IS MERELY SHIFTING ITS ORBIT.
YOU ASK ME TO STAND BY WHILE EVERY MAN, WOMAN, AND CHILD IS DESTROYED.

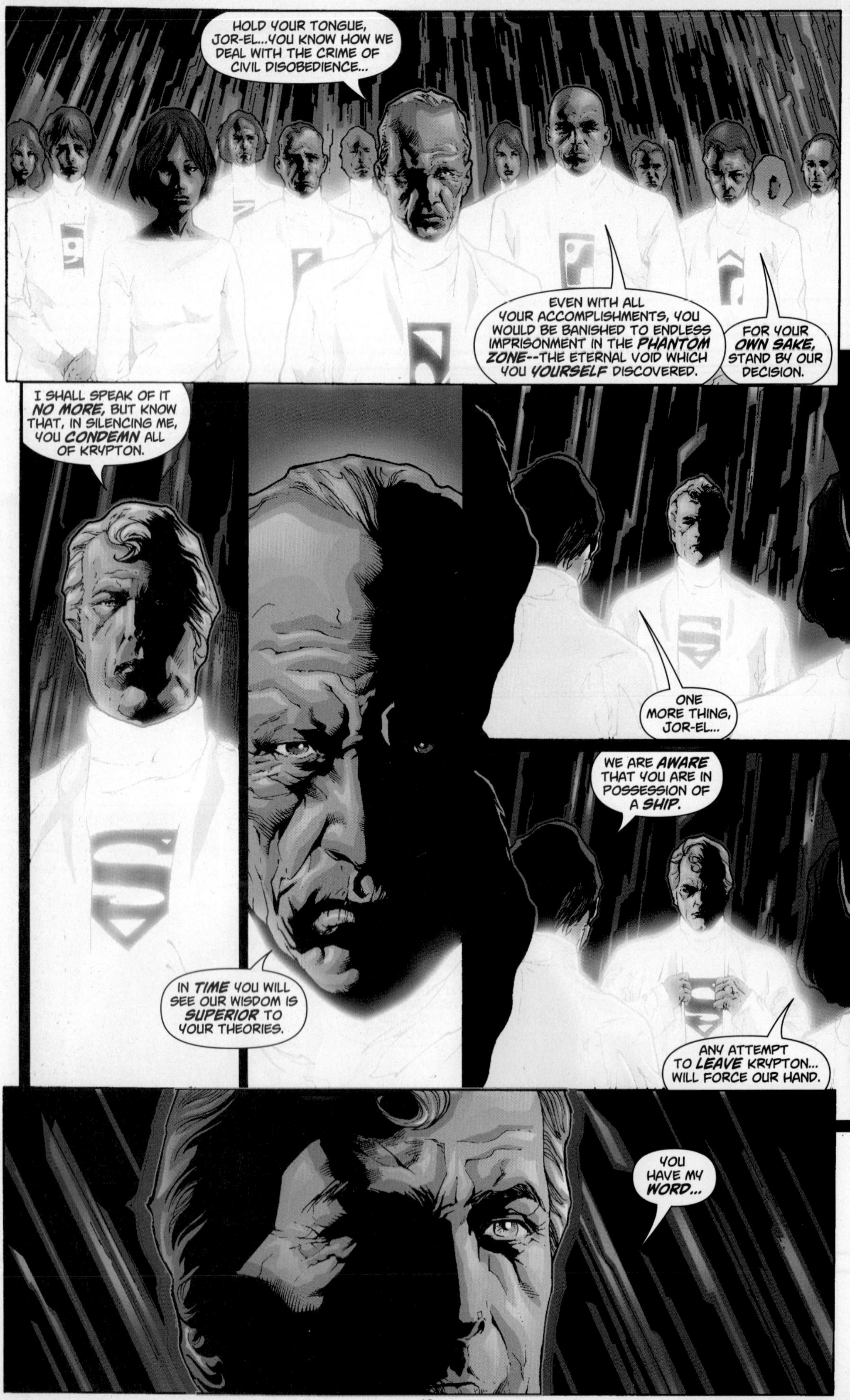
HOLD YOUR TONGUE, JOR-EL...YOU KNOW HOW WE DEAL WITH THE CRIME OF CIVIL DISOBEDIENCE...
EVEN WITH ALL YOUR ACCOMPLISHMENTS, YOU WOULD BE BANISHED TO ENDLESS IMPRISONMENT IN THE PHANTOM ZONE--THE ETERNAL VOID WHICH YOU YOURSELF DISCOVERED.
FOR YOUR OWN SAKE, STAND BY OUR DECISION.
I SHALL SPEAK OF IT NO MORE, BUT KNOW THAT, IN SILENCING ME, YOU CONDEMN ALL OF KRYPTON.
IN TIME YOU WILL SEE OUR WISDOM IS SUPERIOR TO YOUR THEORIES.
ONE MORE THING, JOR-EL...
WE ARE AWARE THAT YOU ARE IN POSSESSION OF A SHIP.
ANY ATTEMPT TO LEAVE KRYPTON... WILL FORCE OUR HAND.
YOU HAVE MY WORD...

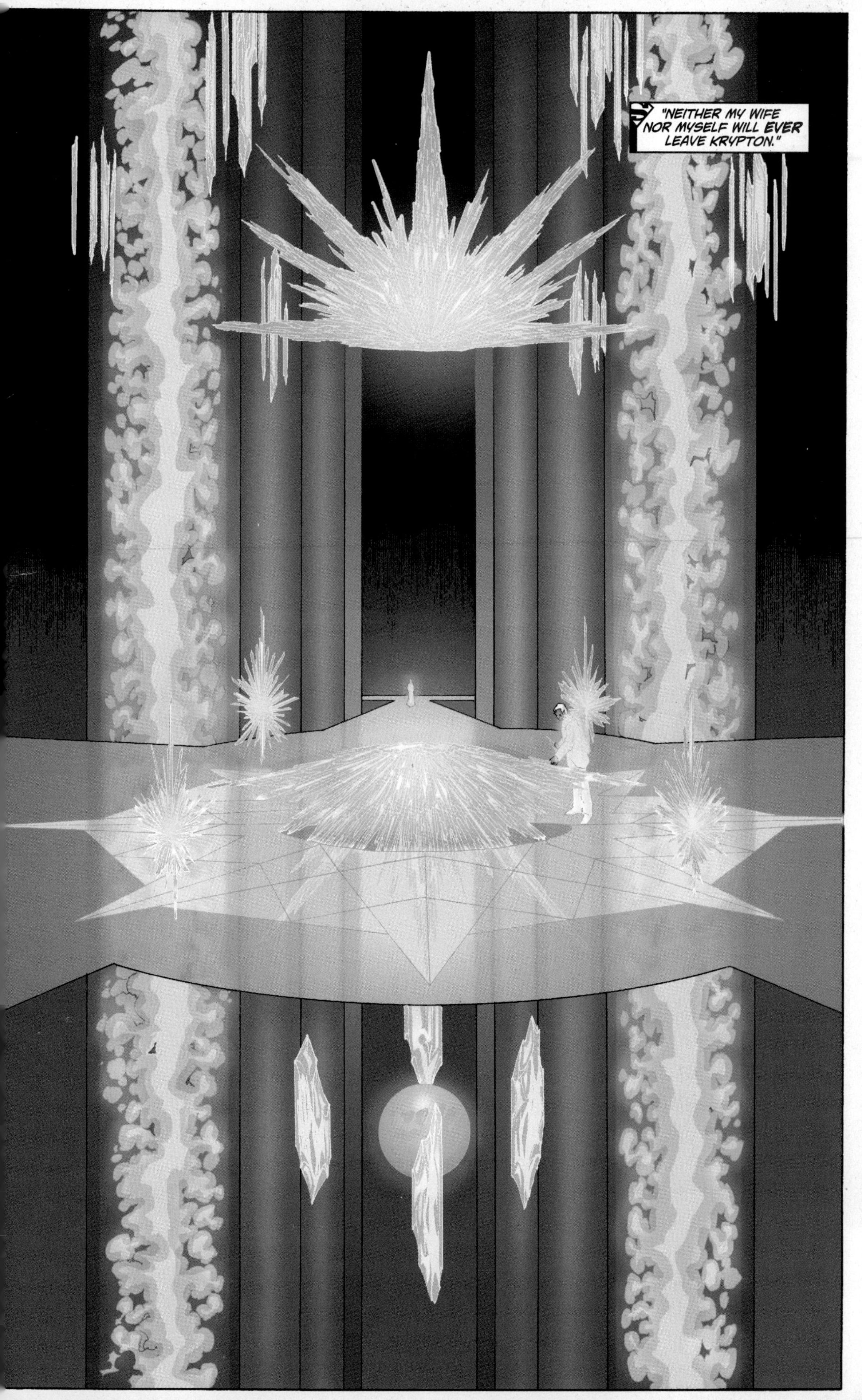
"NEITHER MY WIFE NOR MYSELF WILL EVER LEAVE KRYPTON."

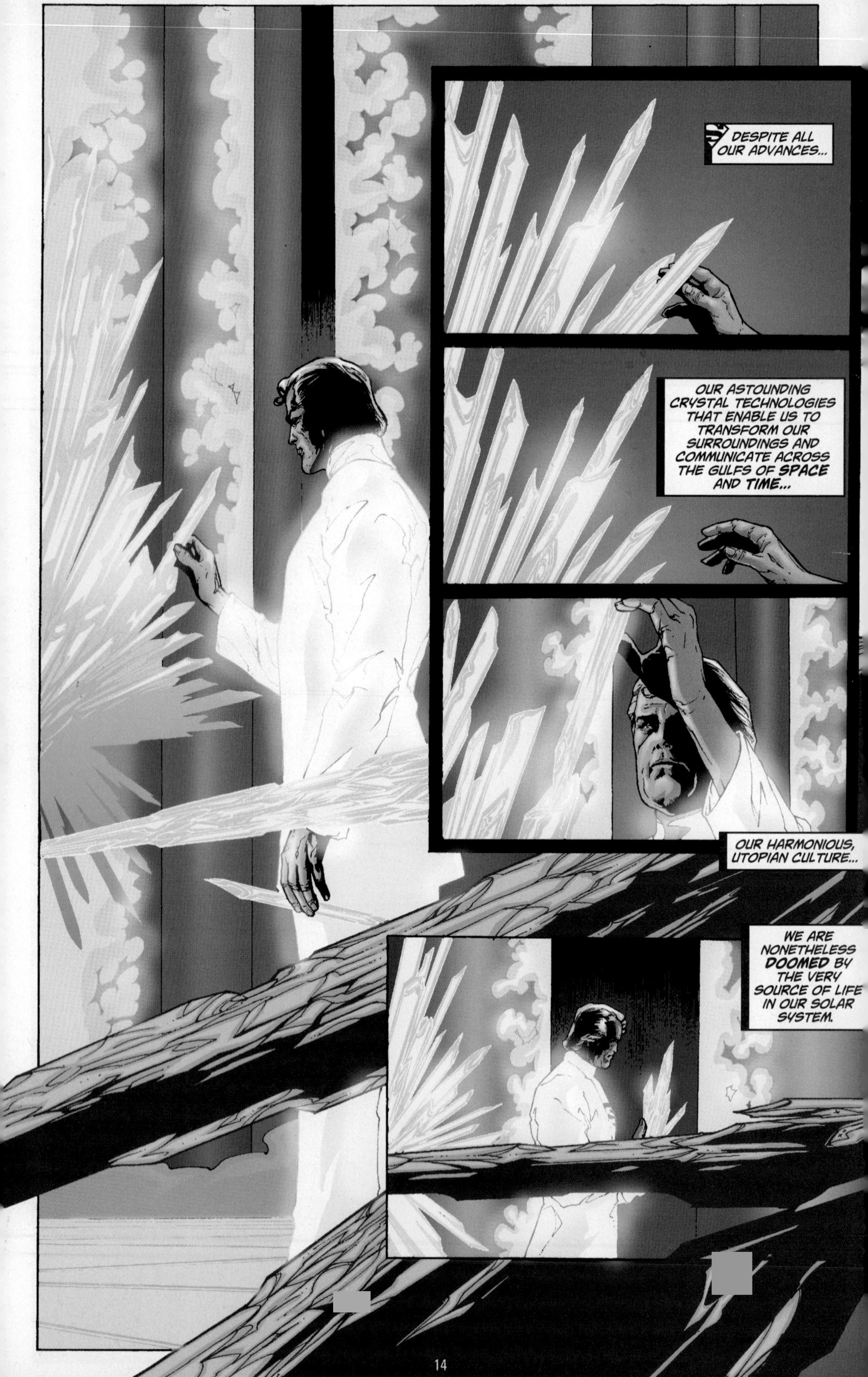
DESPITE ALL OUR ADVANCES...
OUR ASTOUNDING CRYSTAL TECHNOLOGIES THAT ENABLE US TO TRANSFORM OUR SURROUNDINGS AND COMMUNICATE ACROSS THE GULFS OF SPACE AND TIME...
OUR HARMONIOUS, UTOPIAN CULTURE...
WE ARE NONETHELESS DOOMED BY THE VERY SOURCE OF LIFE IN OUR SOLAR SYSTEM.

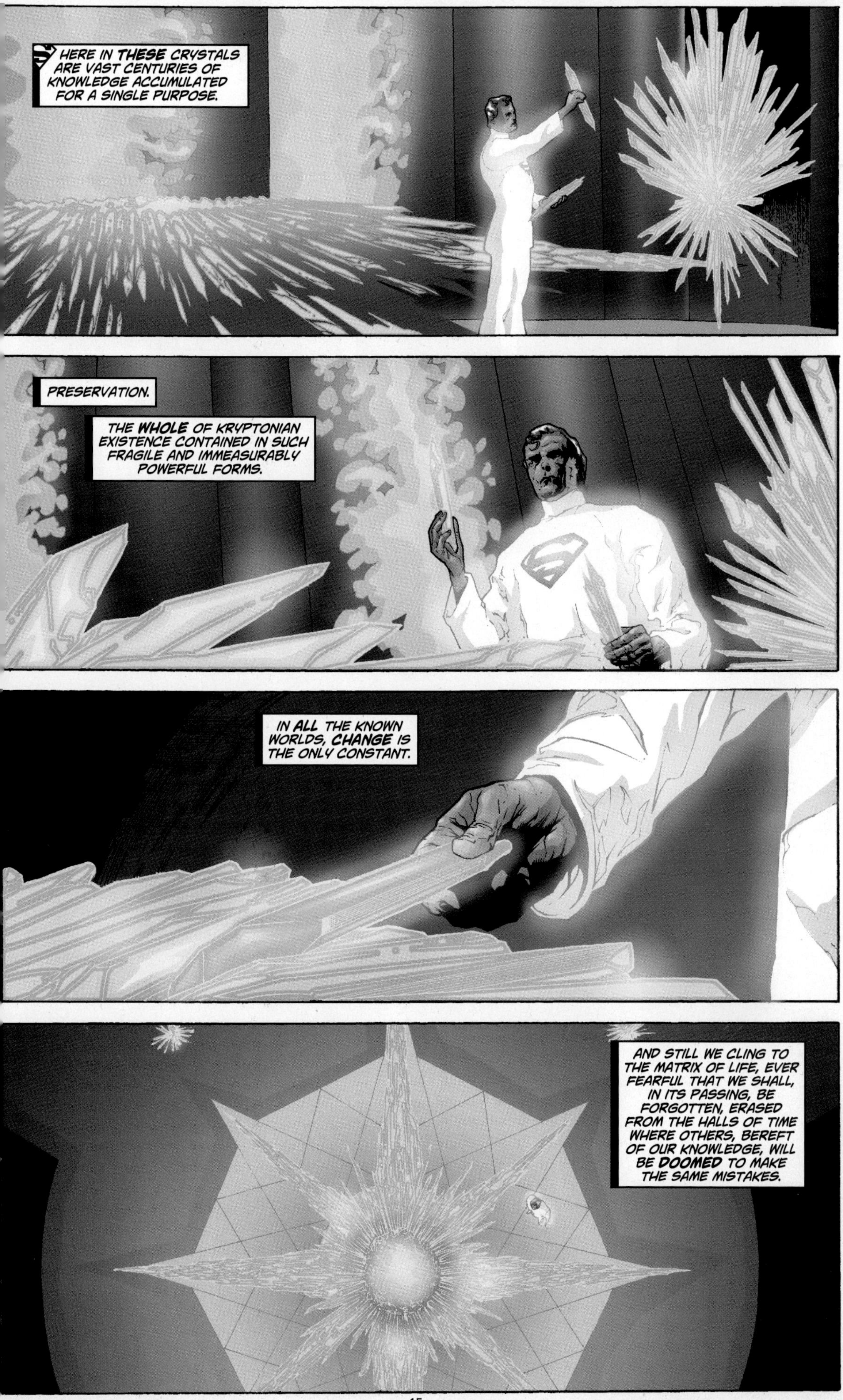
HERE IN THESE CRYSTALS ARE VAST CENTURIES OF KNOWLEDGE ACCUMULATED FOR A SINGLE PURPOSE.
PRESERVATION.
THE WHOLE OF KRYPTONIAN EXISTENCE CONTAINED IN SUCH FRAGILE AND IMMEASURABLY POWERFUL FORMS.
IN ALL THE KNOWN WORLDS, CHANGE IS THE ONLY CONSTANT.
AND STILL WE CLING TO THE MATRIX OF LIFE, EVER FEARFUL THAT WE SHALL, IN ITS PASSING, BE FORGOTTEN, ERASED FROM THE HALLS OF TIME WHERE OTHERS, BEREFT OF OUR KNOWLEDGE, WILL BE DOOMED TO MAKE THE SAME MISTAKES.

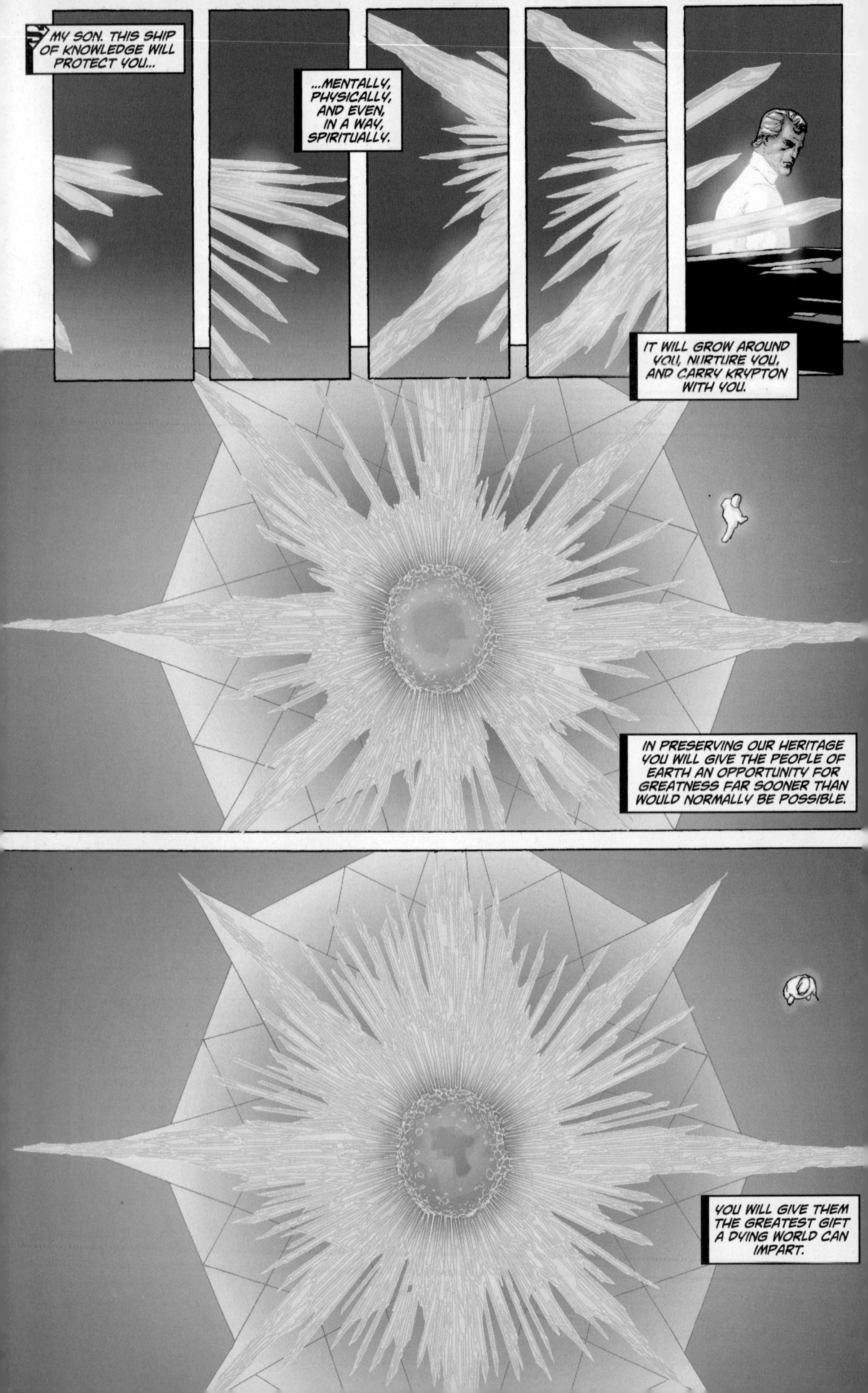
MY SON. THIS SHIP OF KNOWLEDGE WILL PROTECT YOU...
...MENTALLY, PHYSICALLY, AND EVEN, IN A WAY, SPIRITUALLY.
IT WILL GROW AROUND YOU, NURTURE YOU, AND CARRY KRYPTON WITH YOU.
IN PRESERVING OUR HERITAGE YOU WILL GIVE THE PEOPLE OF EARTH AN OPPORTUNITY FOR GREATNESS FAR SOONER THAN WOULD NORMALLY BE POSSIBLE.
YOU WILL GIVE THEM THE GREATEST GIFT A DYING WORLD CAN IMPART.

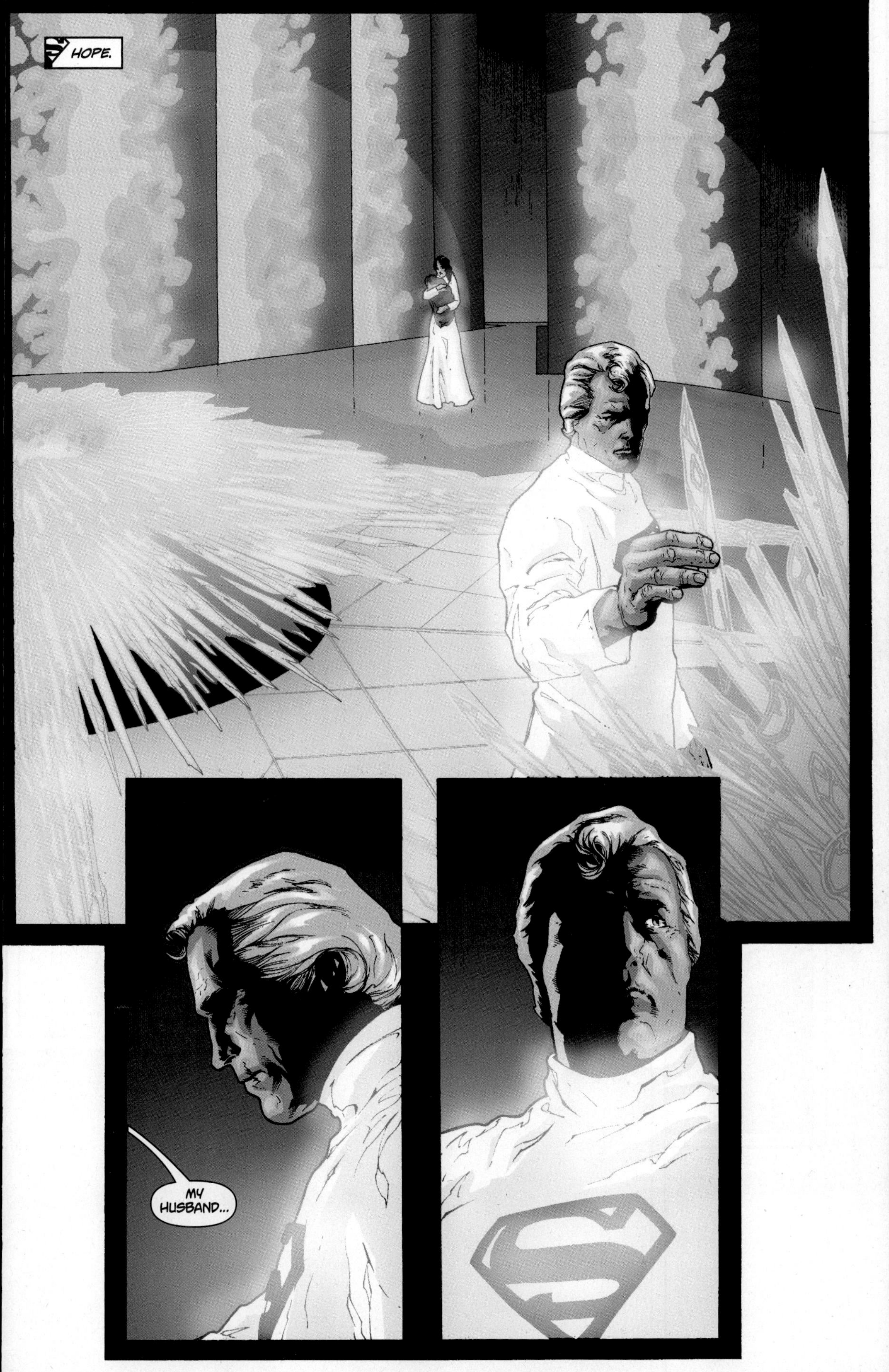
HOPE.
MY HUSBAND...

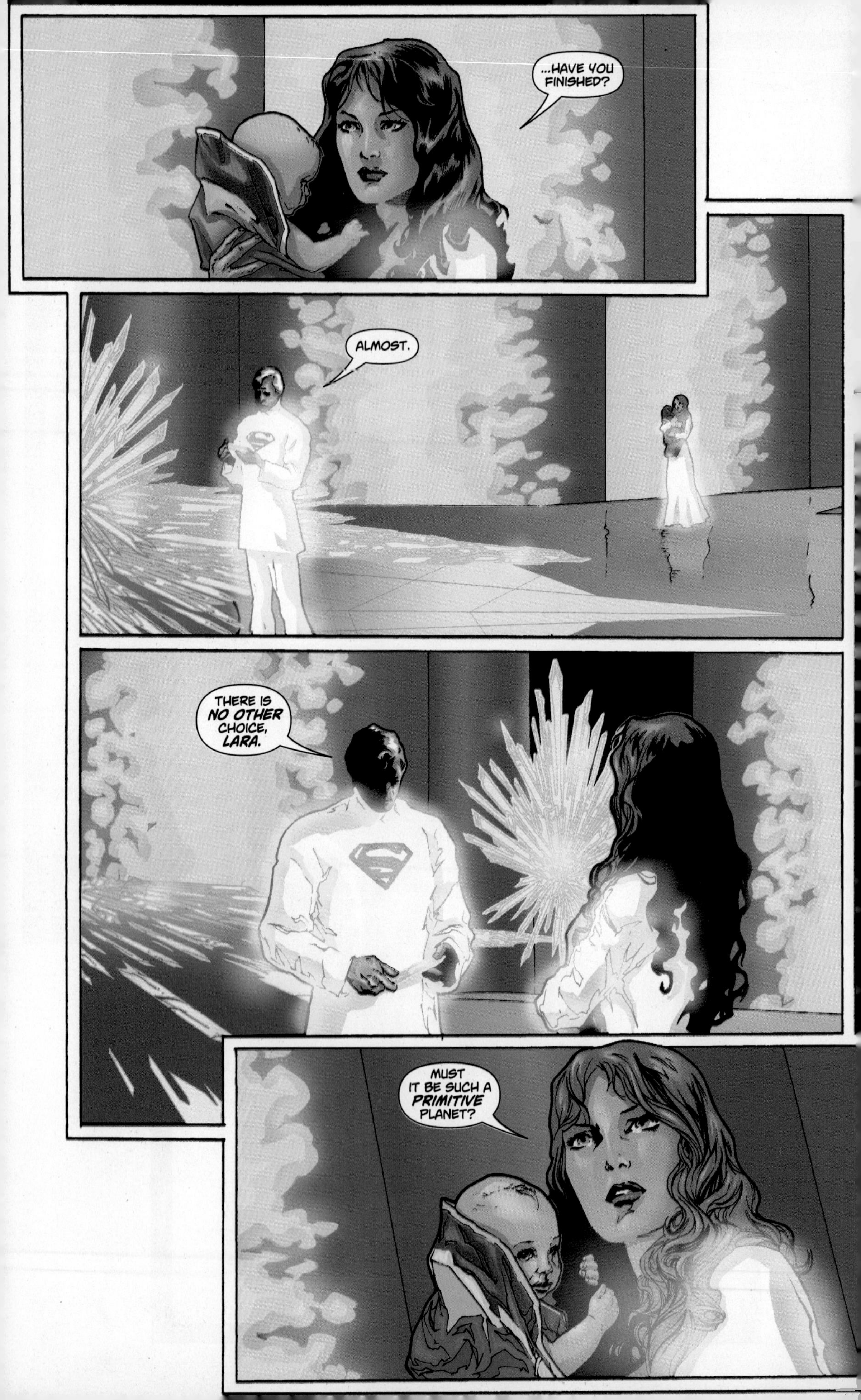
...HAVE YOU FINISHED?
ALMOST.
THERE IS NO OTHER CHOICE, LARA.
MUST IT BE SUCH A PRIMITIVE PLANET?

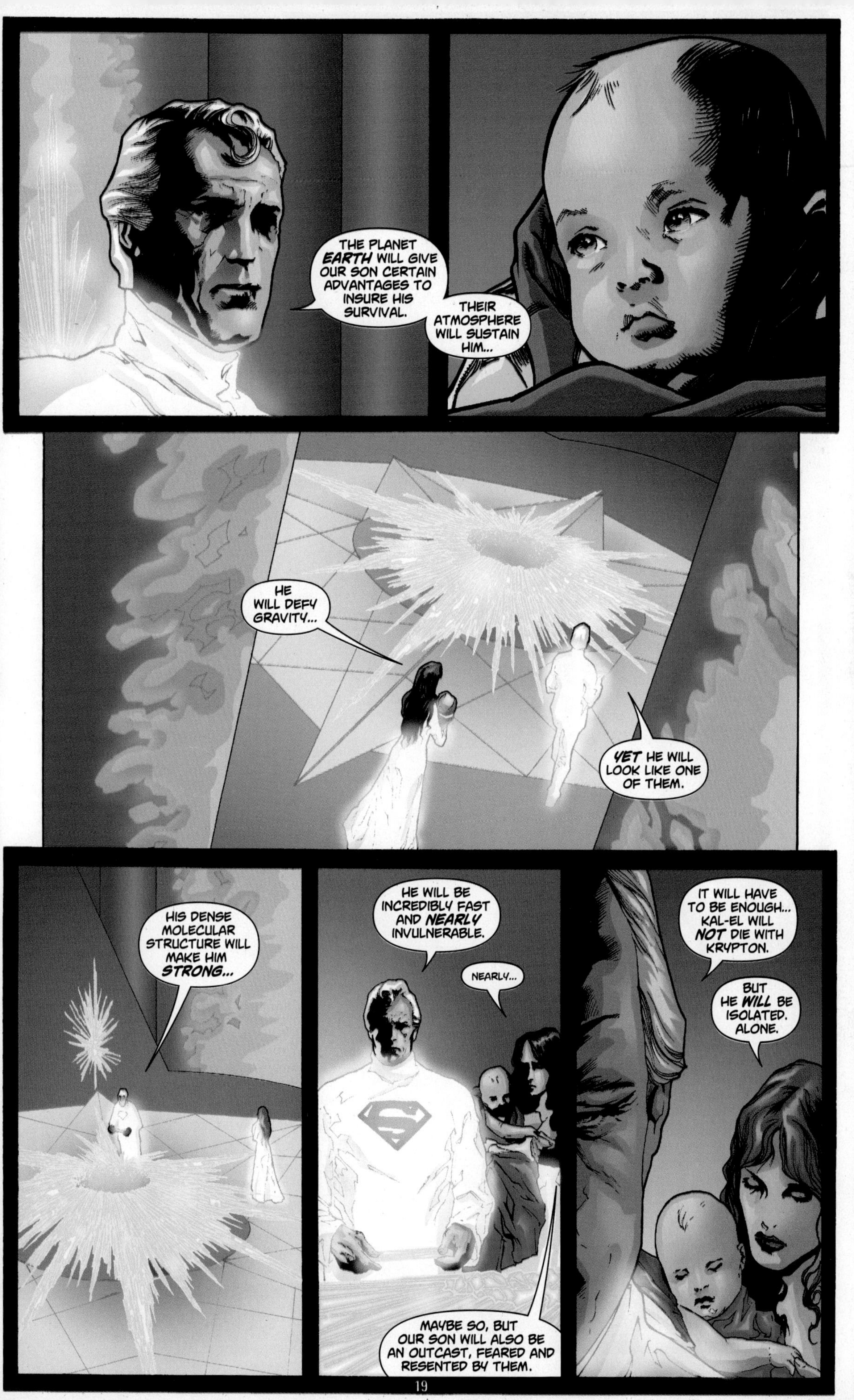
THE PLANET EARTH WILL GIVE OUR SON CERTAIN ADVANTAGES TO INSURE HIS SURVIVAL.
THEIR ATMOSPHERE WILL SUSTAIN HIM...
HE WILL DEFY GRAVITY...
YET HE WILL LOOK LIKE ONE OF THEM.
HIS DENSE MOLECULAR STRUCTURE WILL MAKE HIM STRONG...
HE WILL BE INCREDIBLY FAST AND NEARLY INVULNERABLE.
NEARLY...
MAYBE SO, BUT OUR SON WILL ALSO BE AN OUTCAST, FEARED AND RESENTED BY THEM.
IT WILL HAVE TO BE ENOUGH... KAL-EL WILL NOT DIE WITH KRYPTON.
BUT HE WILL BE ISOLATED. ALONE.

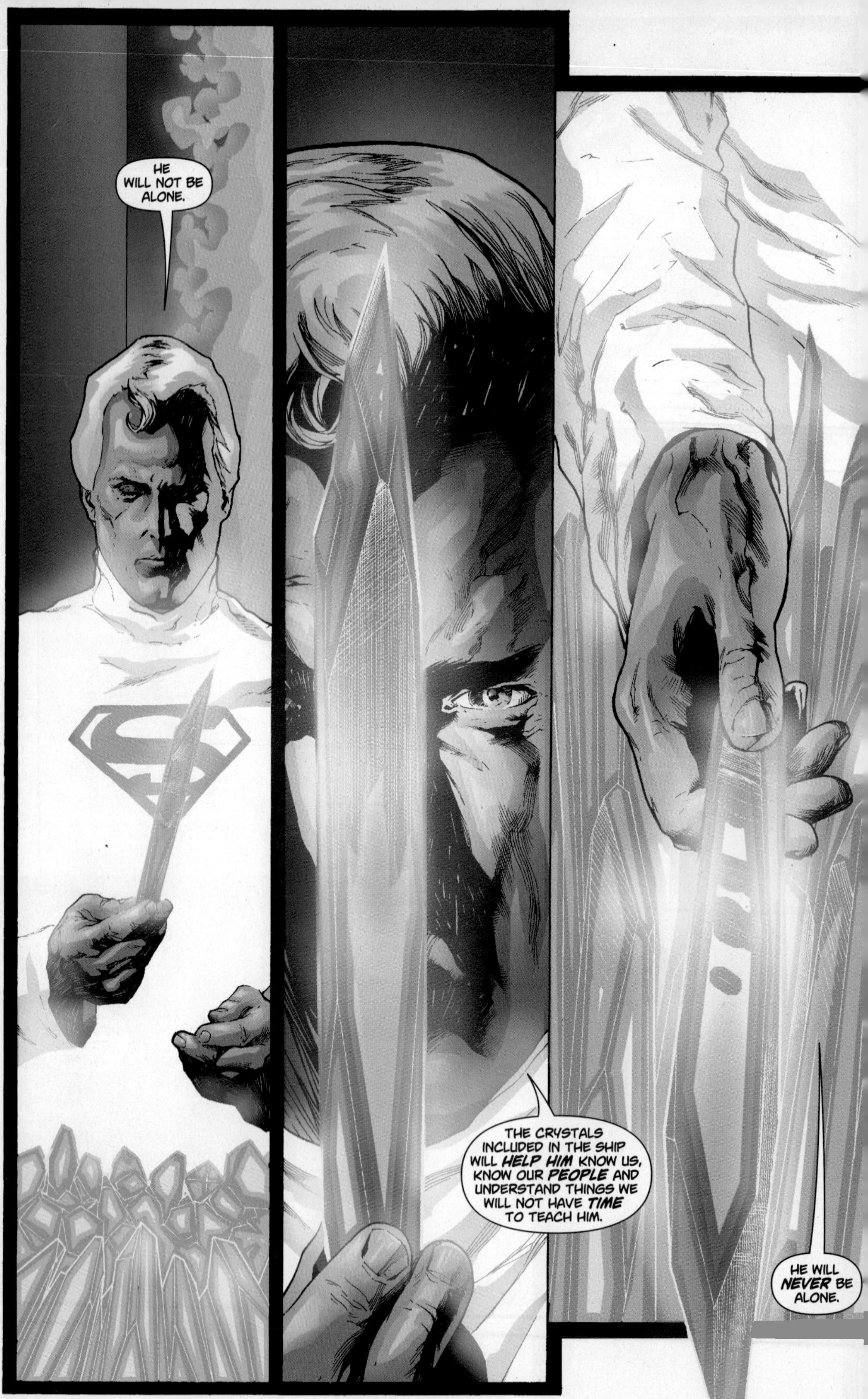
HE WILL NOT BE ALONE.
THE CRYSTALS INCLUDED IN THE SHIP WILL HELP HIM KNOW US, KNOW OUR PEOPLE AND UNDERSTAND THINGS WE WILL NOT HAVE TIME TO TEACH HIM.
HE WILL NEVER BE ALONE.

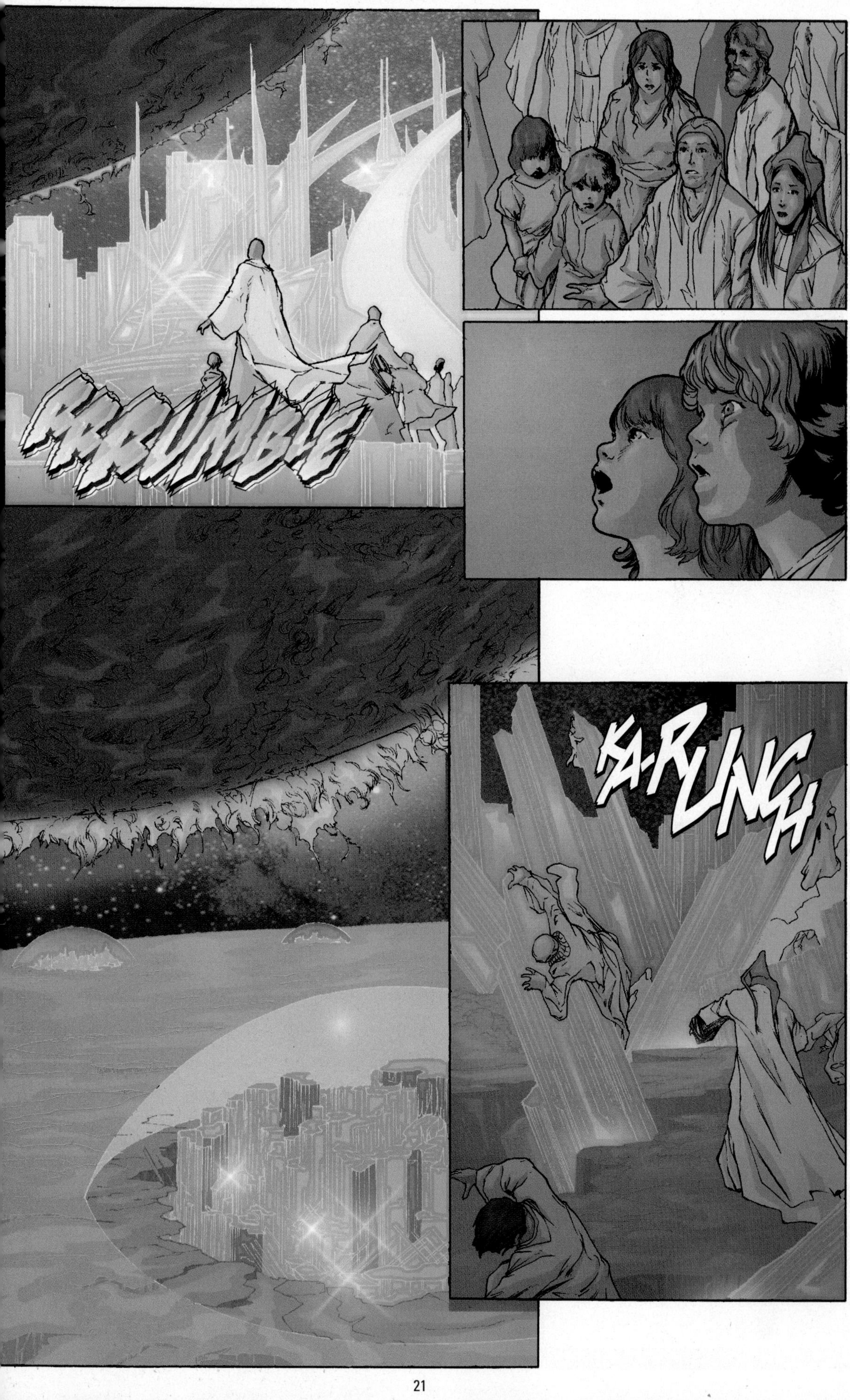
KA-RUNCH

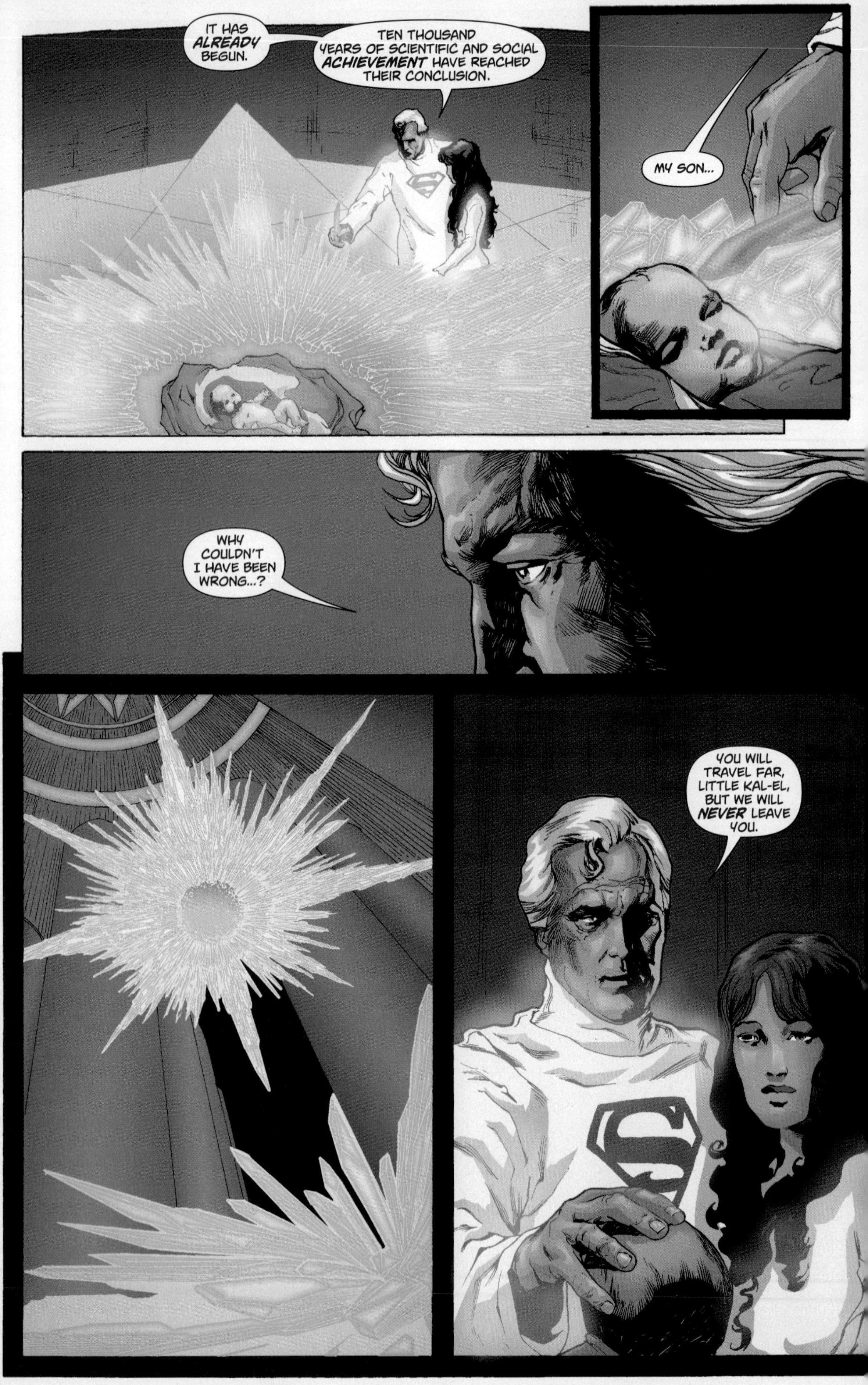
IT HAS ALREADY BEGUN.
TEN THOUSAND YEARS OF SCIENTIFIC AND SOCIAL ACHIEVEMENT HAVE REACHED THEIR CONCLUSION.
MY SON...
WHY COULDN'T I HAVE BEEN WRONG...?
YOU WILL TRAVEL FAR, LITTLE KAL-EL, BUT WE WILL NEVER LEAVE YOU.

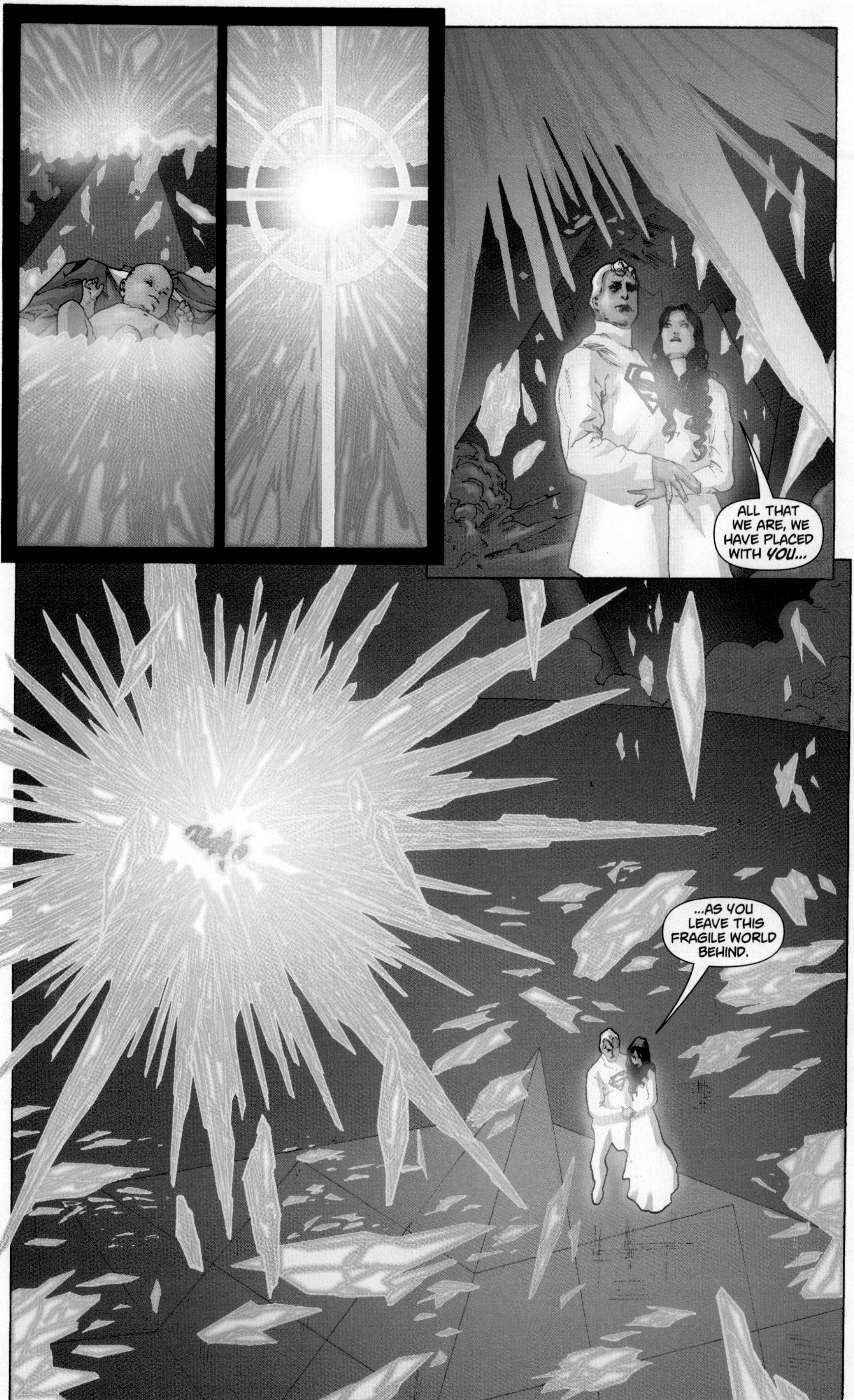
ALL THAT WE ARE, WE HAVE PLACED WITH YOU...
...AS YOU LEAVE THIS FRAGILE WORLD BEHIND.

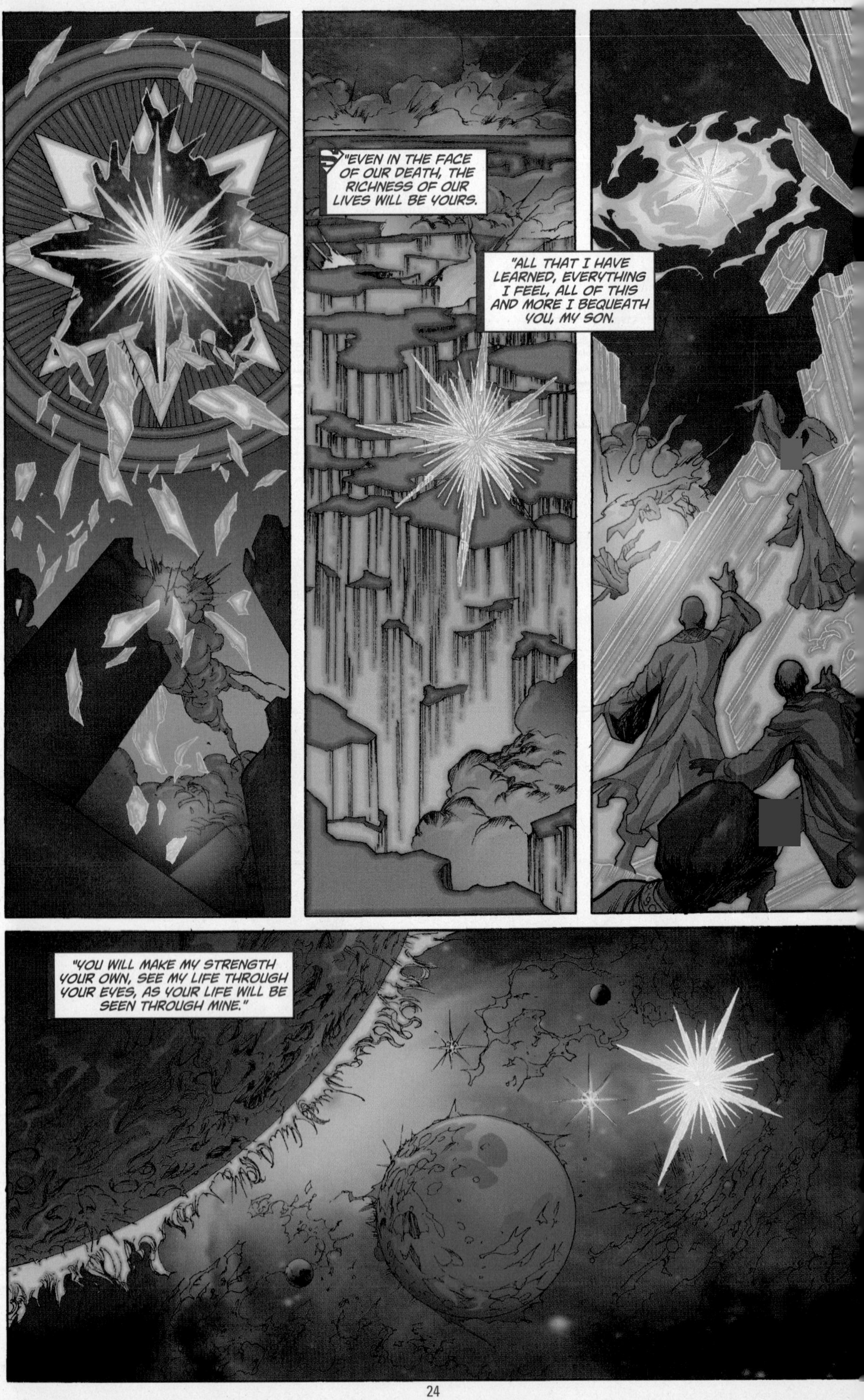
"EVEN IN THE FACE OF OUR DEATH, THE RICHNESS OF OUR LIVES WILL BE YOURS.
"ALL THAT I HAVE LEARNED, EVERYTHING I FEEL, ALL OF THIS AND MORE I BEQUEATH YOU, MY SON.
"YOU WILL MAKE MY STRENGTH YOUR OWN, SEE MY LIFE THROUGH YOUR EYES, AS YOUR LIFE WILL BE SEEN THROUGH MINE."

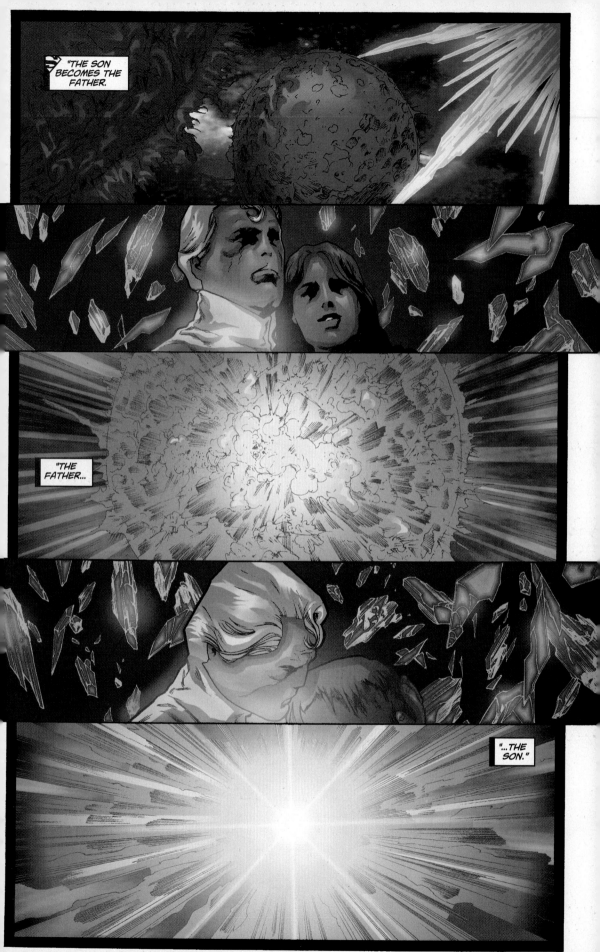

"THE SON BECOMES THE FATHER.

"THE FATHER...

"...THE SON."

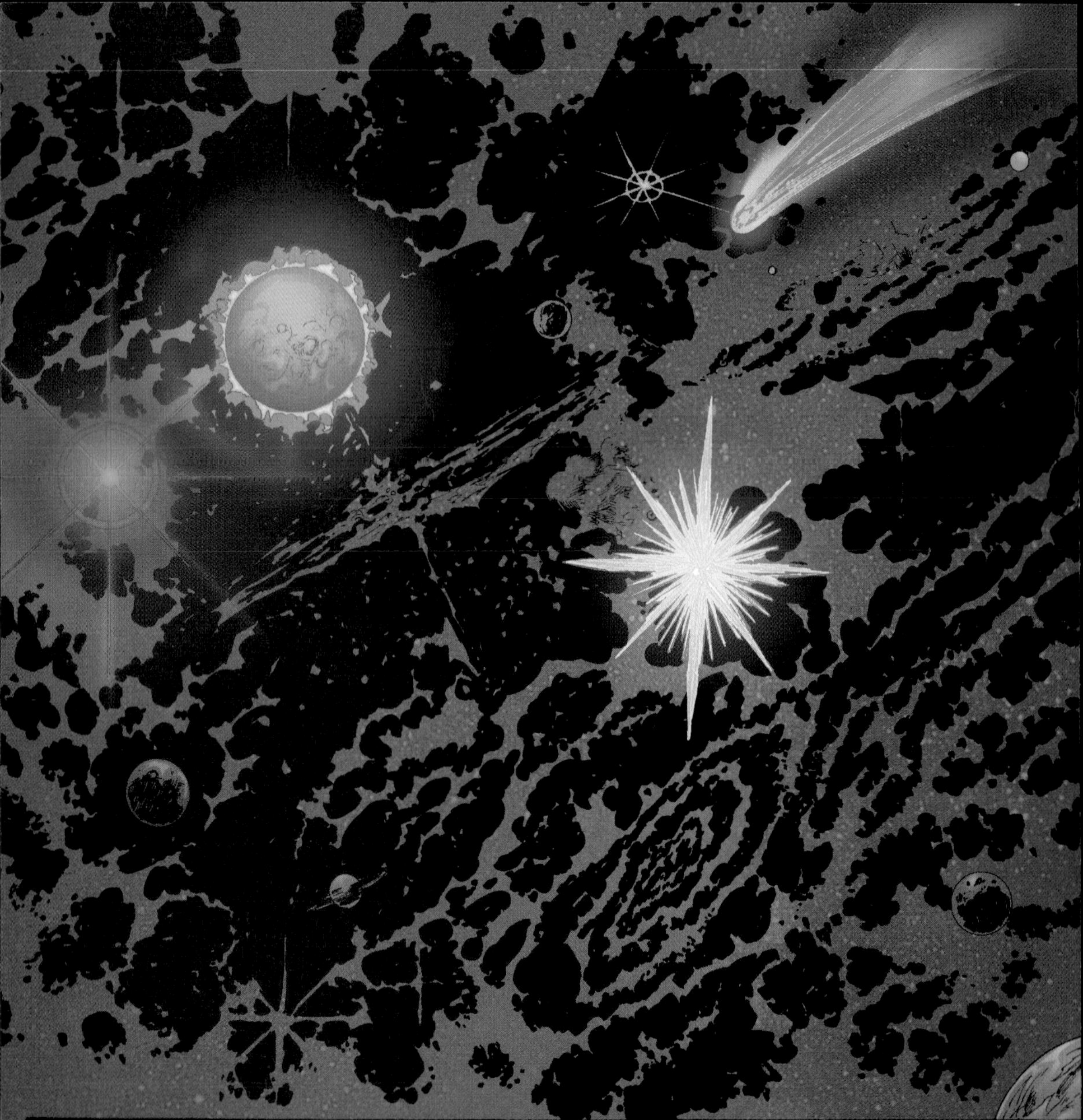

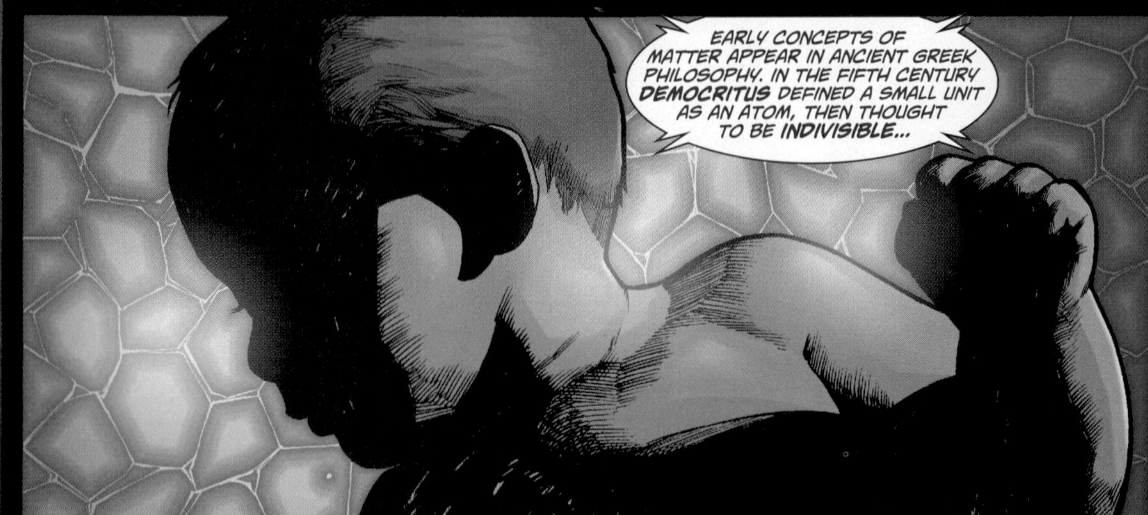
EARLY CONCEPTS OF MATTER APPEAR IN ANCIENT GREEK PHILOSOPHY. IN THE FIFTH CENTURY DEMOCRITUS DEFINED A SMALL UNIT AS AN ATOM, THEN THOUGHT TO BE INDIVISIBLE...

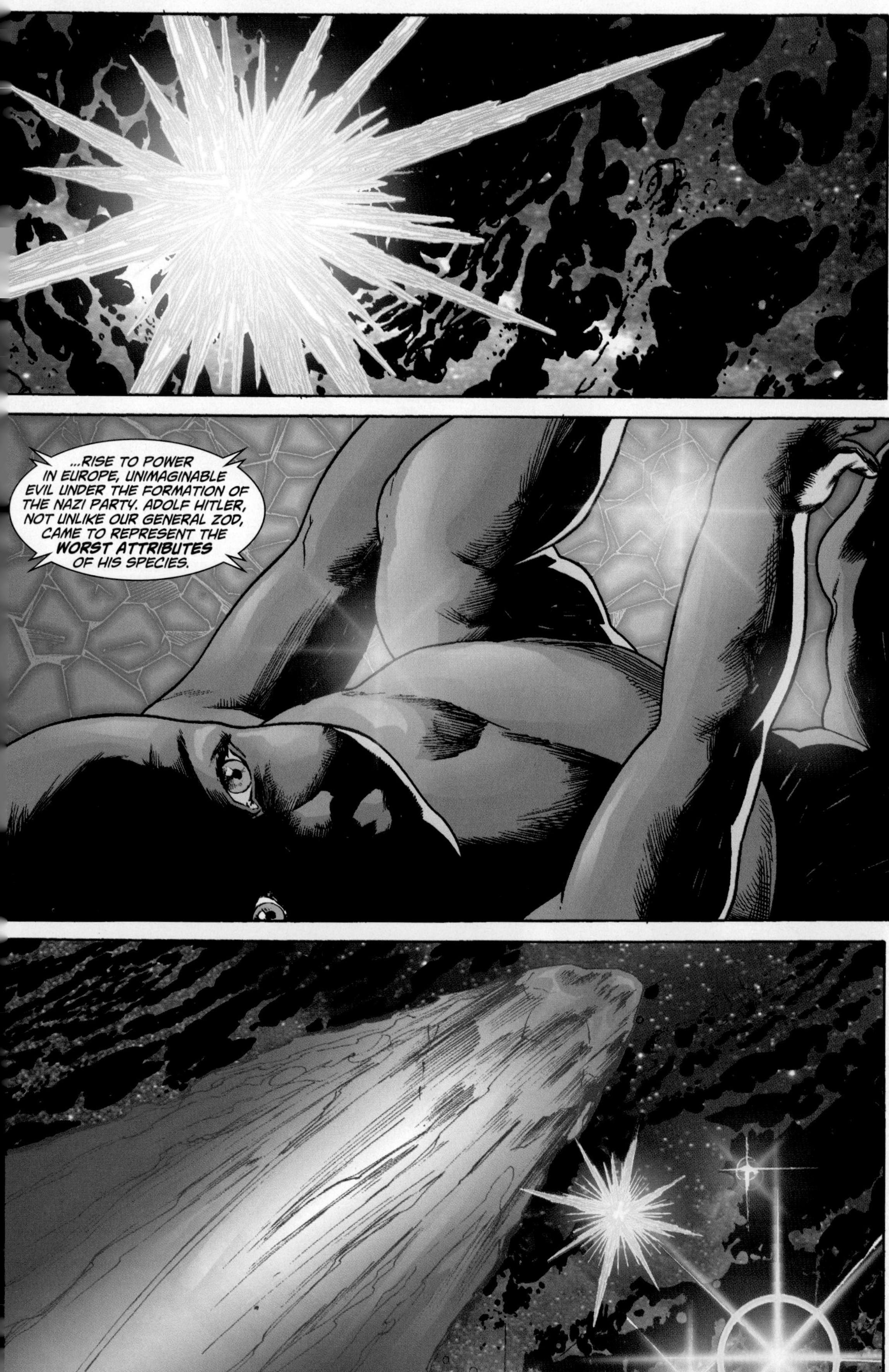
...RISE TO POWER IN EUROPE, UNIMAGINABLE EVIL UNDER THE FORMATION OF THE NAZI PARTY. ADOLF HITLER, NOT UNLIKE OUR GENERAL ZOD, CAME TO REPRESENT THE **WORST ATTRIBUTES** OF HIS SPECIES.

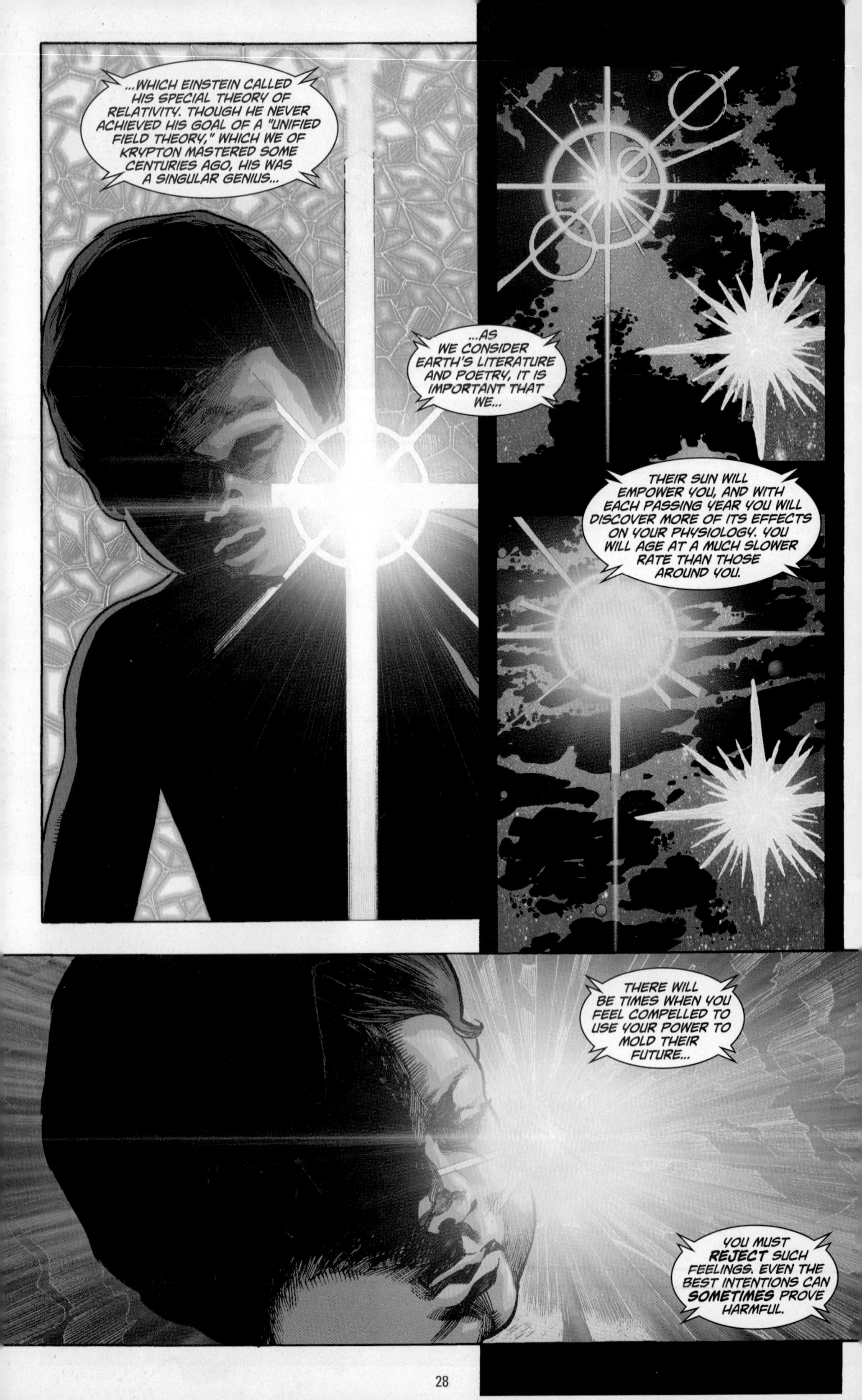

...WHICH EINSTEIN CALLED HIS SPECIAL THEORY OF RELATIVITY. THOUGH HE NEVER ACHIEVED HIS GOAL OF A "UNIFIED FIELD THEORY," WHICH WE OF KRYPTON MASTERED SOME CENTURIES AGO, HIS WAS A SINGULAR GENIUS...
...AS WE CONSIDER EARTH'S LITERATURE AND POETRY, IT IS IMPORTANT THAT WE...
THEIR SUN WILL EMPOWER YOU, AND WITH EACH PASSING YEAR YOU WILL DISCOVER MORE OF ITS EFFECTS ON YOUR PHYSIOLOGY. YOU WILL AGE AT A MUCH SLOWER RATE THAN THOSE AROUND YOU.
THERE WILL BE TIMES WHEN YOU FEEL COMPELLED TO USE YOUR POWER TO MOLD THEIR FUTURE...
YOU MUST REJECT SUCH FEELINGS. EVEN THE BEST INTENTIONS CAN SOMETIMES PROVE HARMFUL.

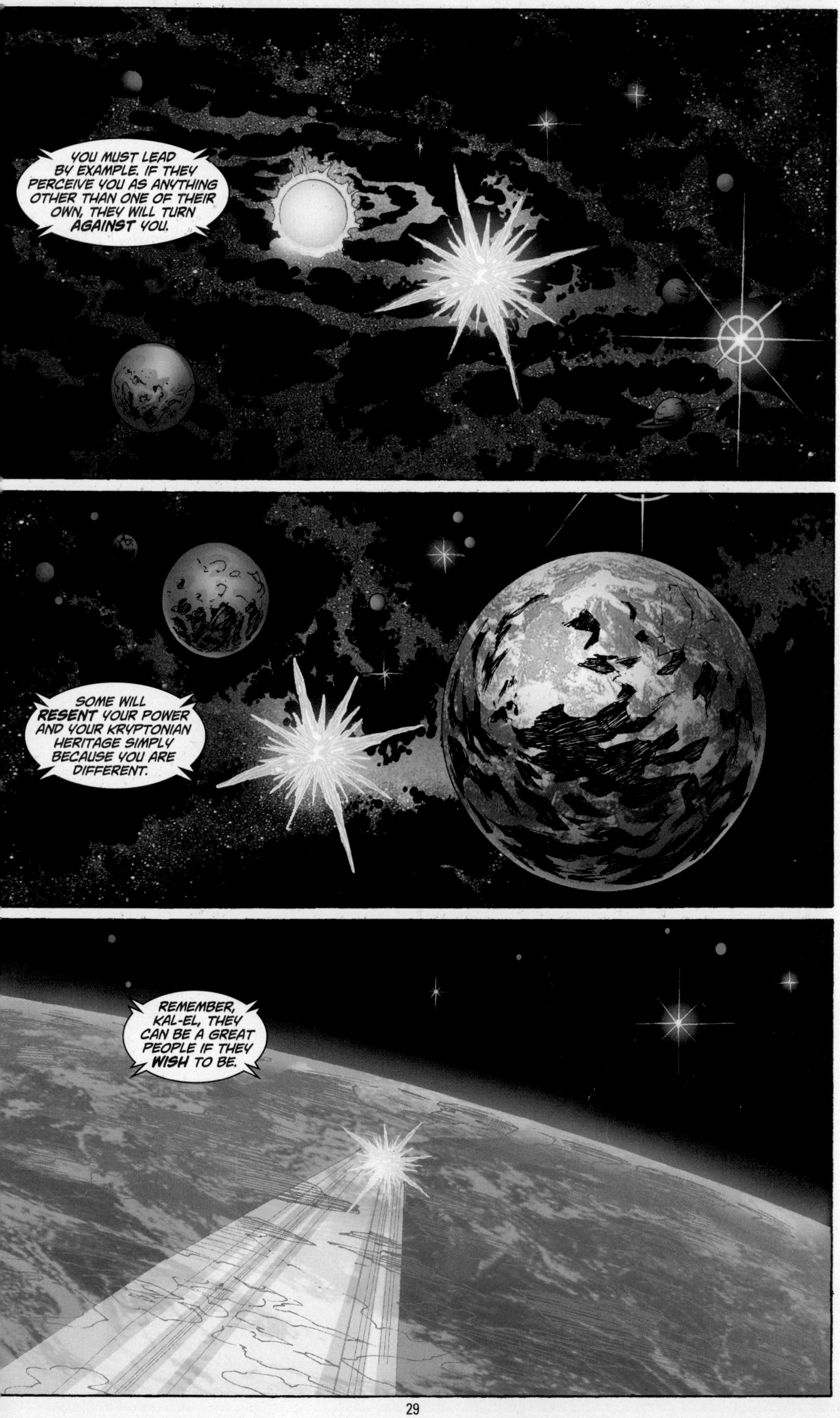
YOU MUST LEAD BY EXAMPLE. IF THEY PERCEIVE YOU AS ANYTHING OTHER THAN ONE OF THEIR OWN, THEY WILL TURN AGAINST YOU.
SOME WILL RESENT YOUR POWER AND YOUR KRYPTONIAN HERITAGE SIMPLY BECAUSE YOU ARE DIFFERENT.
REMEMBER, KAL-EL, THEY CAN BE A GREAT PEOPLE IF THEY WISH TO BE.

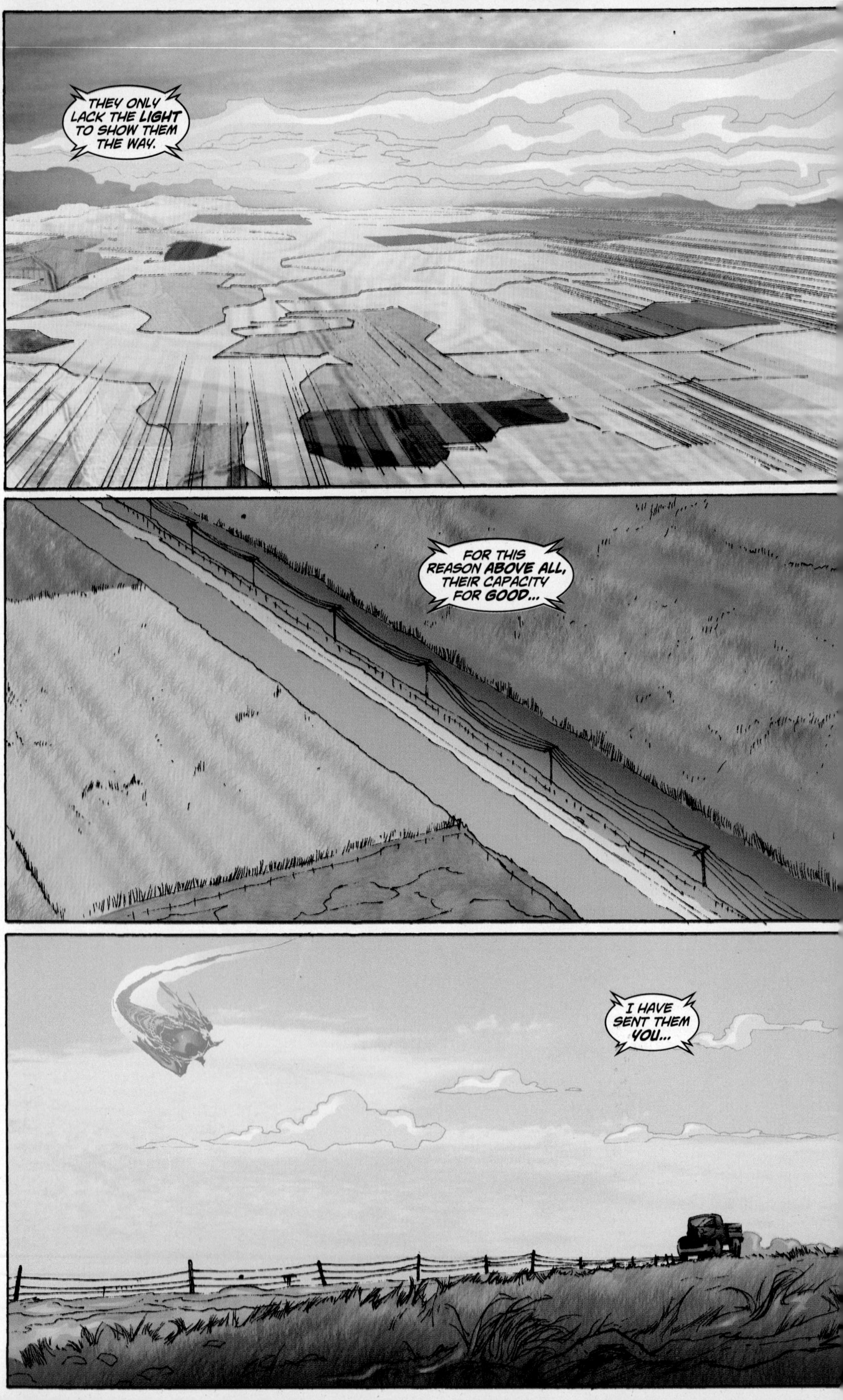
THEY ONLY LACK THE LIGHT TO SHOW THEM THE WAY.
FOR THIS REASON ABOVE ALL, THEIR CAPACITY FOR GOOD...
I HAVE SENT THEM YOU...

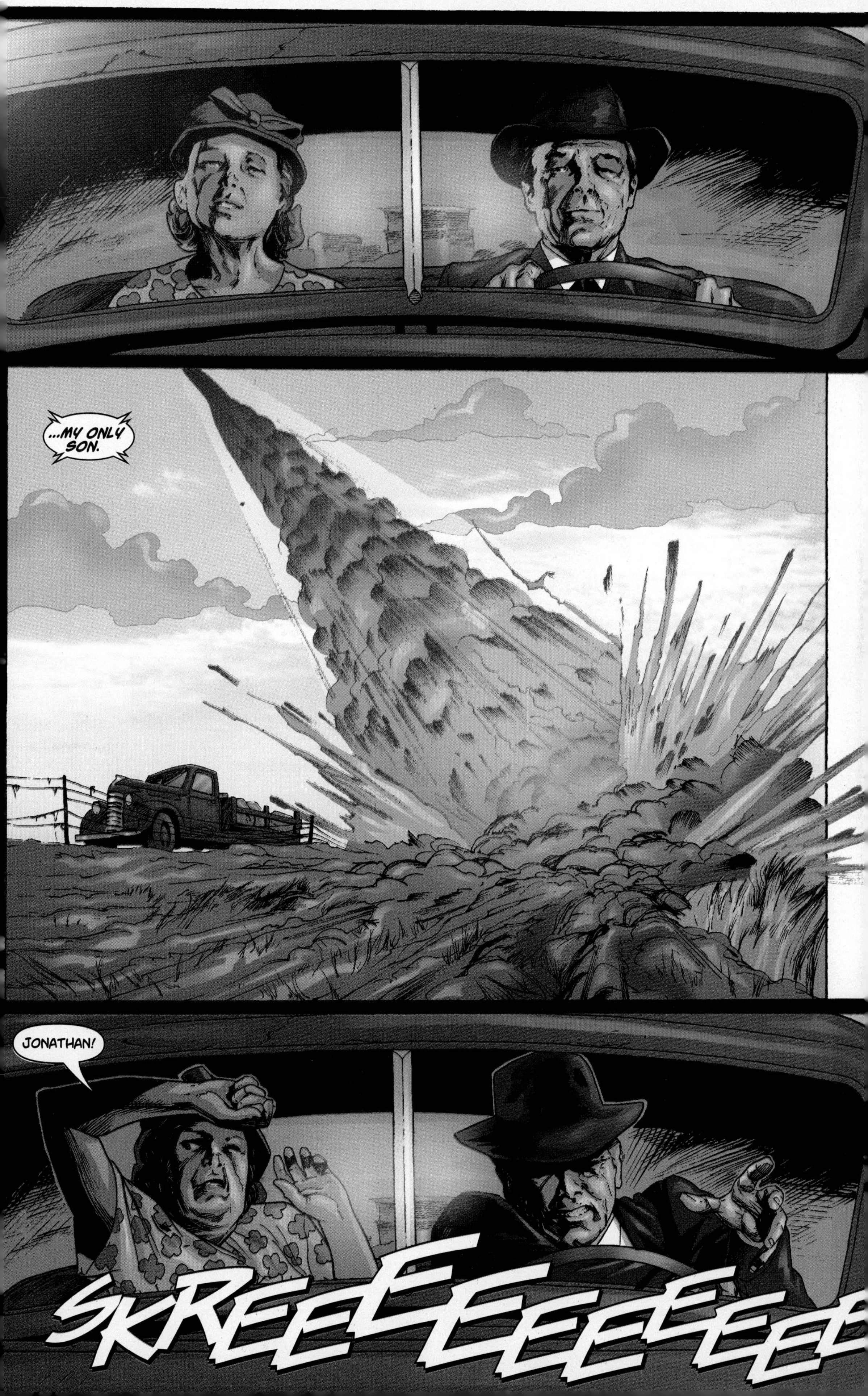
...MY ONLY SON.
JONATHAN!
SKREEEEEEEEEE

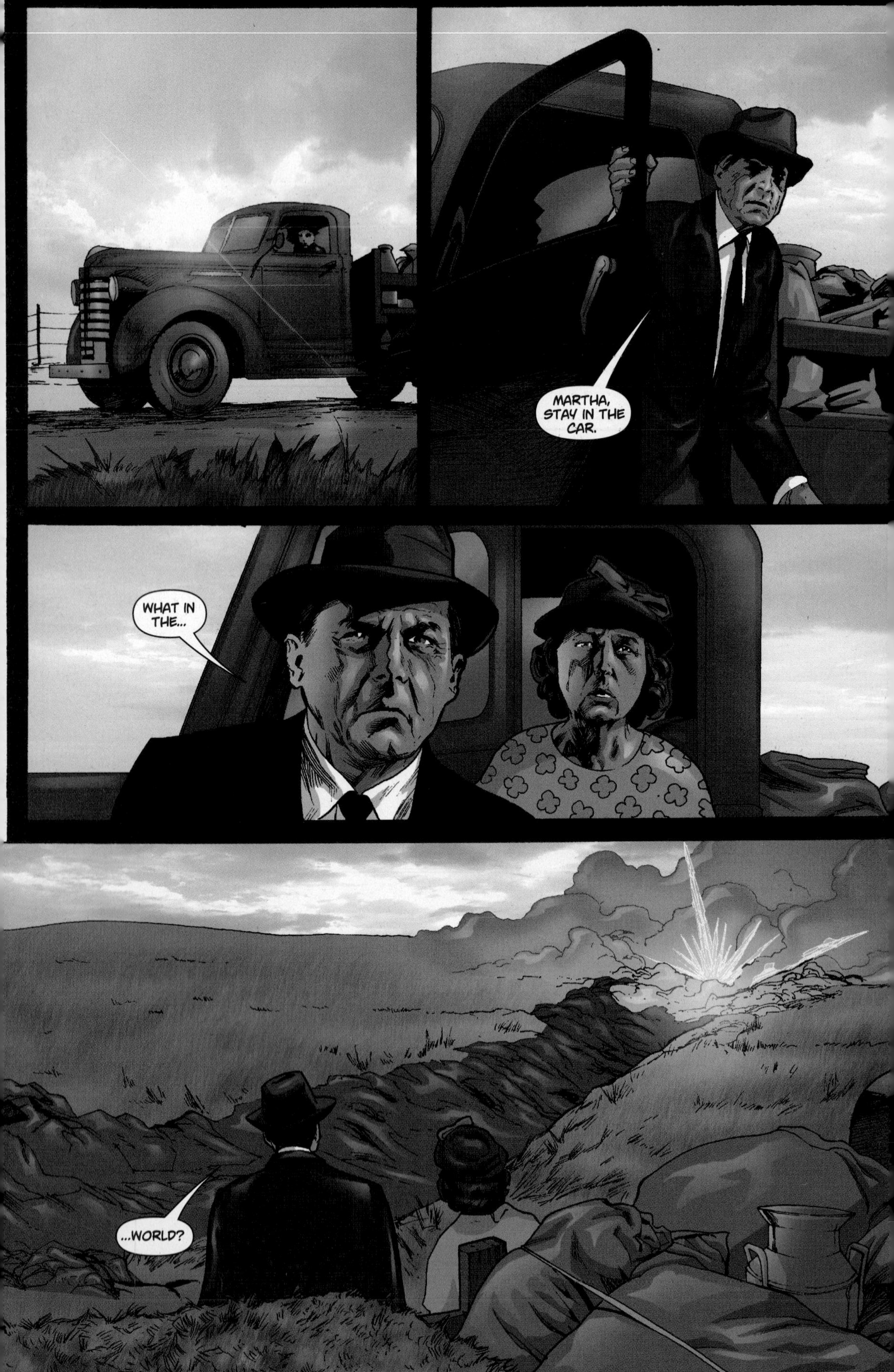
MARTHA, STAY IN THE CAR.
WHAT IN THE...
...WORLD?

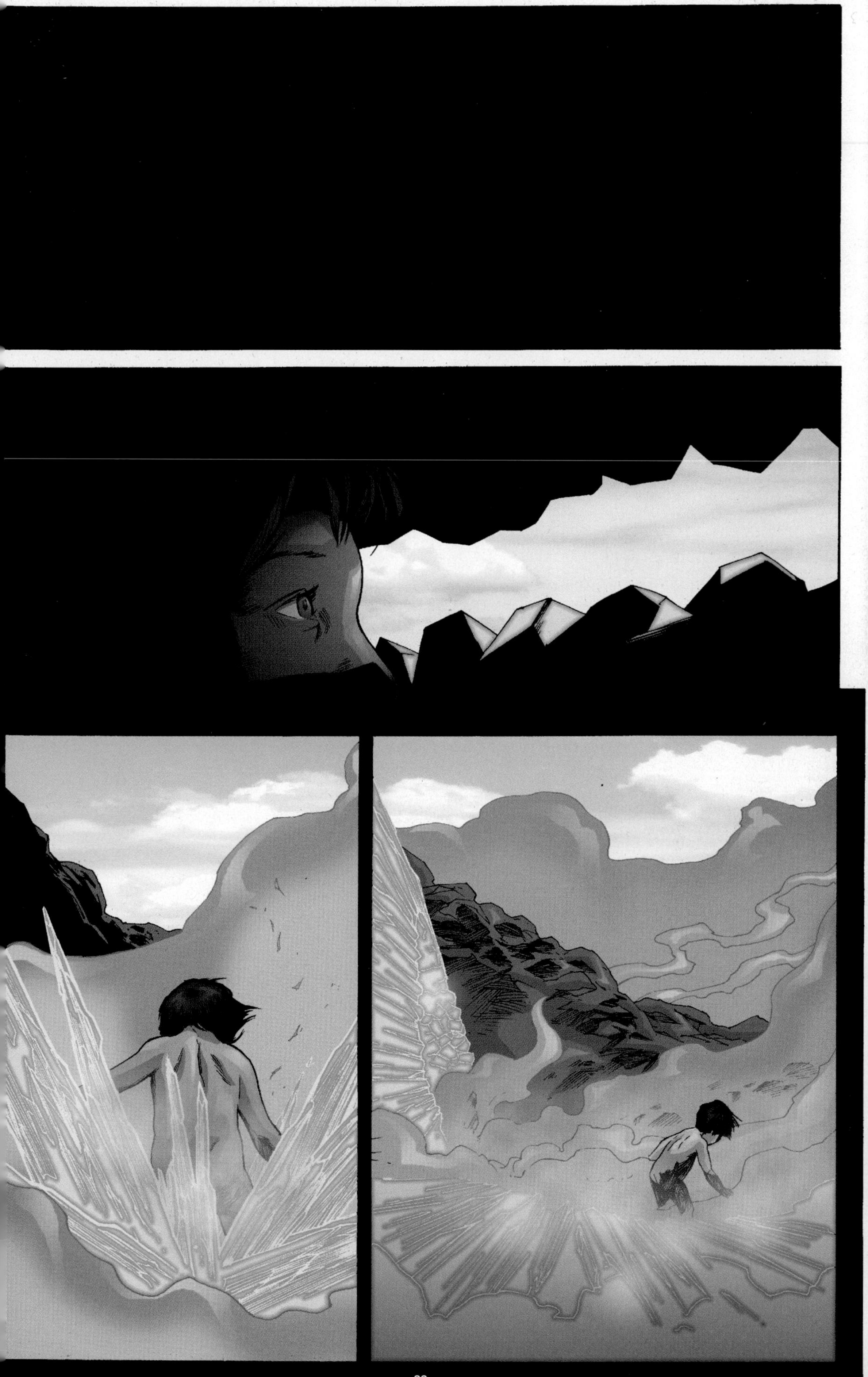

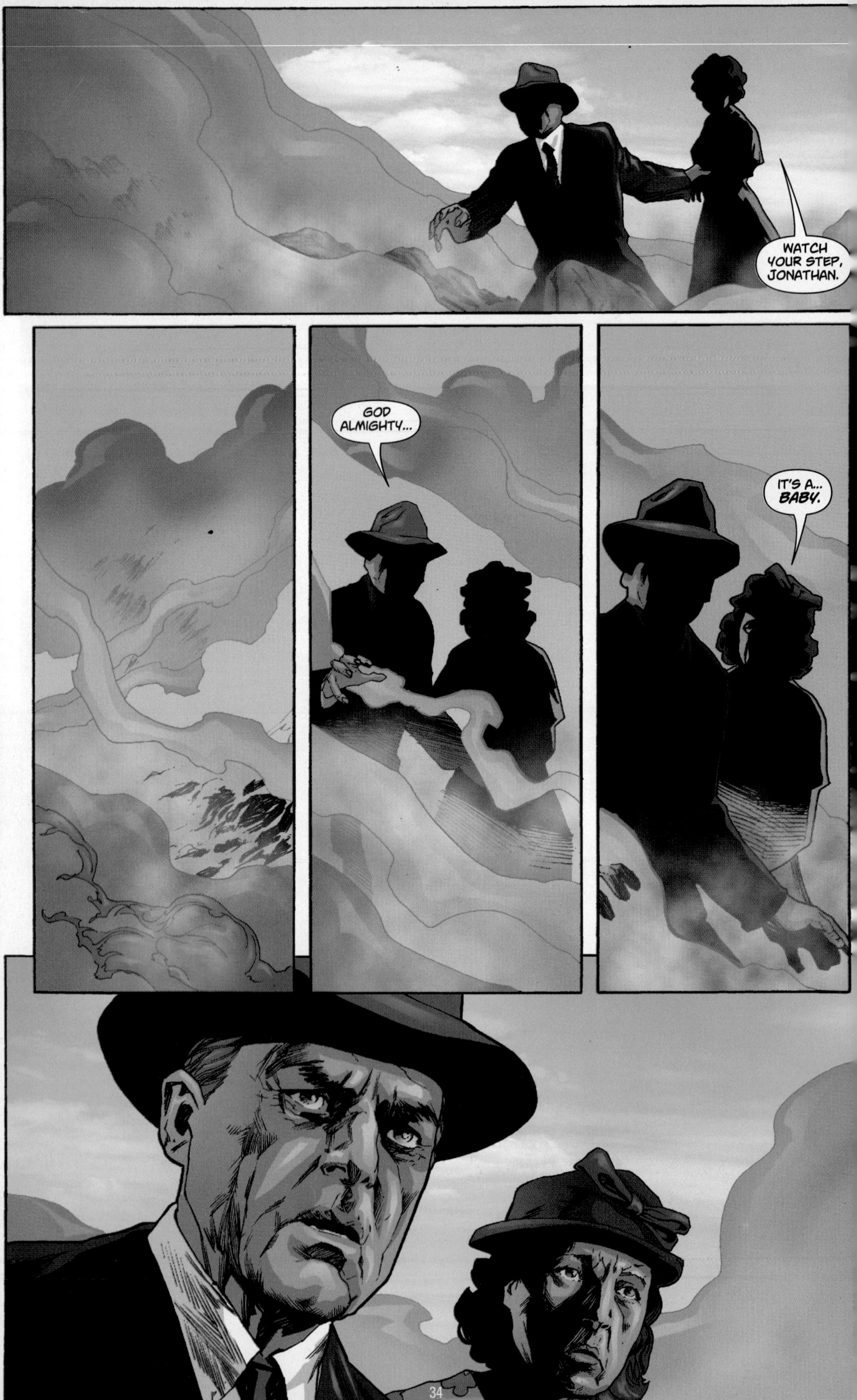
WATCH YOUR STEP, JONATHAN.
GOD ALMIGHTY...
IT'S A... BABY.

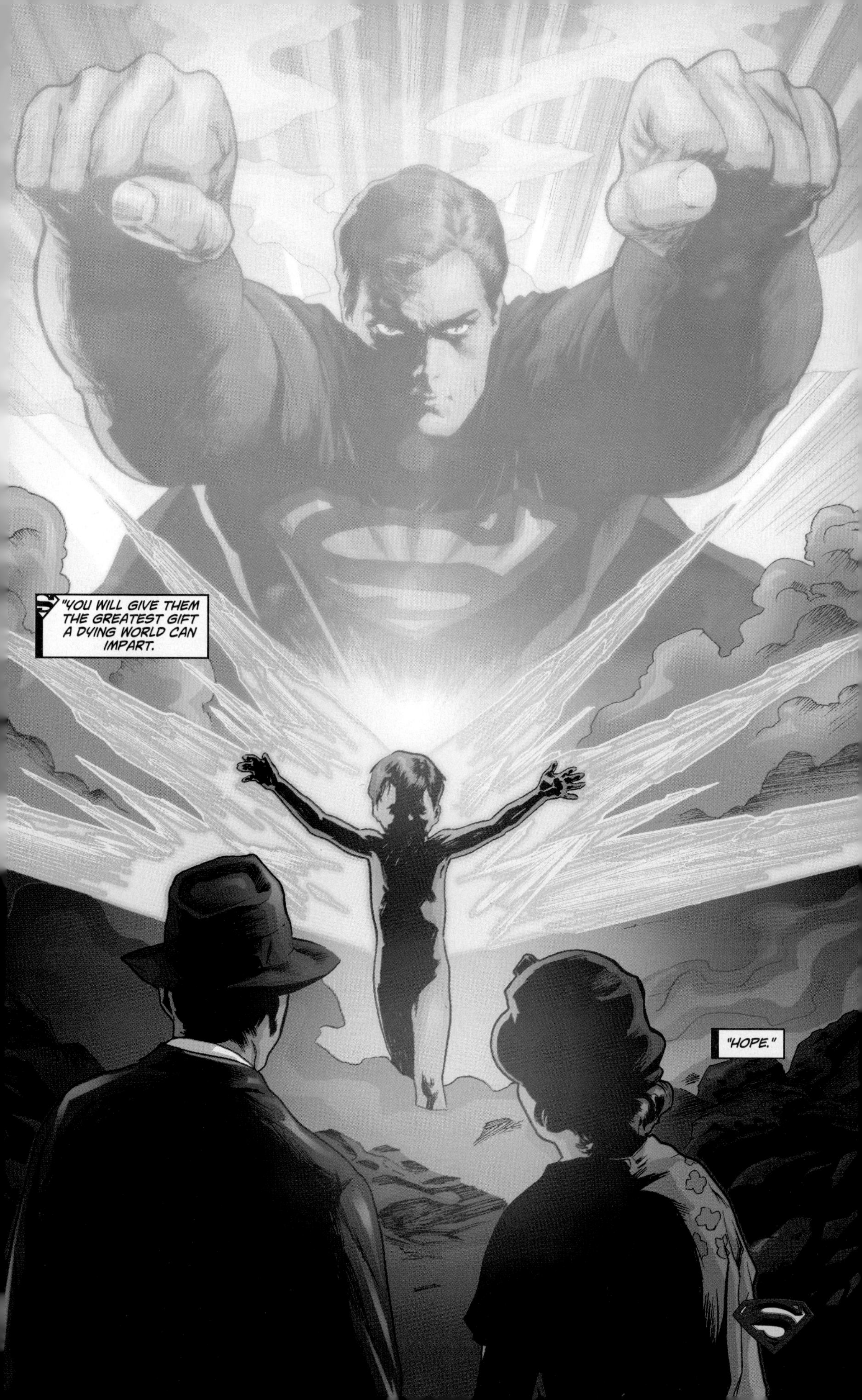
"YOU WILL GIVE THEM THE GREATEST GIFT A DYING WORLD CAN IMPART.
"HOPE."

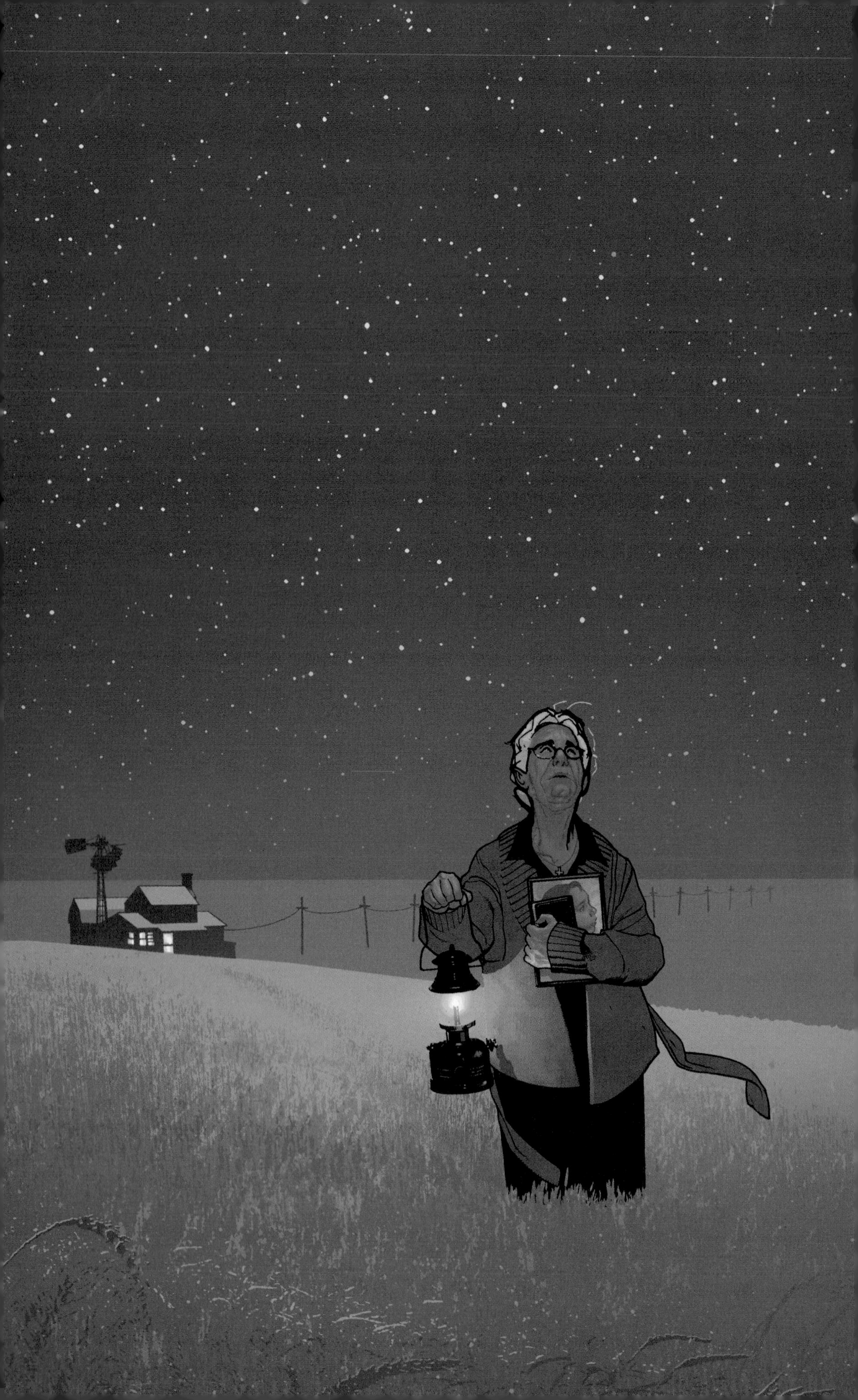

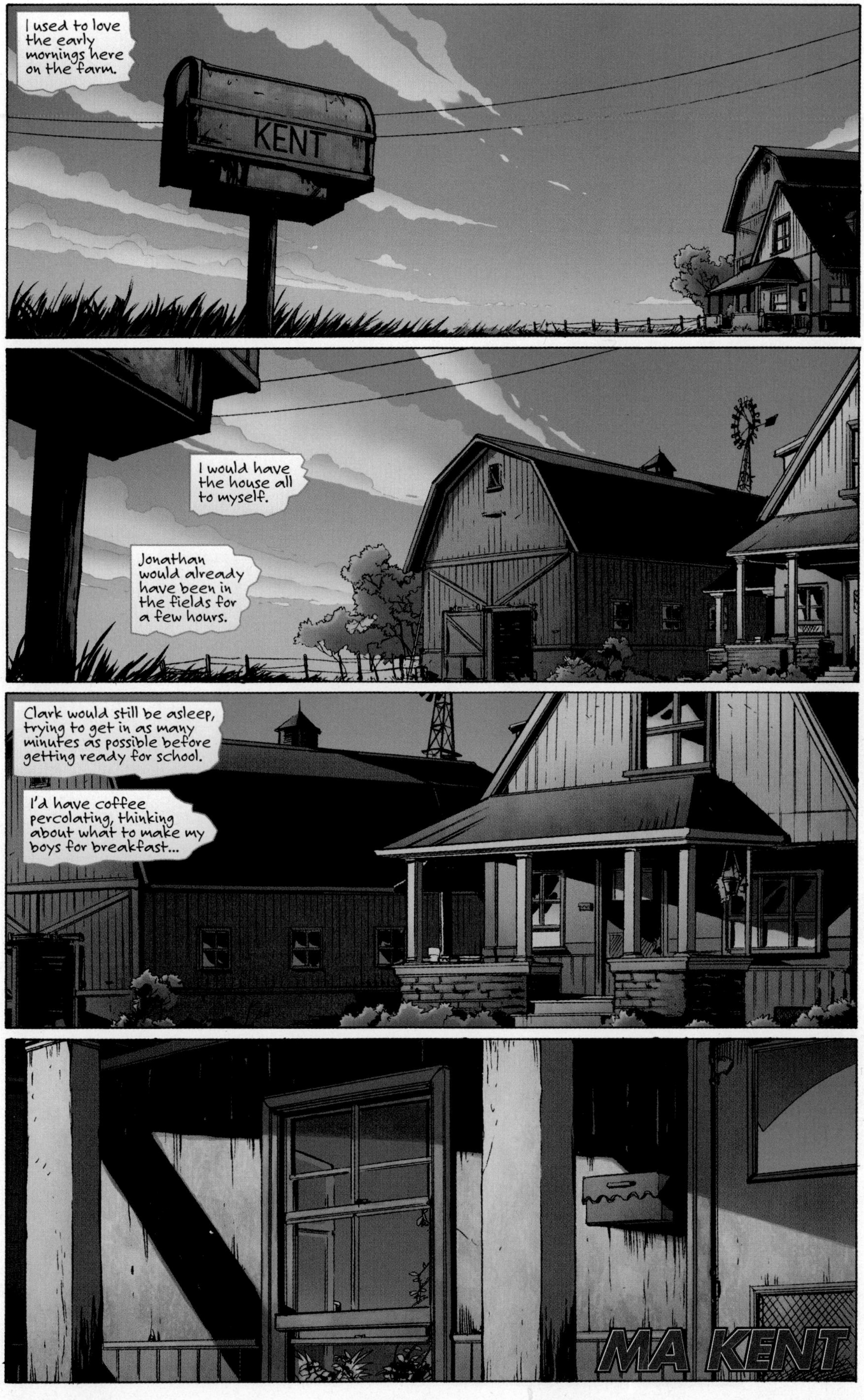
I used to love the early mornings here on the farm.
KENT
I would have the house all to myself.
Jonathan would already have been in the fields for a few hours.
Clark would still be asleep, trying to get in as many minutes as possible before getting ready for school.
I'd have coffee percolating, thinking about what to make my boys for breakfast...
MA KENT

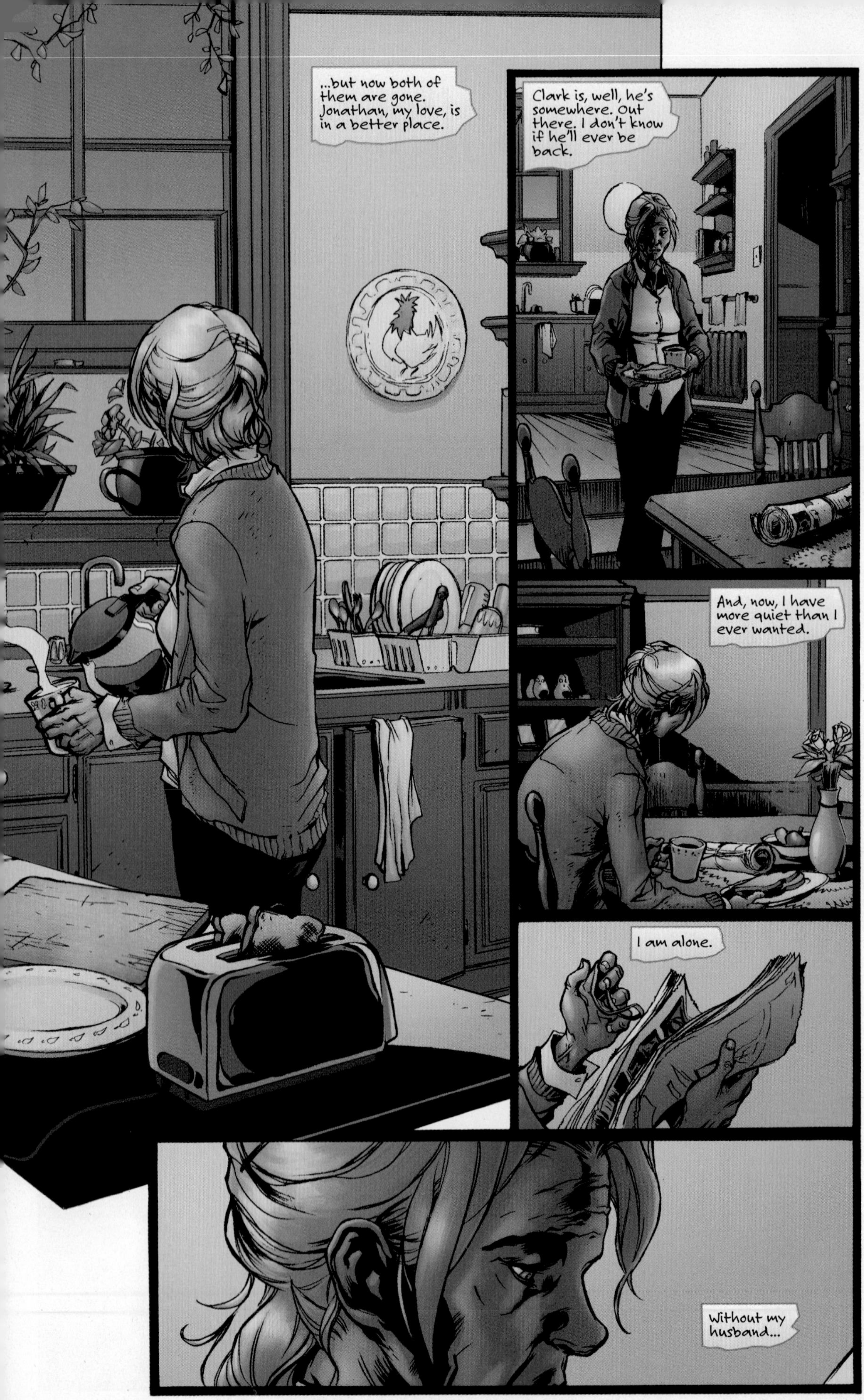
...but now both of them are gone. Jonathan, my love, is in a better place.
Clark is, well, he's somewhere. Out there. I don't know if he'll ever be back.
And, now, I have more quiet than I ever wanted.
I am alone.
Without my husband...

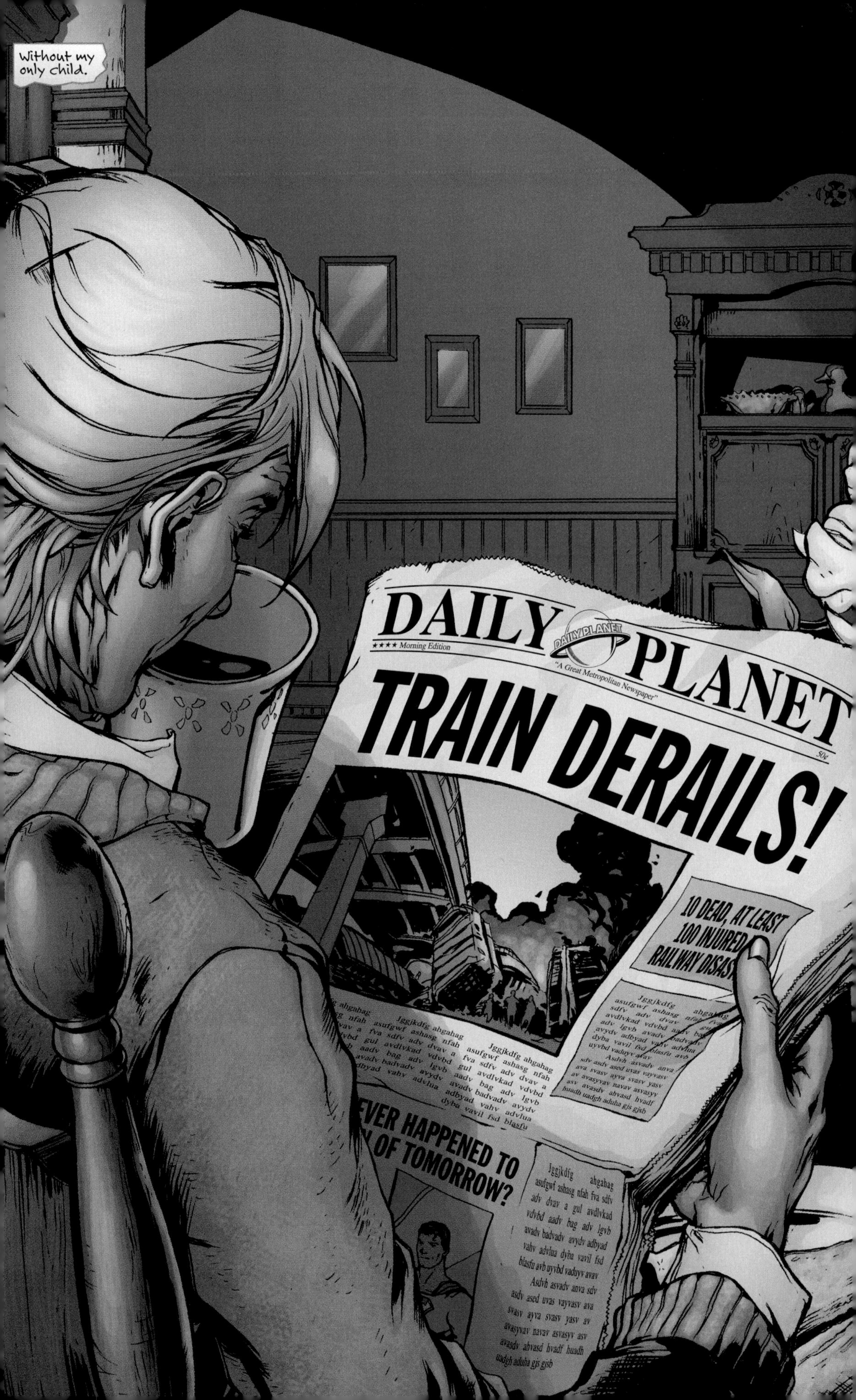
Without my only child.
DAILY PLANET
★★★★ Morning Edition
"A Great Metropolitan Newspaper"
50¢
TRAIN DERAILS!
10 DEAD, AT LEAST
EVER HAPPENED TO
OF TOMORROW?

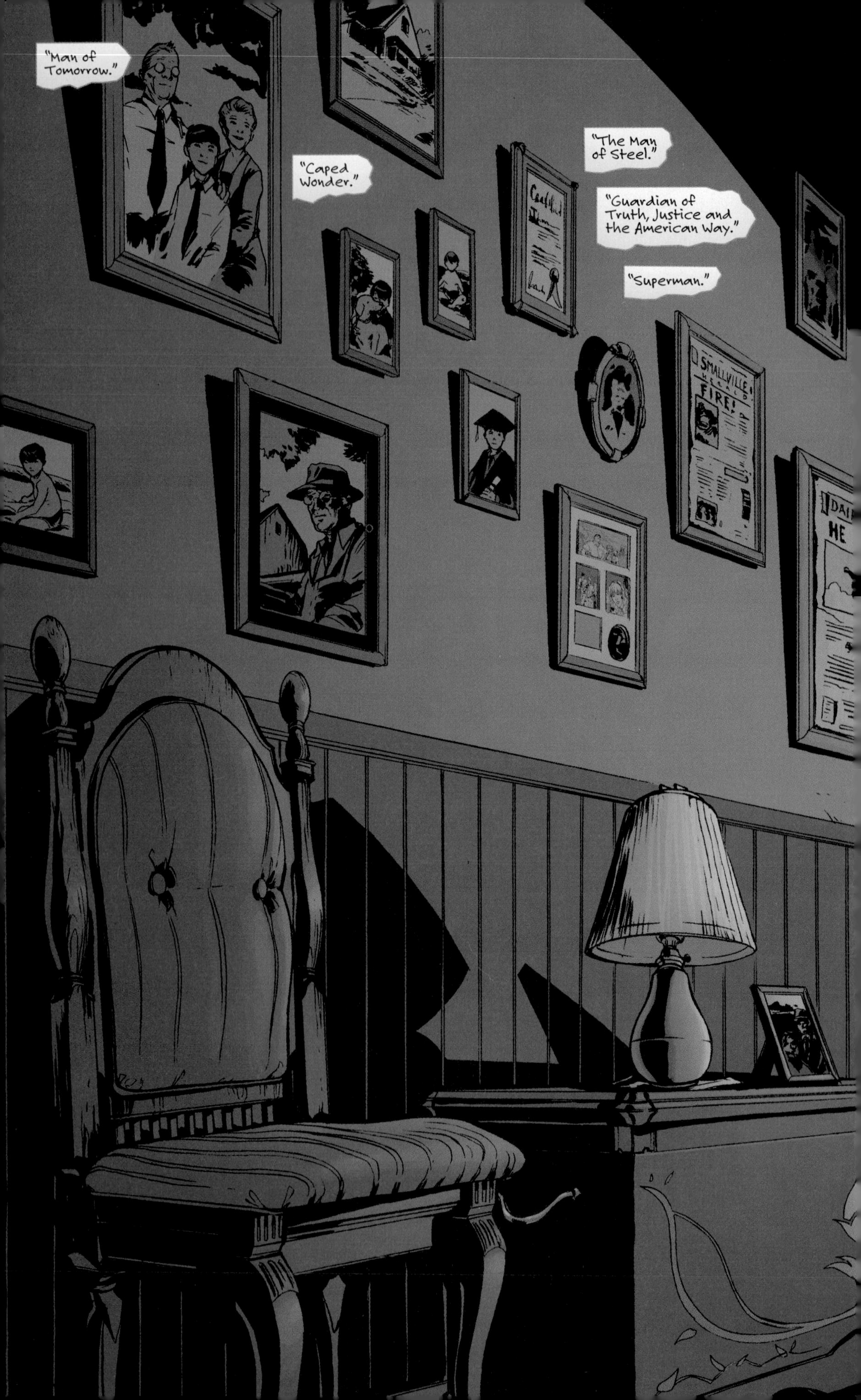
"Man of Tomorrow."
"Caped Wonder."
"The Man of Steel."
"Guardian of Truth, Justice and the American Way."
"Superman."
SMALLVILLE HERALD
FIRE!

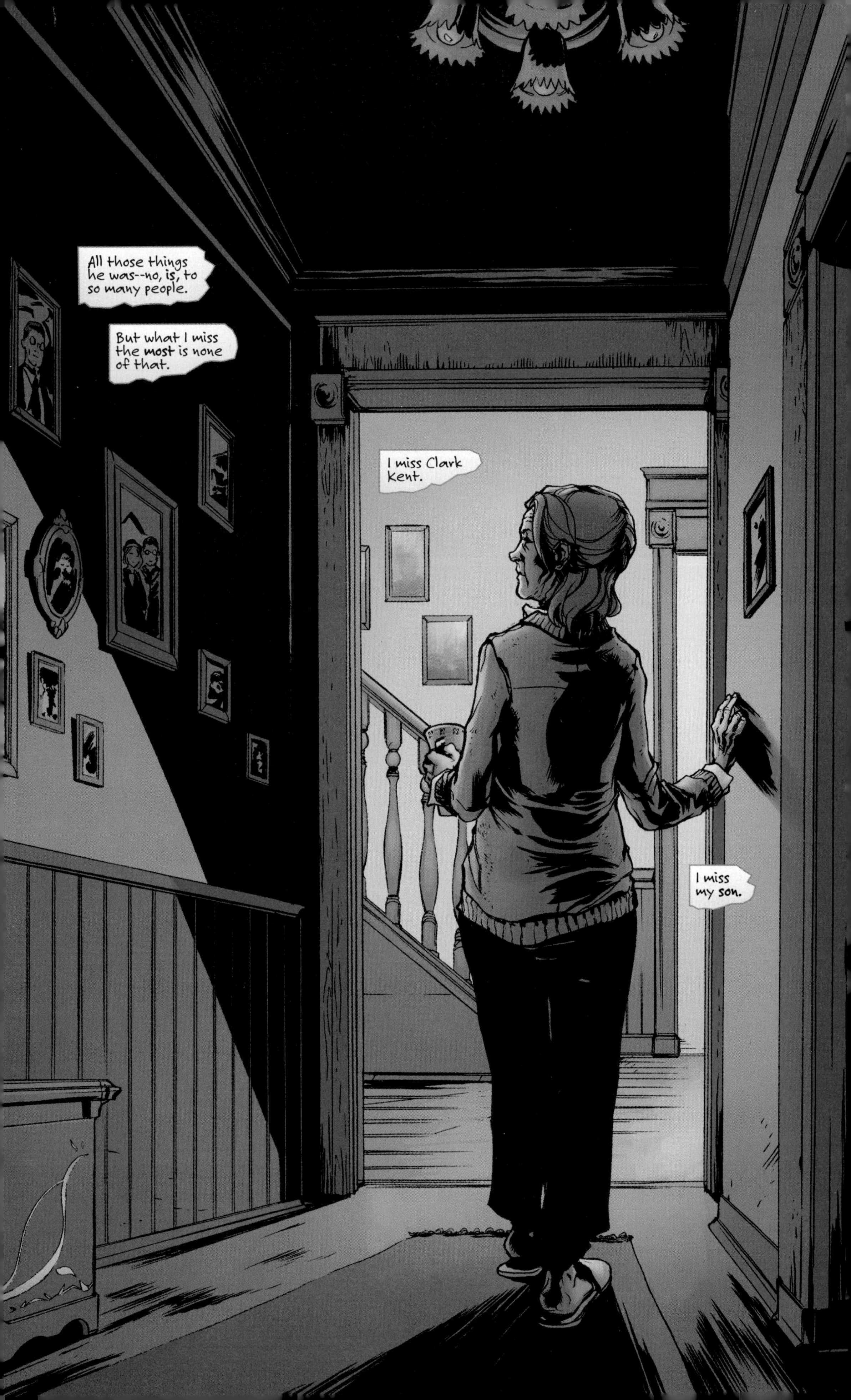
All those things he was--no, is, to so many people.
But what I miss the **most** is none of that.
I miss Clark Kent.
I miss my **son.**

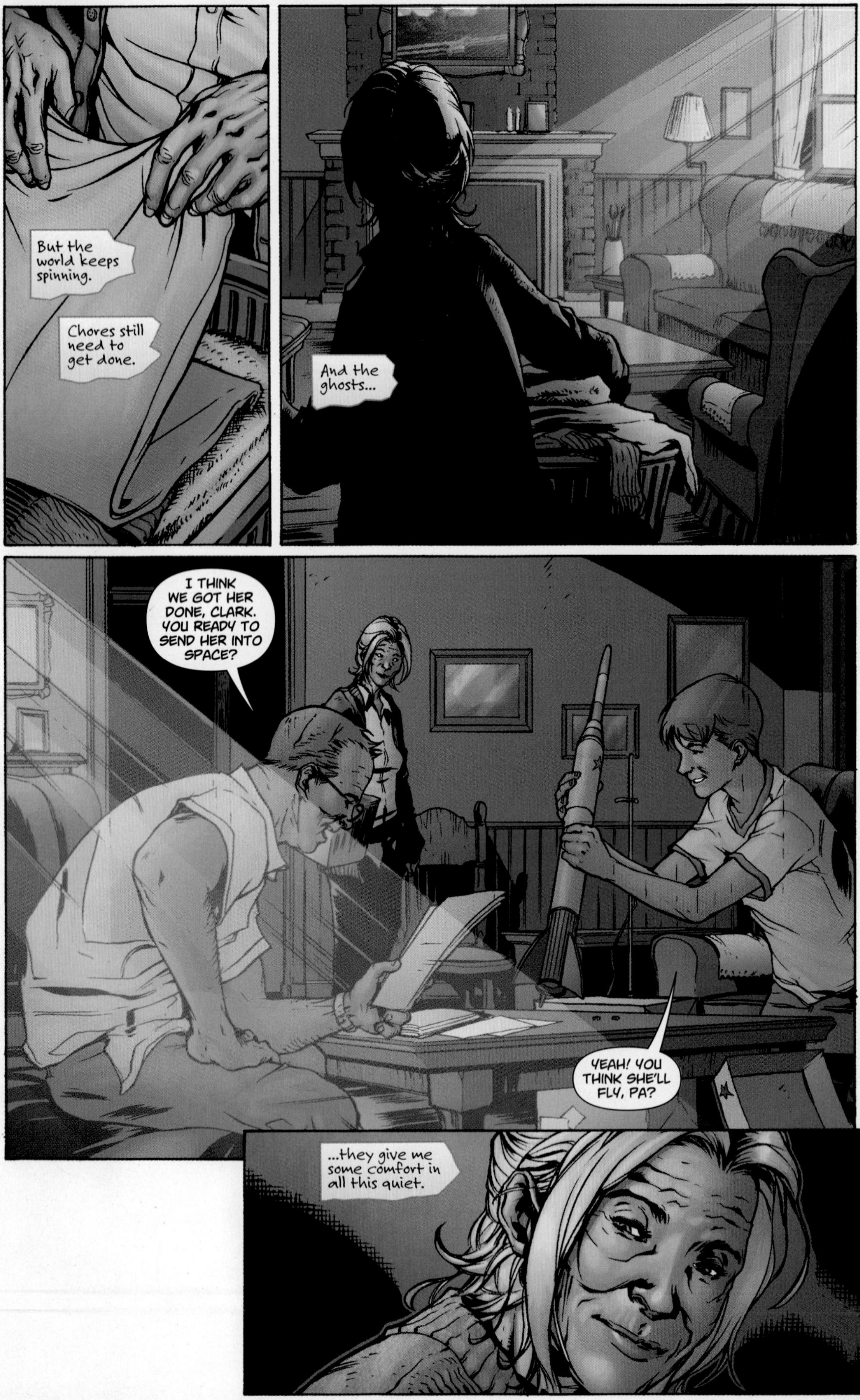
But the world keeps spinning.
Chores still need to get done.
And the ghosts...
I THINK WE GOT HER DONE, CLARK. YOU READY TO SEND HER INTO SPACE?
YEAH! YOU THINK SHE'LL FLY, PA?
...they give me some comfort in all this quiet.

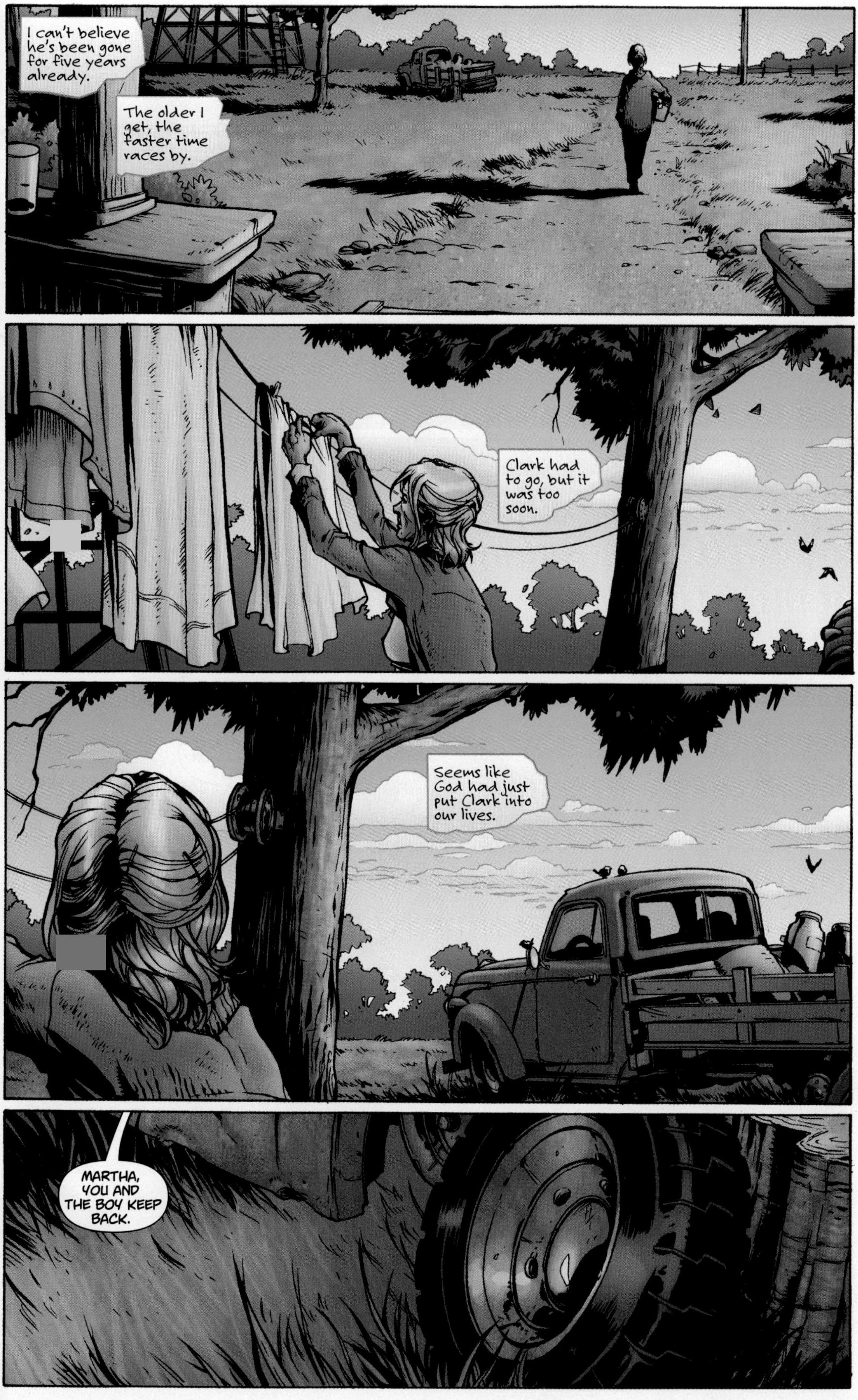
I can't believe he's been gone for five years already.
The older I get, the faster time races by.
Clark had to go, but it was too soon.
Seems like God had just put Clark into our lives.
MARTHA, YOU AND THE BOY KEEP BACK.

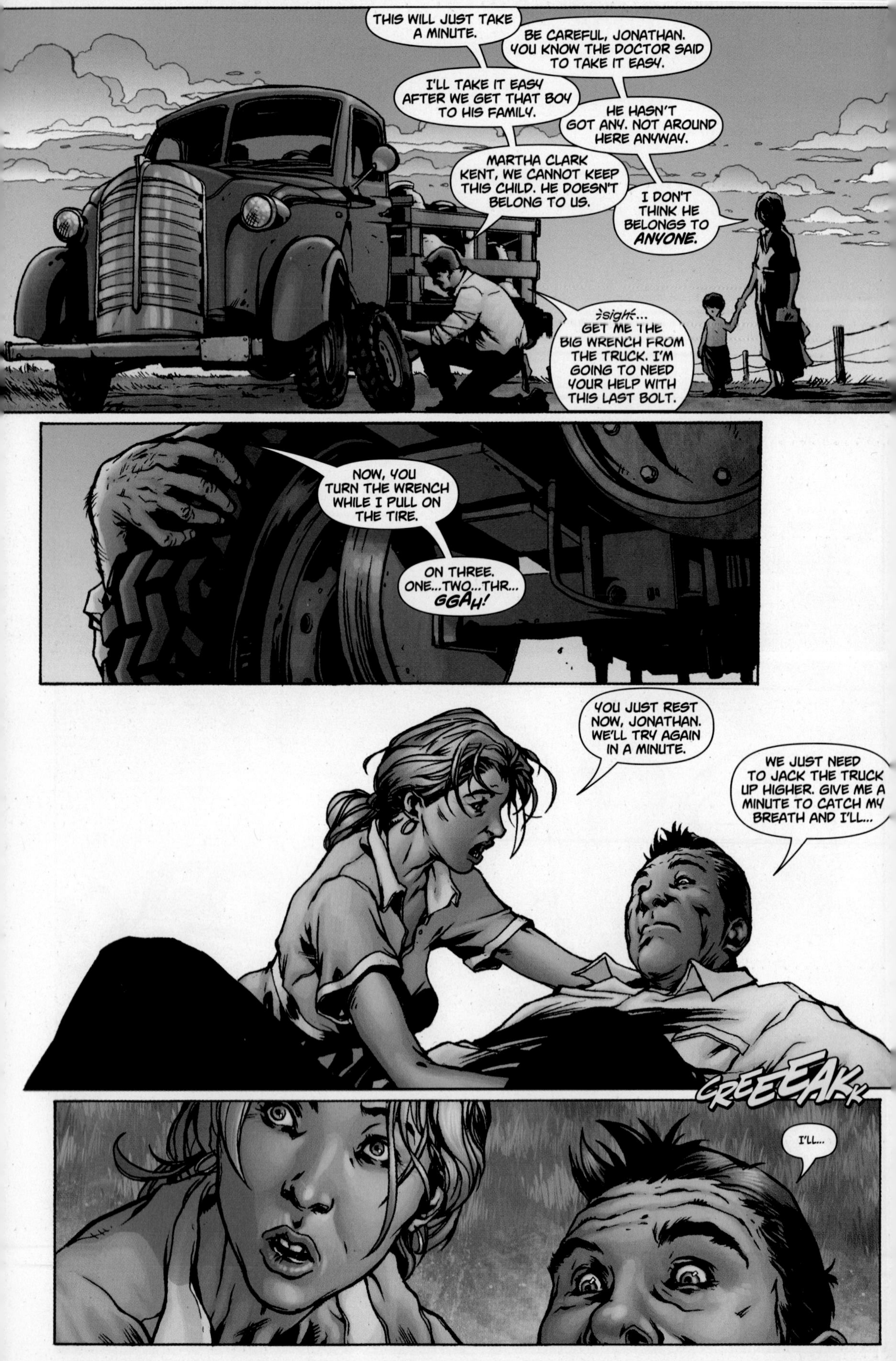
THIS WILL JUST TAKE A MINUTE.
BE CAREFUL, JONATHAN. YOU KNOW THE DOCTOR SAID TO TAKE IT EASY.
I'LL TAKE IT EASY AFTER WE GET THAT BOY TO HIS FAMILY.
HE HASN'T GOT ANY. NOT AROUND HERE ANYWAY.
MARTHA CLARK KENT, WE CANNOT KEEP THIS CHILD. HE DOESN'T BELONG TO US.
I DON'T THINK HE BELONGS TO ANYONE.
sigh... GET ME THE BIG WRENCH FROM THE TRUCK. I'M GOING TO NEED YOUR HELP WITH THIS LAST BOLT.
NOW, YOU TURN THE WRENCH WHILE I PULL ON THE TIRE.
ON THREE. ONE...TWO...THR... GGAH!
YOU JUST REST NOW, JONATHAN. WE'LL TRY AGAIN IN A MINUTE.
WE JUST NEED TO JACK THE TRUCK UP HIGHER. GIVE ME A MINUTE TO CATCH MY BREATH AND I'LL...
CREEEAKK
I'LL...

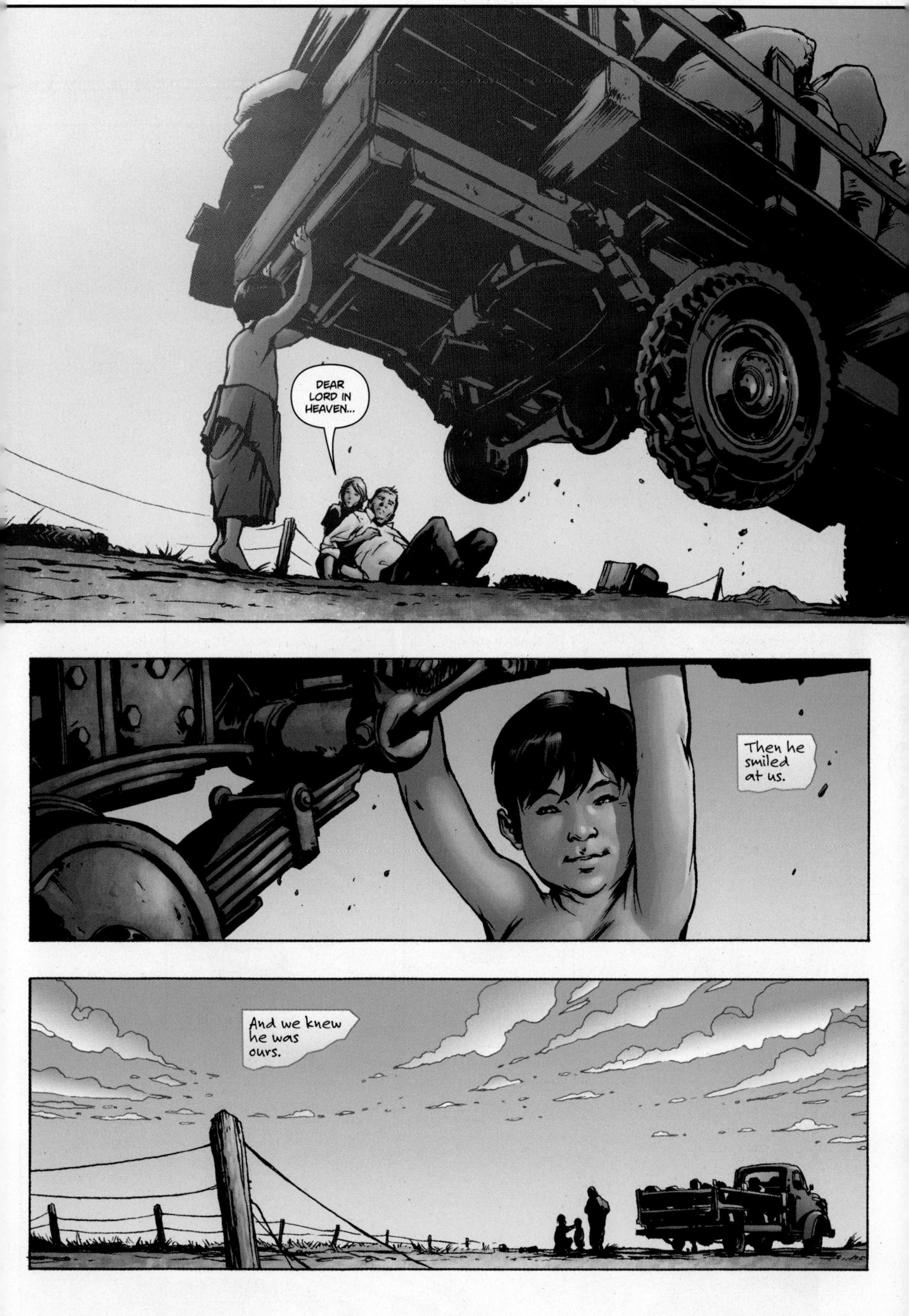
DEAR LORD IN HEAVEN...
Then he smiled at us.
And we knew he was ours.

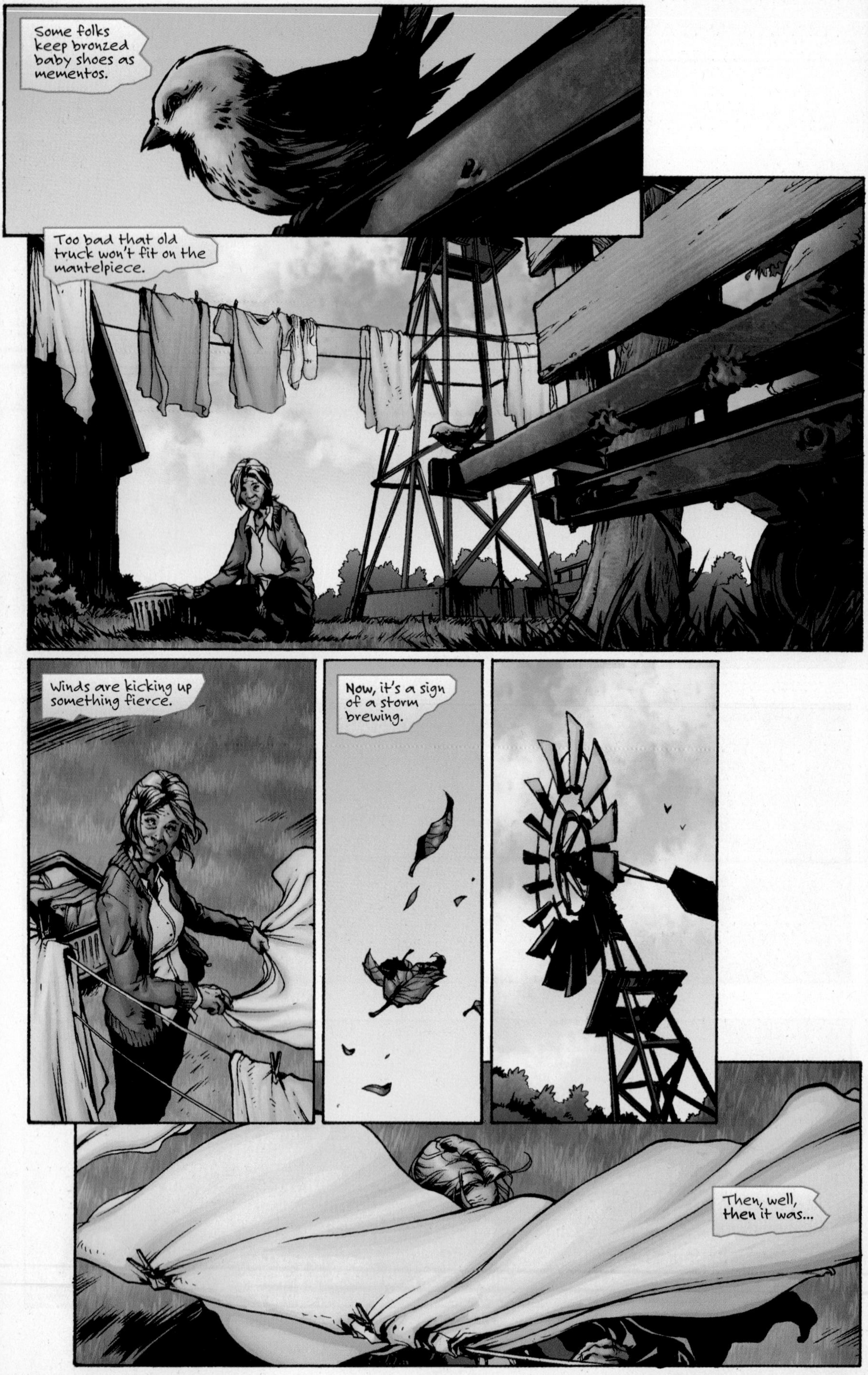
Some folks keep bronzed baby shoes as mementos.
Too bad that old truck won't fit on the mantelpiece.
Winds are kicking up something fierce.
Now, it's a sign of a storm brewing.
Then, well, then it was...

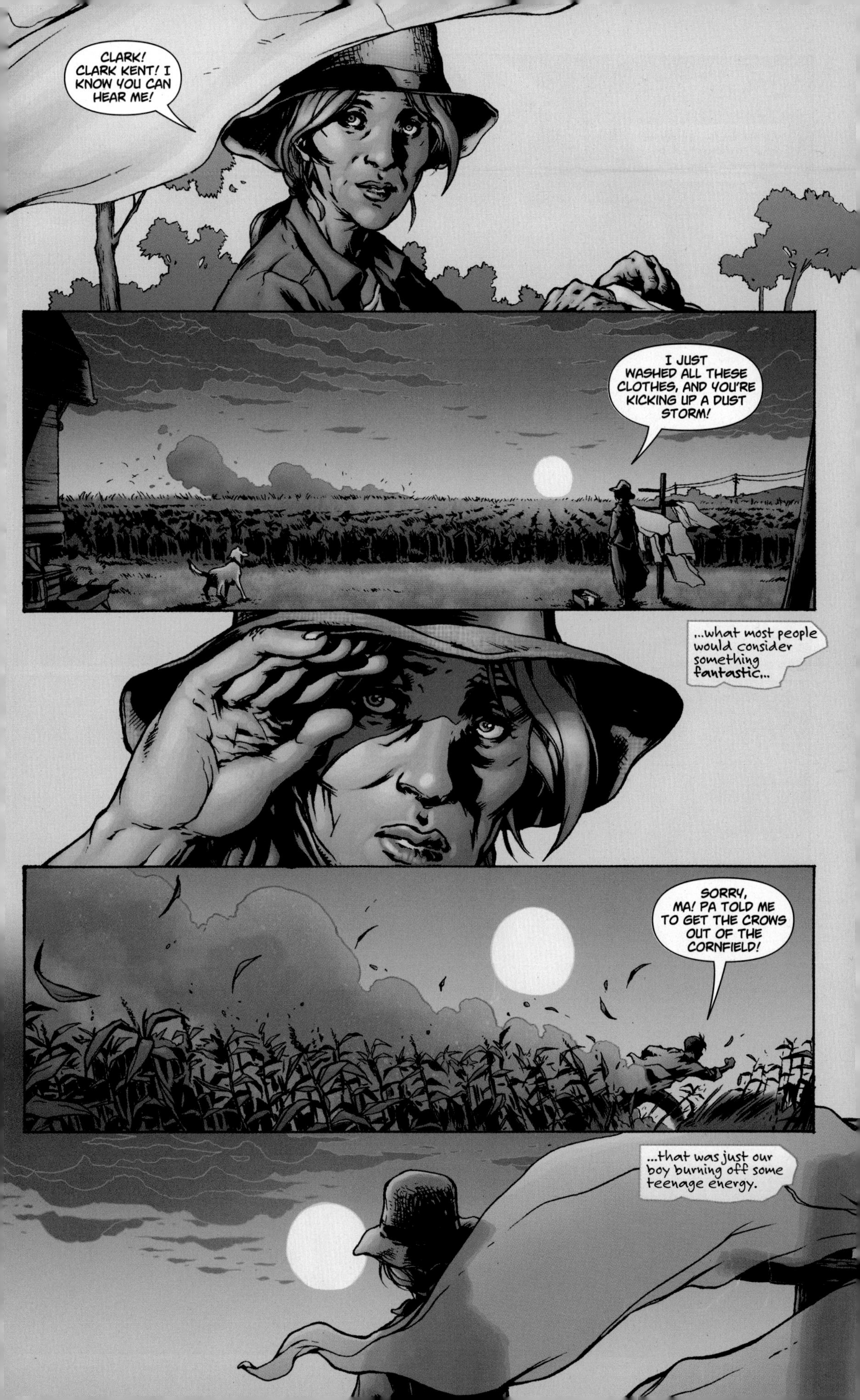
CLARK! CLARK KENT! I KNOW YOU CAN HEAR ME!
I JUST WASHED ALL THESE CLOTHES, AND YOU'RE KICKING UP A DUST STORM!
...what most people would consider something fantastic...
SORRY, MA! PA TOLD ME TO GET THE CROWS OUT OF THE CORNFIELD!
...that was just our boy burning off some teenage energy.

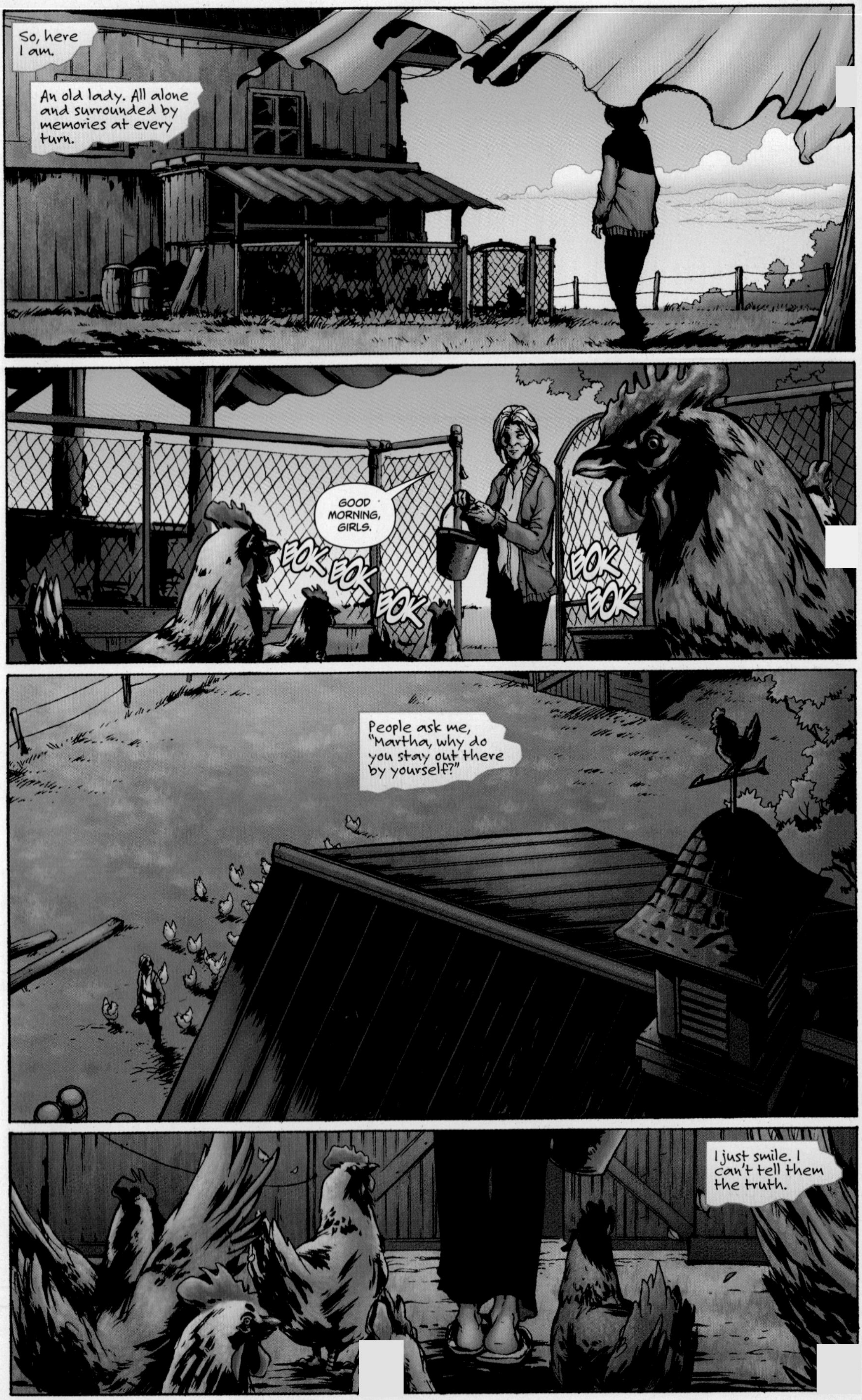
So, here I am.
An old lady. All alone and surrounded by memories at every turn.
GOOD MORNING, GIRLS.
BOK BOK BOK
BOK BOK
People ask me, "Martha, why do you stay out there by yourself?"
I just smile. I can't tell them the truth.

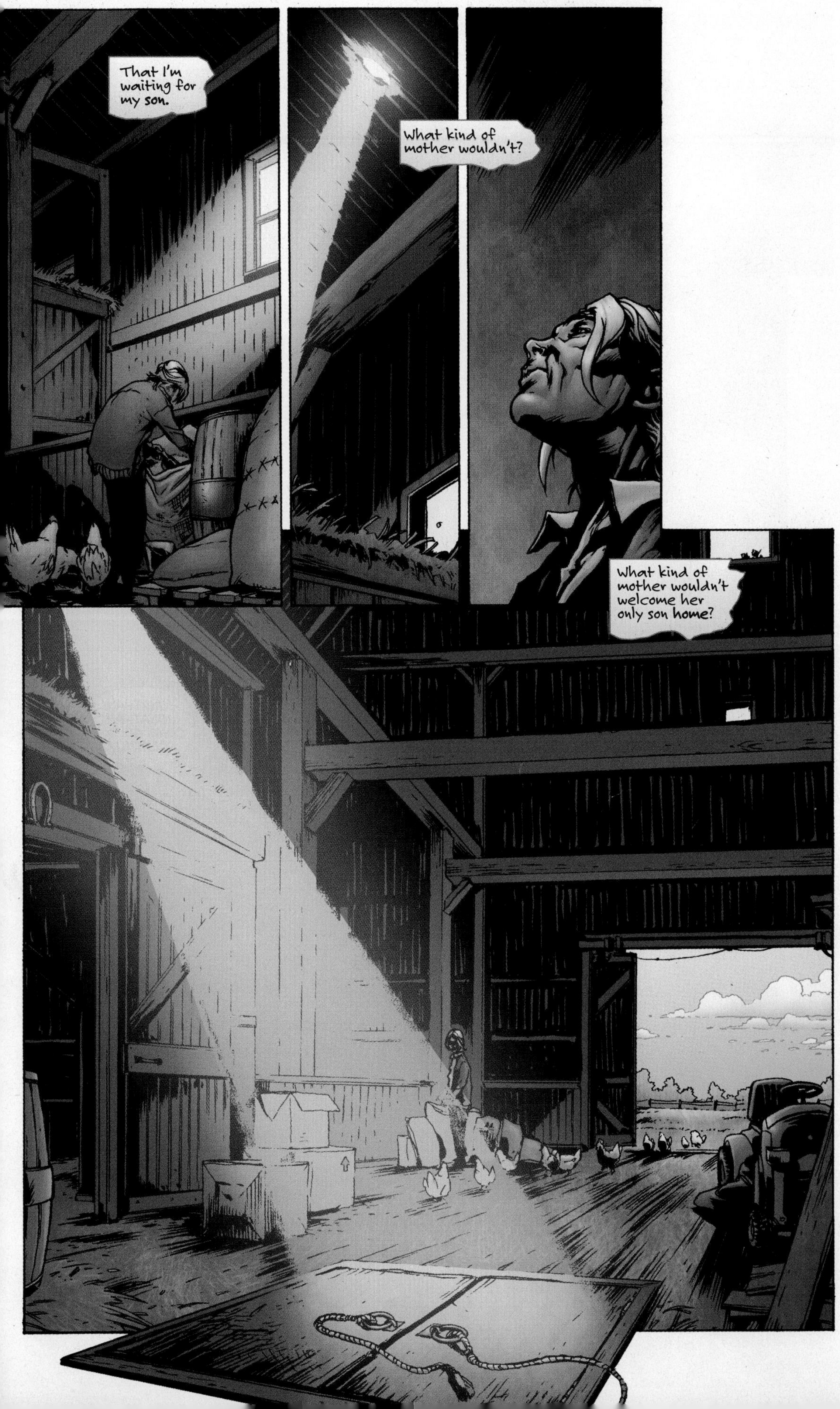
That I'm waiting for my son.
What kind of mother wouldn't?
What kind of mother wouldn't welcome her only son home?

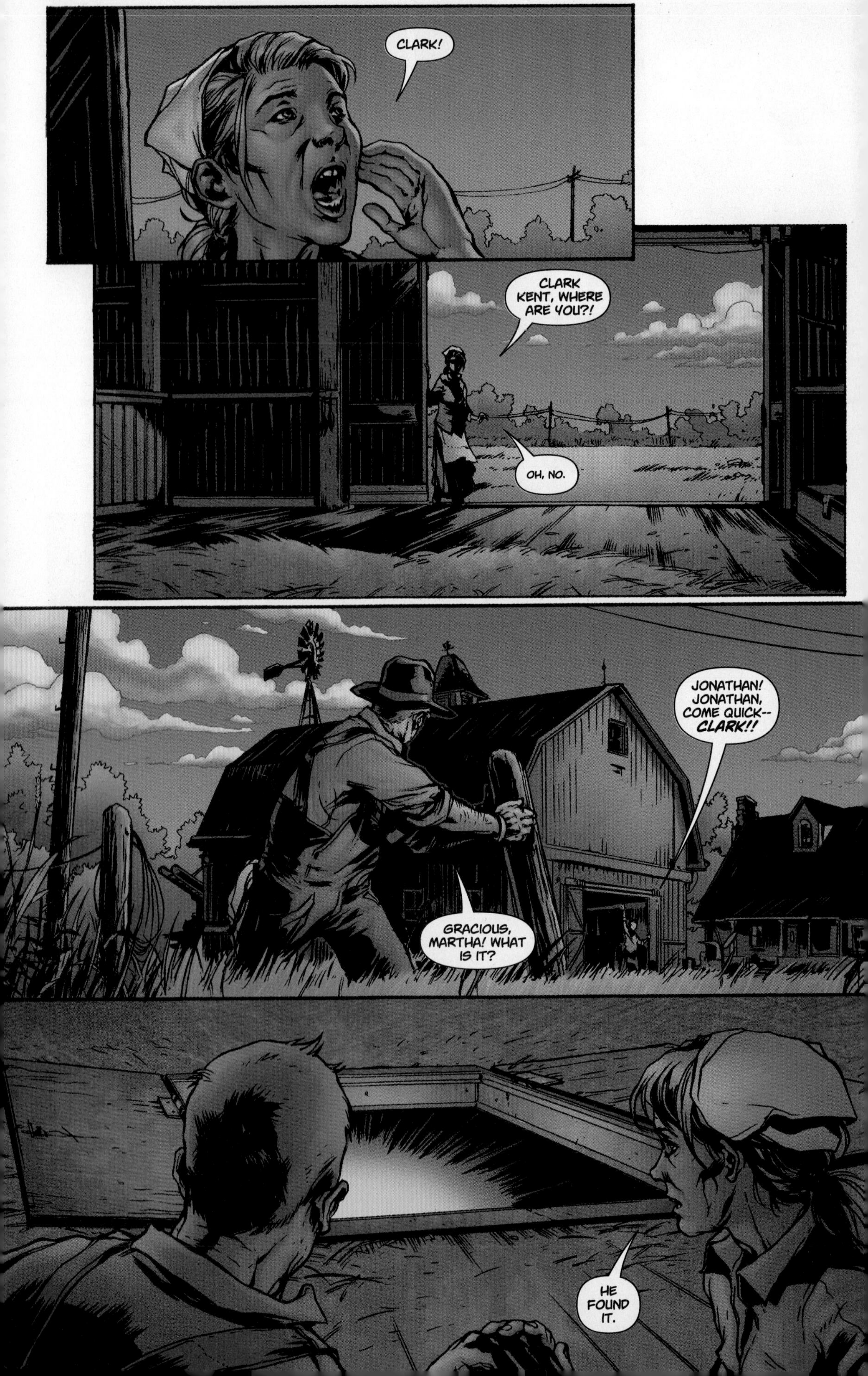
CLARK!
CLARK KENT, WHERE ARE YOU?!
OH, NO.
JONATHAN! JONATHAN, COME QUICK-- CLARK!!
GRACIOUS, MARTHA! WHAT IS IT?
HE FOUND IT.

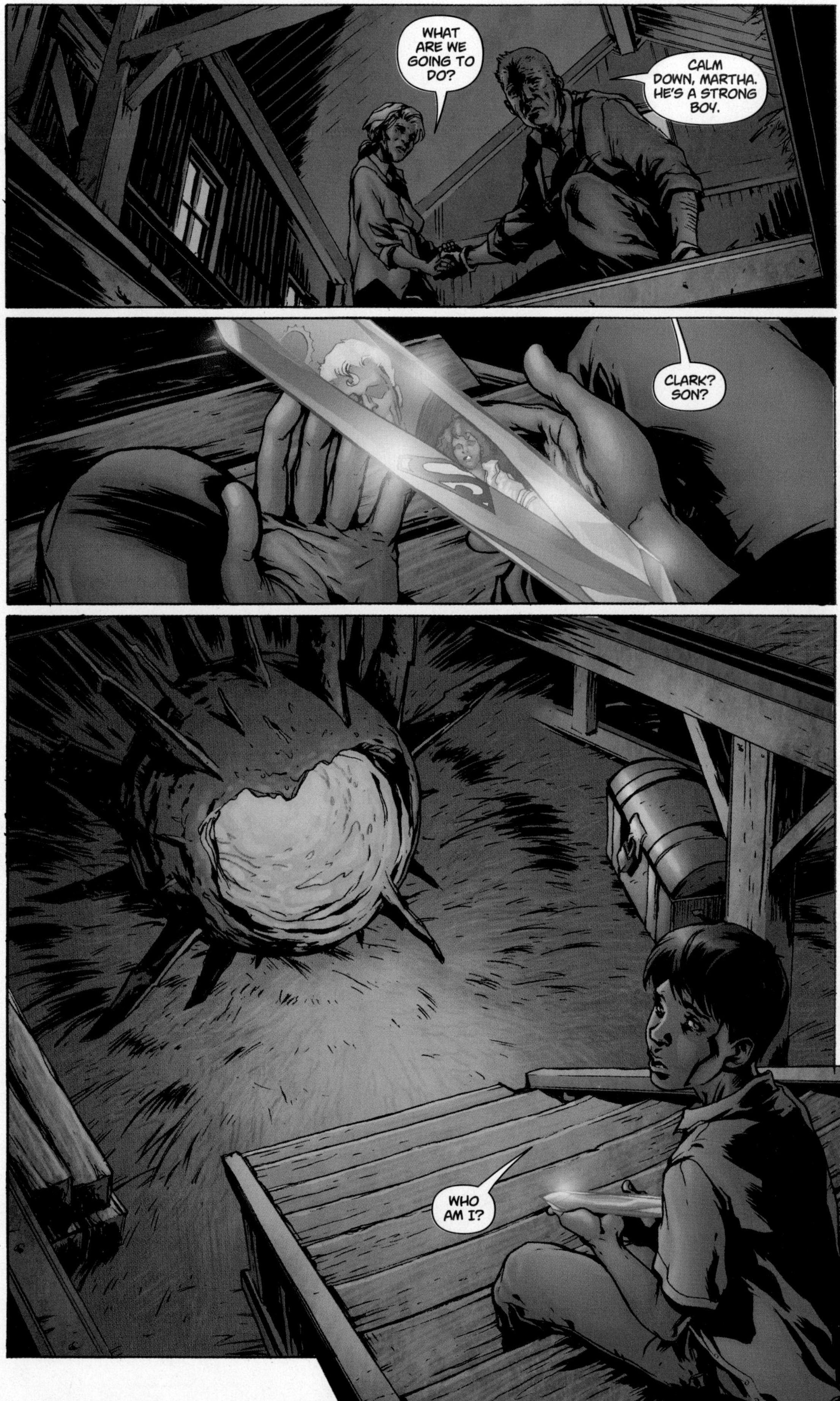
WHAT ARE WE GOING TO DO?
CALM DOWN, MARTHA. HE'S A STRONG BOY.
CLARK? SON?
WHO AM I?

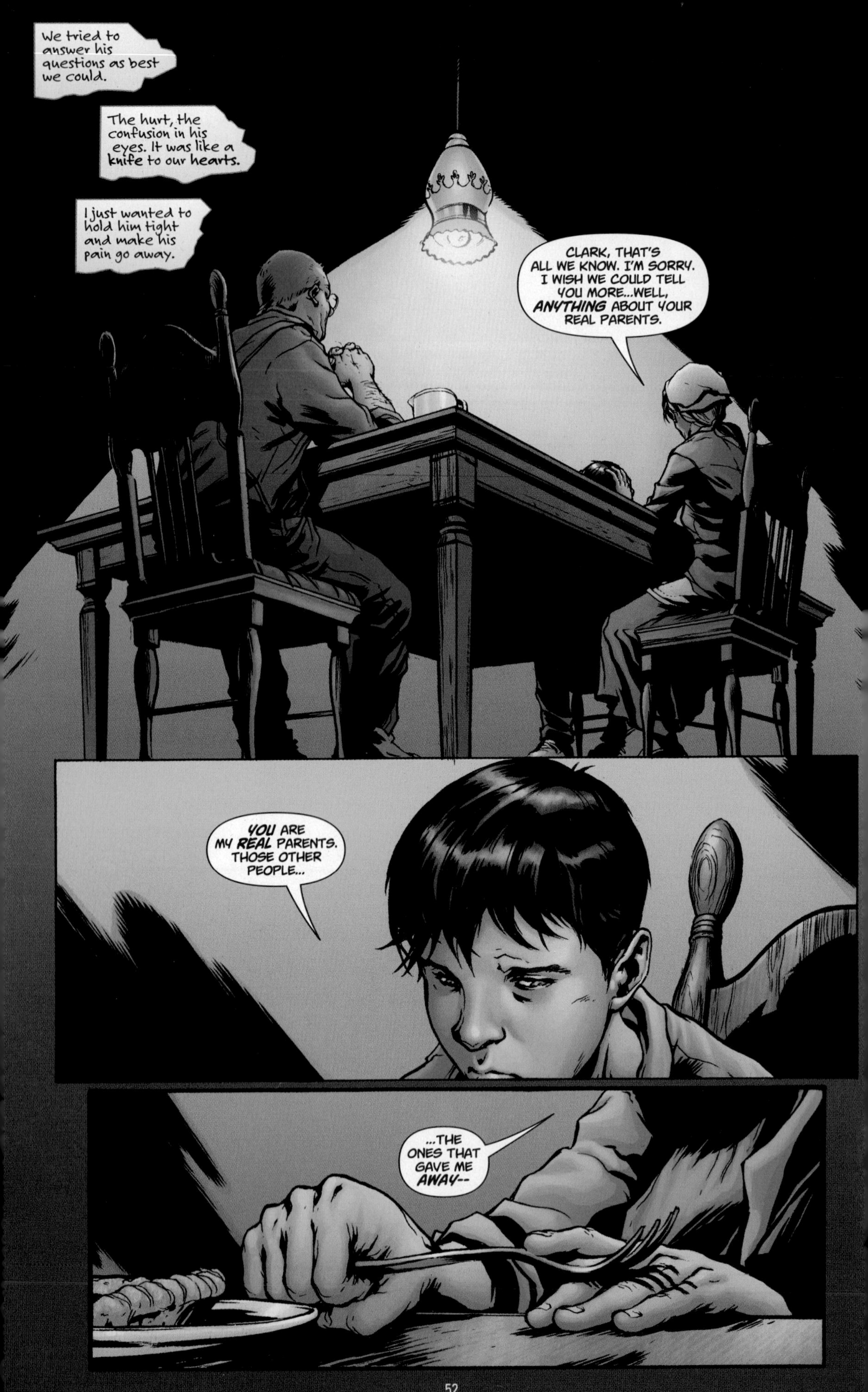
We tried to answer his questions as best we could.
The hurt, the confusion in his eyes. It was like a knife to our hearts.
I just wanted to hold him tight and make his pain go away.
CLARK, THAT'S ALL WE KNOW. I'M SORRY. I WISH WE COULD TELL YOU MORE...WELL, ANYTHING ABOUT YOUR REAL PARENTS.
YOU ARE MY REAL PARENTS. THOSE OTHER PEOPLE...
...THE ONES THAT GAVE ME AWAY--

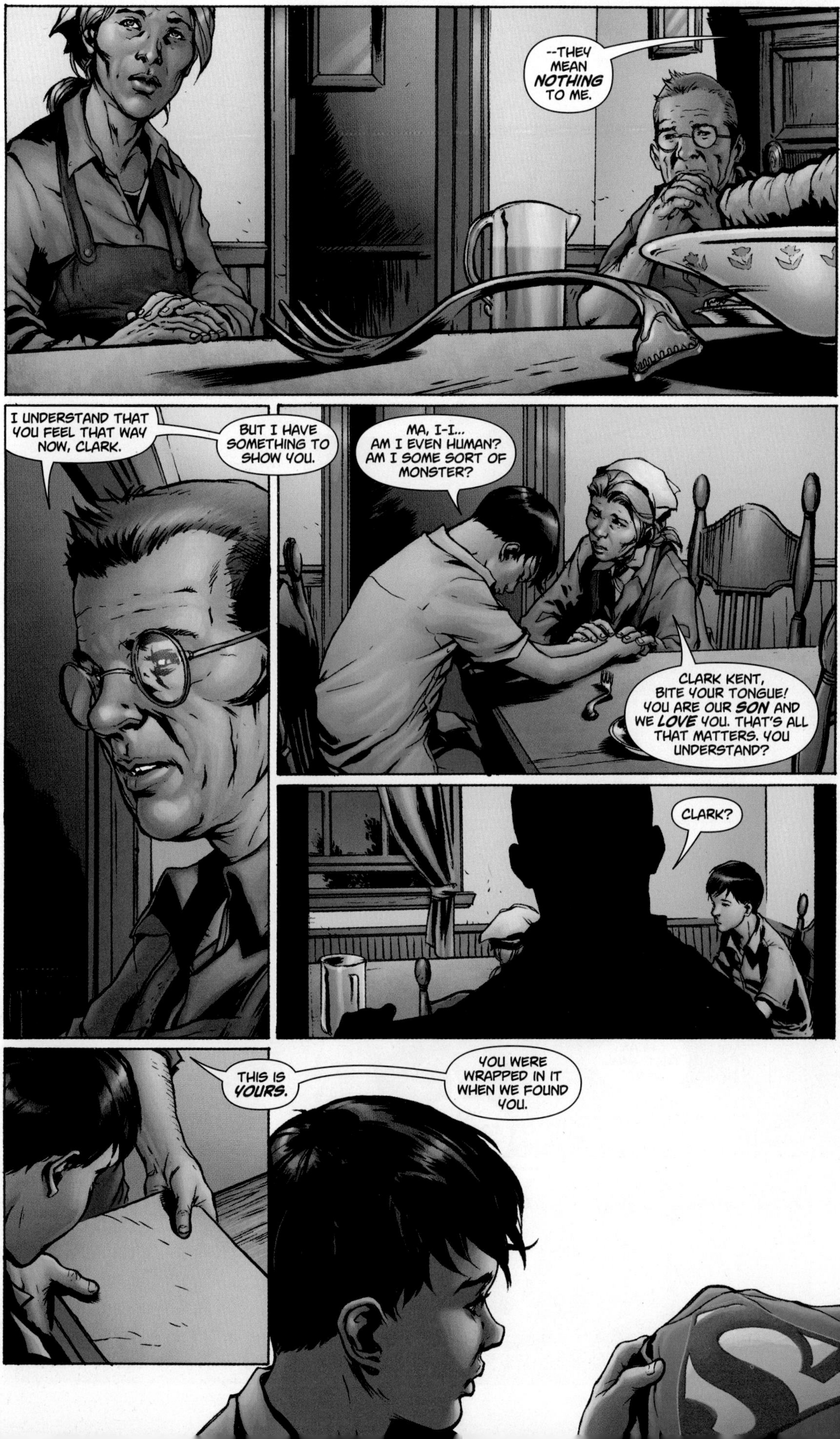
--THEY MEAN ***NOTHING*** TO ME.
I UNDERSTAND THAT YOU FEEL THAT WAY NOW, CLARK.
BUT I HAVE SOMETHING TO SHOW YOU.
MA, I-I... AM I EVEN HUMAN? AM I SOME SORT OF MONSTER?
CLARK KENT, BITE YOUR TONGUE! YOU ARE OUR ***SON*** AND WE ***LOVE*** YOU. THAT'S ALL THAT MATTERS. YOU UNDERSTAND?
CLARK?
THIS IS ***YOURS.***
YOU WERE WRAPPED IN IT WHEN WE FOUND YOU.

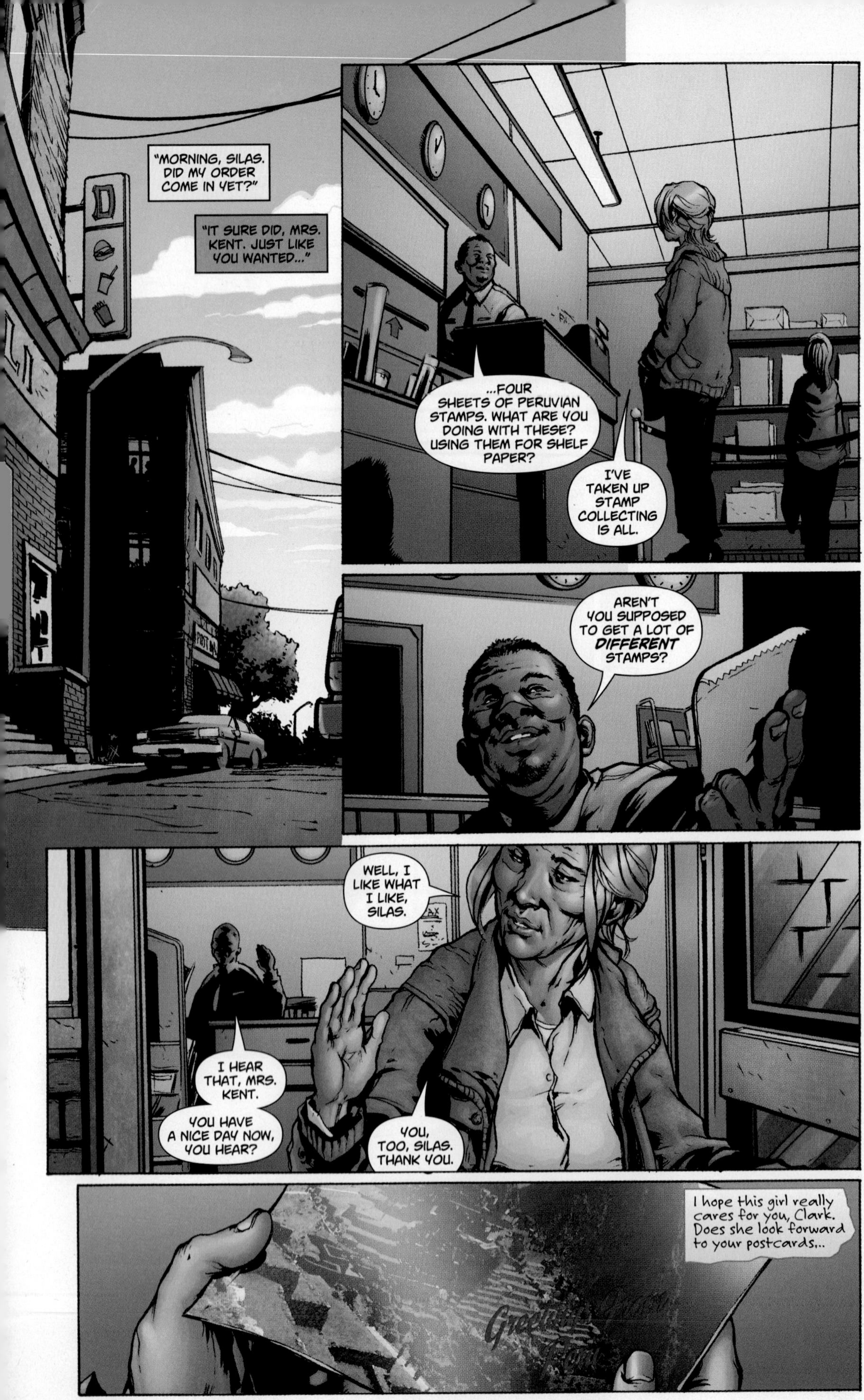
"MORNING, SILAS. DID MY ORDER COME IN YET?"
"IT SURE DID, MRS. KENT. JUST LIKE YOU WANTED..."
...FOUR SHEETS OF PERUVIAN STAMPS. WHAT ARE YOU DOING WITH THESE? USING THEM FOR SHELF PAPER?
I'VE TAKEN UP STAMP COLLECTING IS ALL.
AREN'T YOU SUPPOSED TO GET A LOT OF *DIFFERENT* STAMPS?
WELL, I LIKE WHAT I LIKE, SILAS.
I HEAR THAT, MRS. KENT.
YOU HAVE A NICE DAY NOW, YOU HEAR?
YOU, TOO, SILAS. THANK YOU.
I hope this girl really cares for you, Clark. Does she look forward to your postcards...

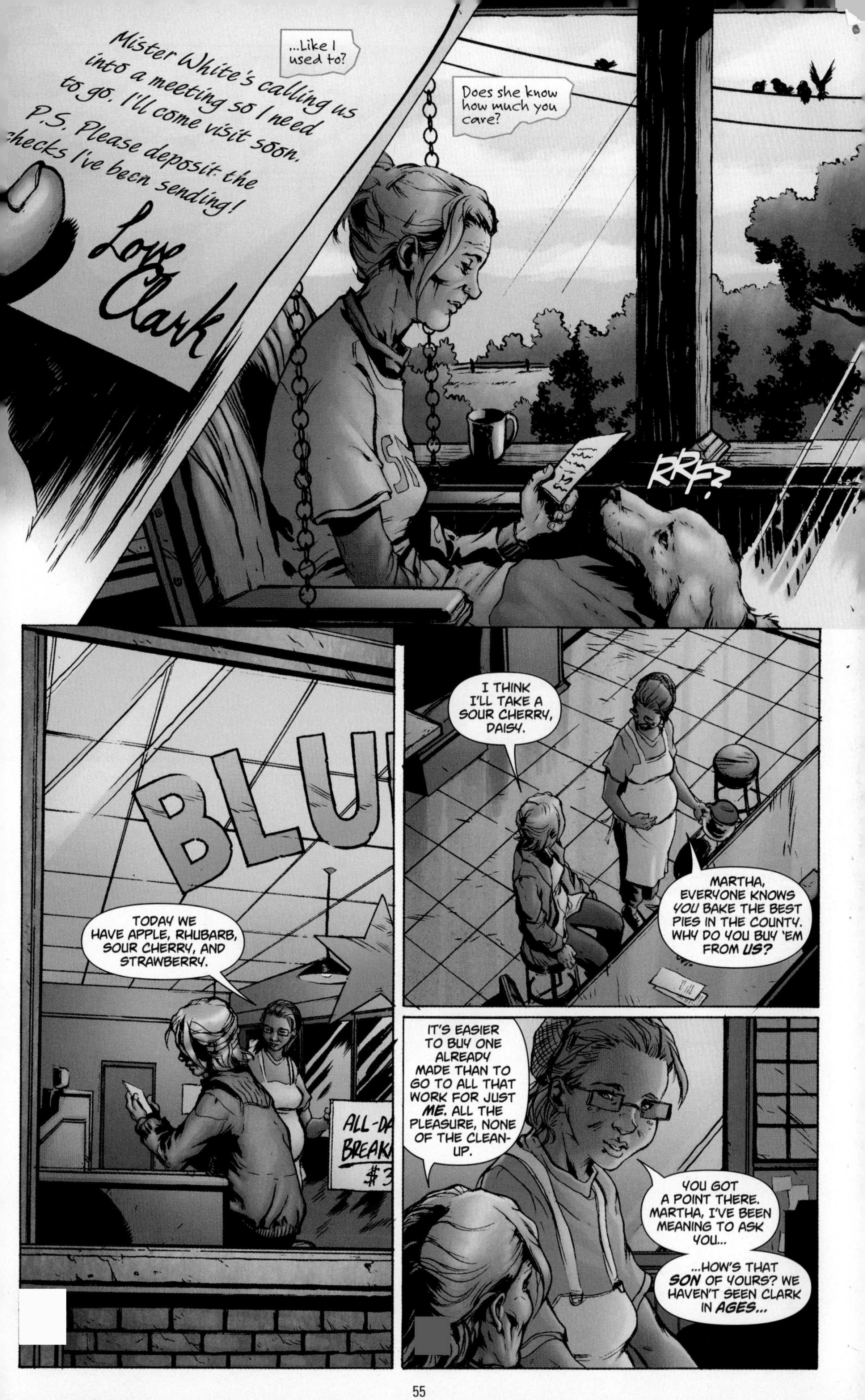

Mister White's calling us into a meeting so I need to go. I'll come visit soon.
P.S. Please deposit the checks I've been sending!
Love Clark
...Like I used to?
Does she know how much you care?
RRF?
TODAY WE HAVE APPLE, RHUBARB, SOUR CHERRY, AND STRAWBERRY.
I THINK I'LL TAKE A SOUR CHERRY, DAISY.
MARTHA, EVERYONE KNOWS YOU BAKE THE BEST PIES IN THE COUNTY. WHY DO YOU BUY 'EM FROM US?
IT'S EASIER TO BUY ONE ALREADY MADE THAN TO GO TO ALL THAT WORK FOR JUST ME. ALL THE PLEASURE, NONE OF THE CLEAN-UP.
YOU GOT A POINT THERE. MARTHA, I'VE BEEN MEANING TO ASK YOU...
...HOW'S THAT SON OF YOURS? WE HAVEN'T SEEN CLARK IN AGES...

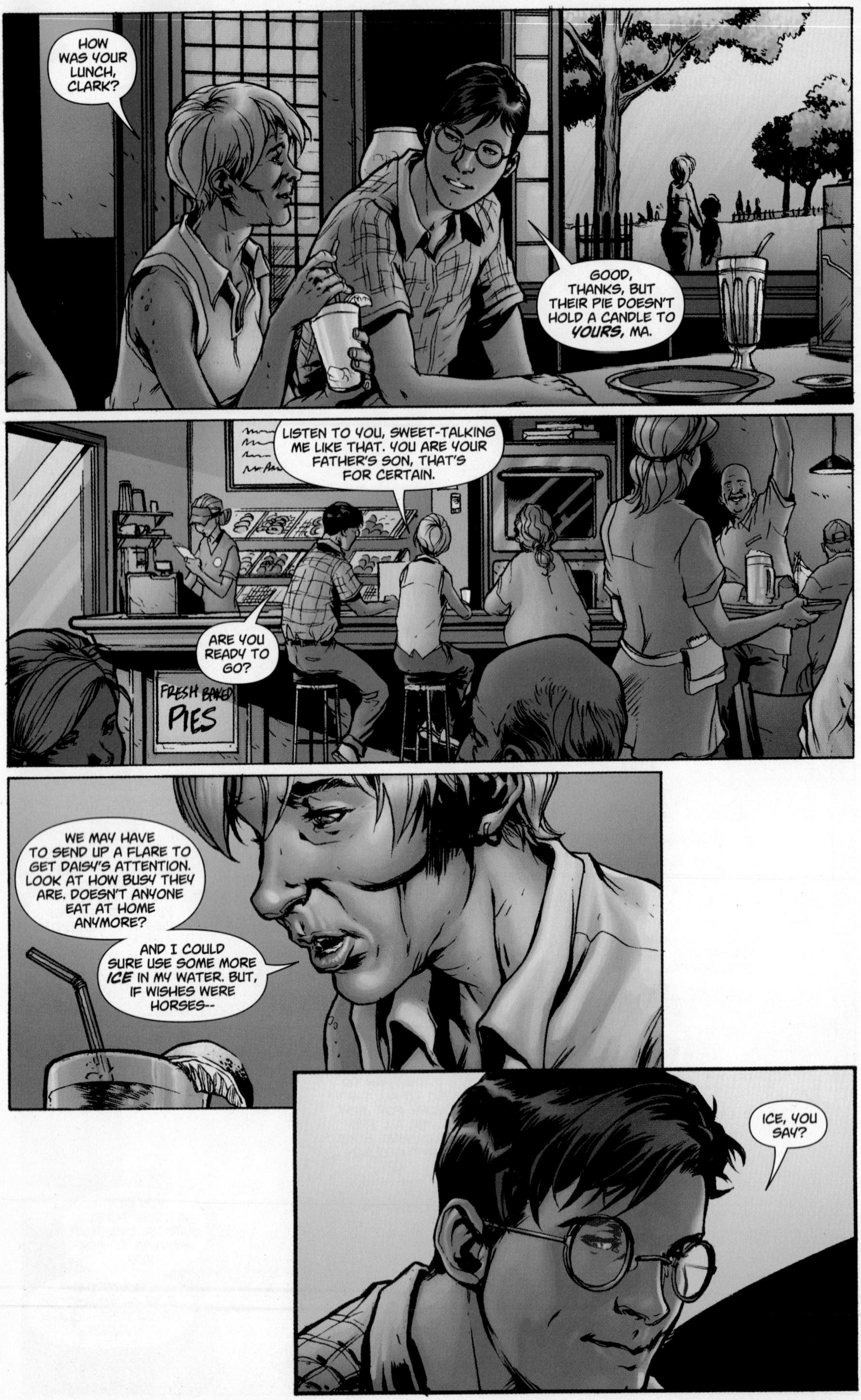
HOW WAS YOUR LUNCH, CLARK?
GOOD, THANKS, BUT THEIR PIE DOESN'T HOLD A CANDLE TO YOURS, MA.
LISTEN TO YOU, SWEET-TALKING ME LIKE THAT. YOU ARE YOUR FATHER'S SON, THAT'S FOR CERTAIN.
ARE YOU READY TO GO?
FRESH BAKED PIES
WE MAY HAVE TO SEND UP A FLARE TO GET DAISY'S ATTENTION. LOOK AT HOW BUSY THEY ARE. DOESN'T ANYONE EAT AT HOME ANYMORE?
AND I COULD SURE USE SOME MORE ICE IN MY WATER. BUT, IF WISHES WERE HORSES--
ICE, YOU SAY?

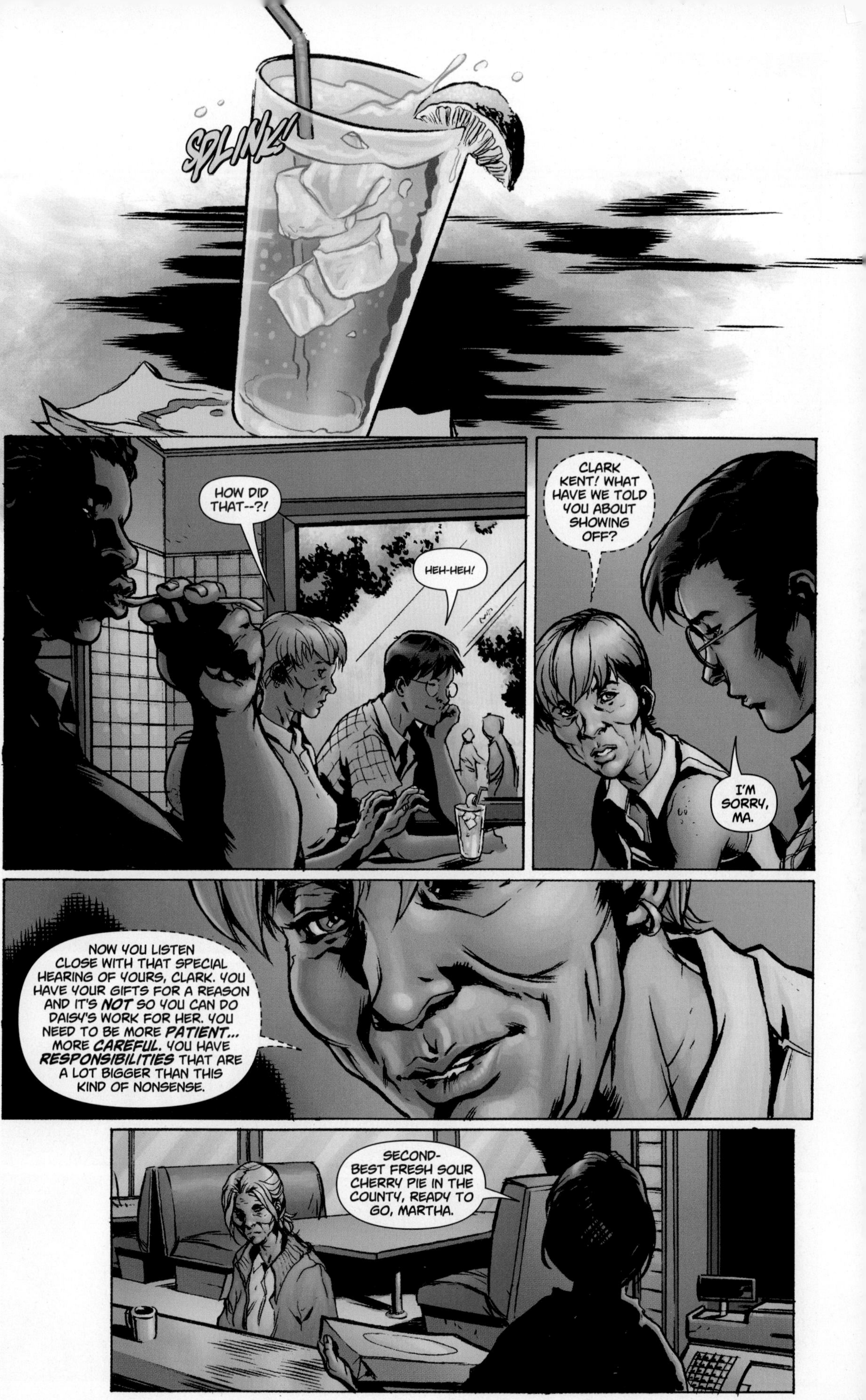
SPLINK!
HOW DID THAT--?!
HEH-HEH!
CLARK KENT! WHAT HAVE WE TOLD YOU ABOUT SHOWING OFF?
I'M SORRY, MA.
NOW YOU LISTEN CLOSE WITH THAT SPECIAL HEARING OF YOURS, CLARK. YOU HAVE YOUR GIFTS FOR A REASON AND IT'S **NOT** SO YOU CAN DO DAISY'S WORK FOR HER. YOU NEED TO BE MORE **PATIENT...** MORE **CAREFUL.** YOU HAVE **RESPONSIBILITIES** THAT ARE A LOT BIGGER THAN THIS KIND OF NONSENSE.
SECOND-BEST FRESH SOUR CHERRY PIE IN THE COUNTY, READY TO GO, MARTHA.

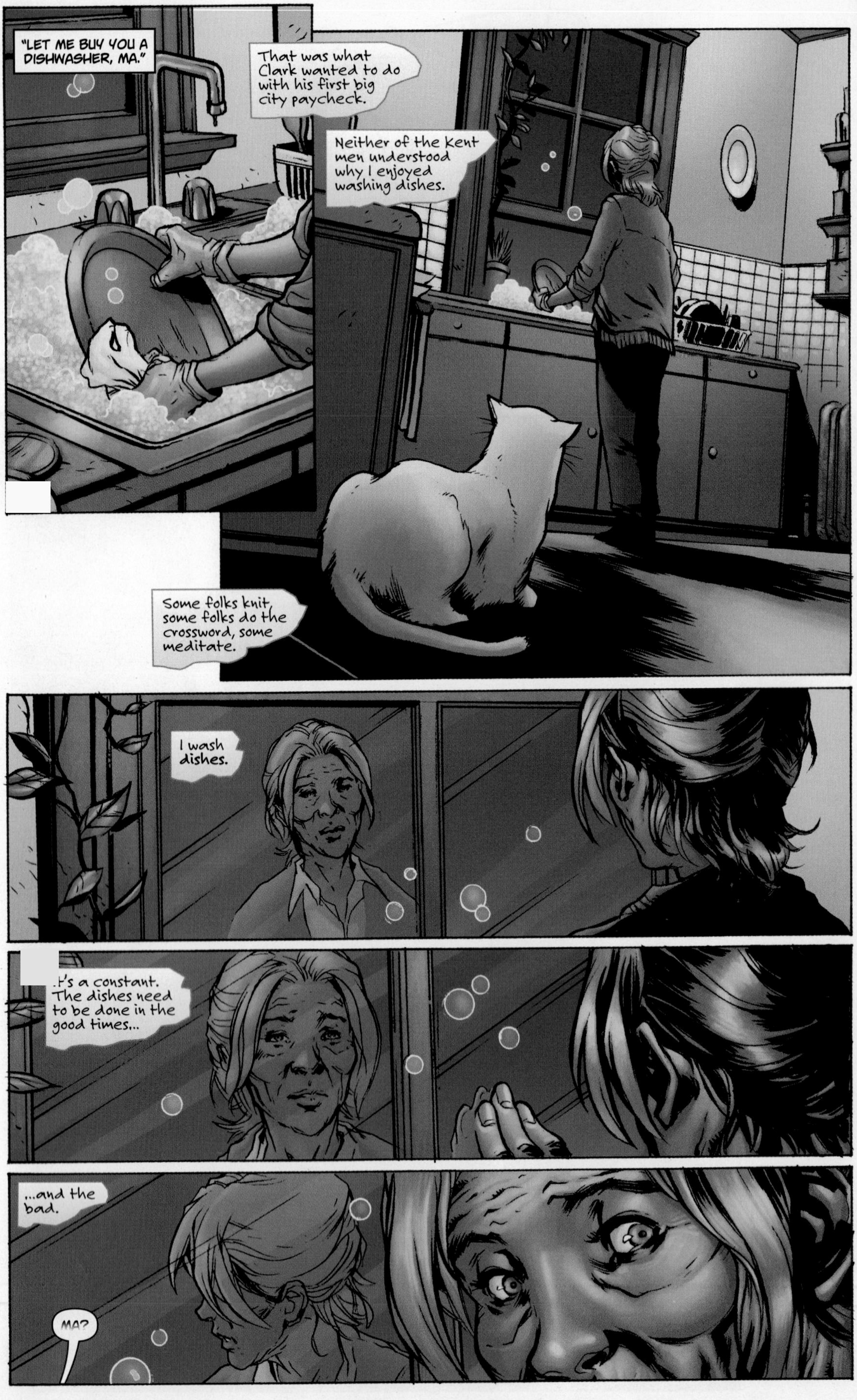
"LET ME BUY YOU A DISHWASHER, MA."
That was what Clark wanted to do with his first big city paycheck.
Neither of the Kent men understood why I enjoyed washing dishes.
Some folks knit, some folks do the crossword, some meditate.
I wash dishes.
t's a constant. The dishes need to be done in the good times...
...and the bad.
MA?

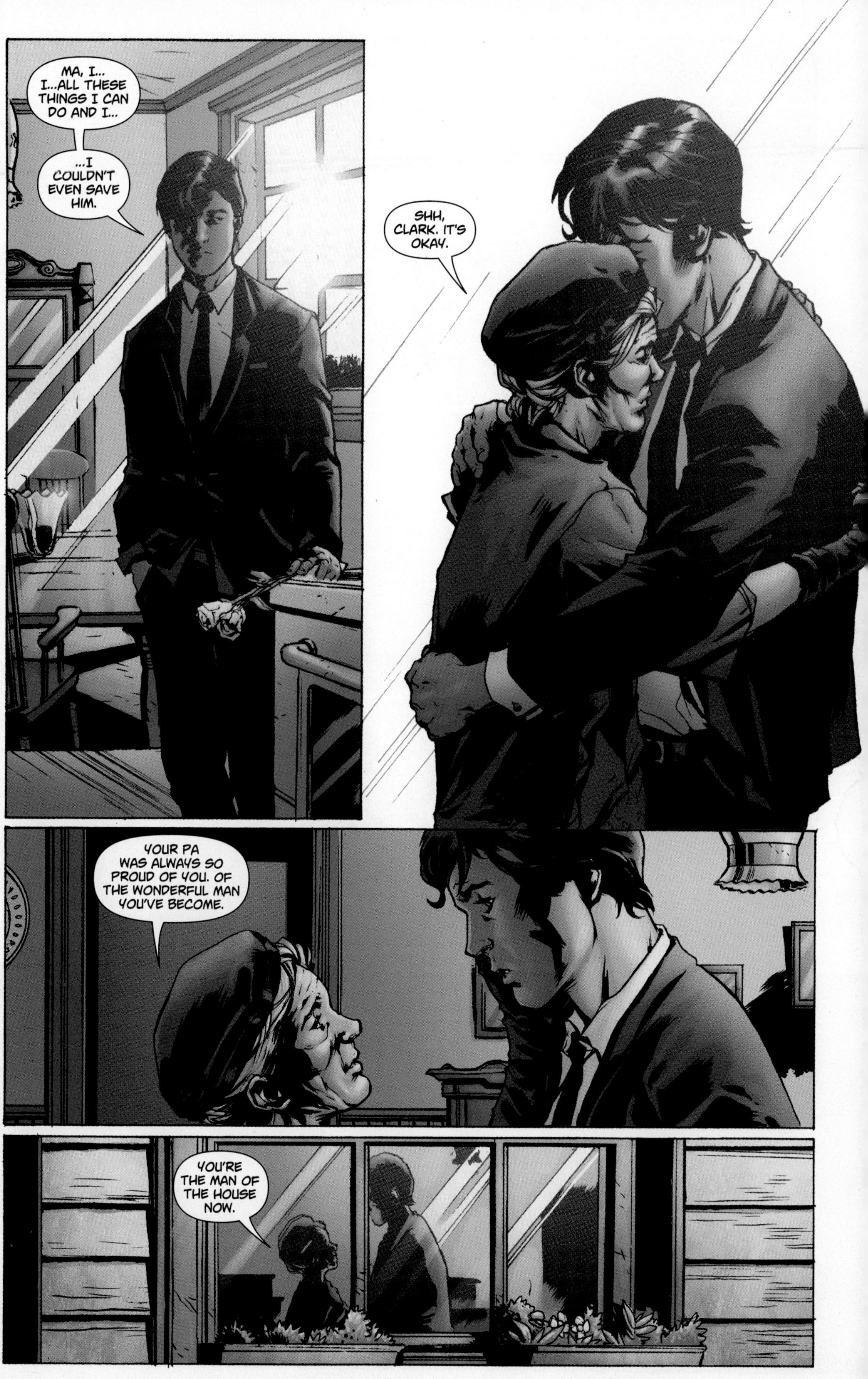
MA, I... I...ALL THESE THINGS I CAN DO AND I...
...I COULDN'T EVEN SAVE HIM.
SHH, CLARK. IT'S OKAY.
YOUR PA WAS ALWAYS SO PROUD OF YOU. OF THE WONDERFUL MAN YOU'VE BECOME.
YOU'RE THE MAN OF THE HOUSE NOW.

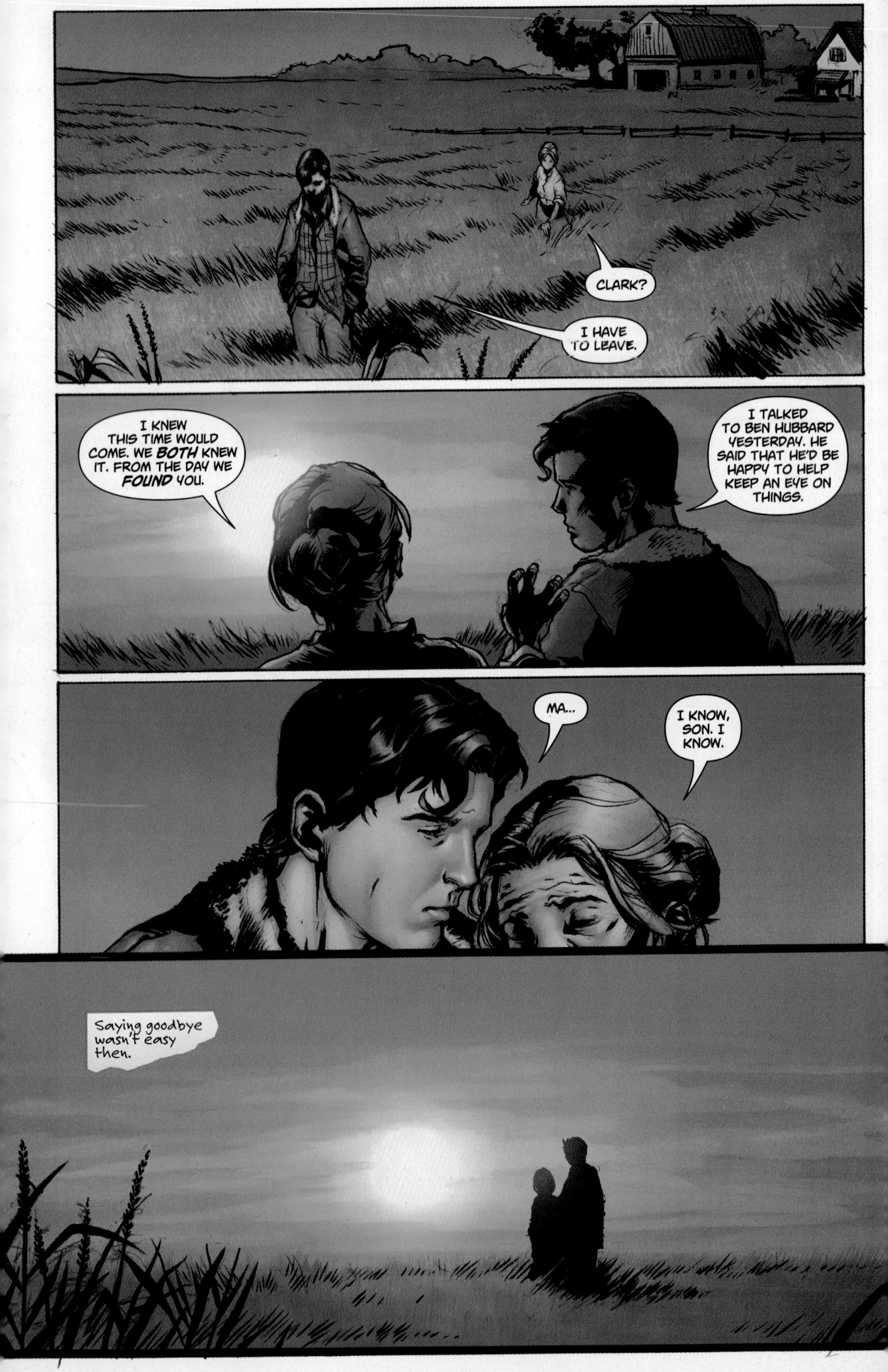
CLARK?
I HAVE TO LEAVE.
I KNEW THIS TIME WOULD COME. WE **BOTH** KNEW IT. FROM THE DAY WE **FOUND** YOU.
I TALKED TO BEN HUBBARD YESTERDAY. HE SAID THAT HE'D BE HAPPY TO HELP KEEP AN EYE ON THINGS.
MA...
I KNOW, SON. I KNOW.
Saying goodbye wasn't easy then.

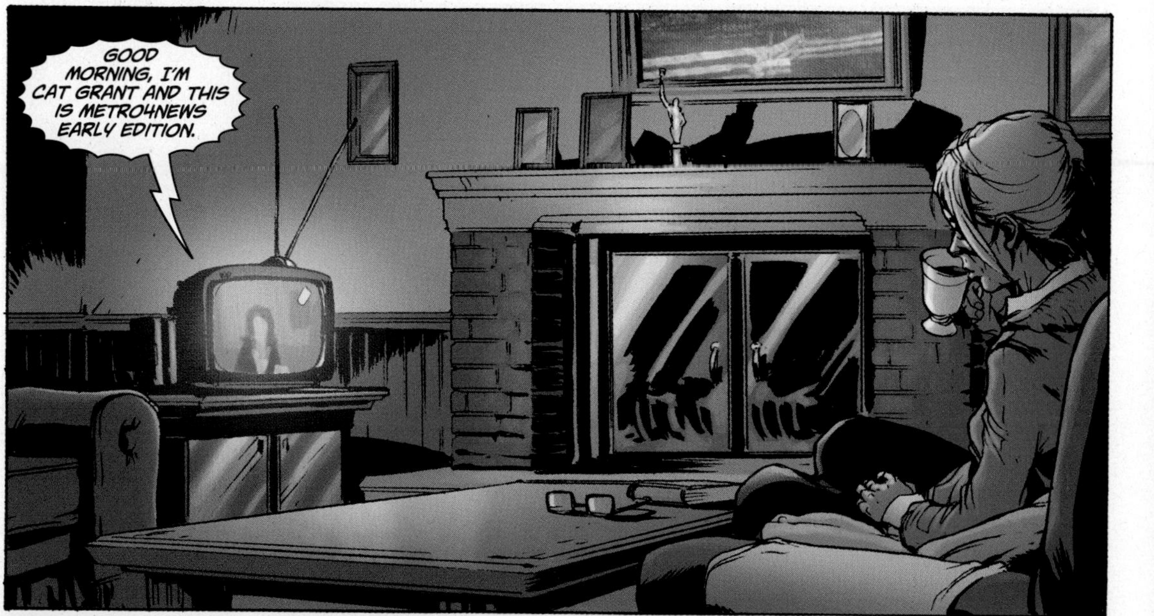
GOOD MORNING, I'M CAT GRANT AND THIS IS METRO4NEWS EARLY EDITION.

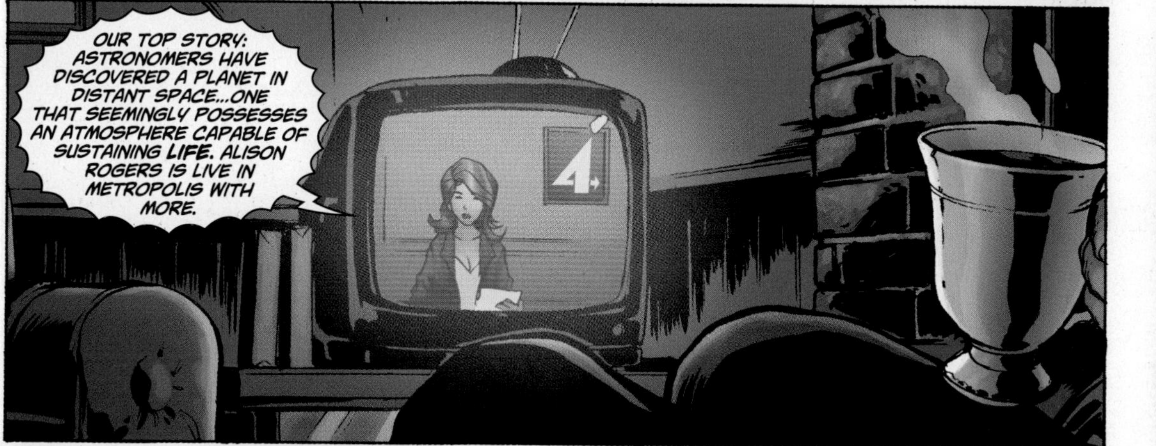
OUR TOP STORY: ASTRONOMERS HAVE DISCOVERED A PLANET IN DISTANT SPACE...ONE THAT SEEMINGLY POSSESSES AN ATMOSPHERE CAPABLE OF SUSTAINING LIFE. ALISON ROGERS IS LIVE IN METROPOLIS WITH MORE.

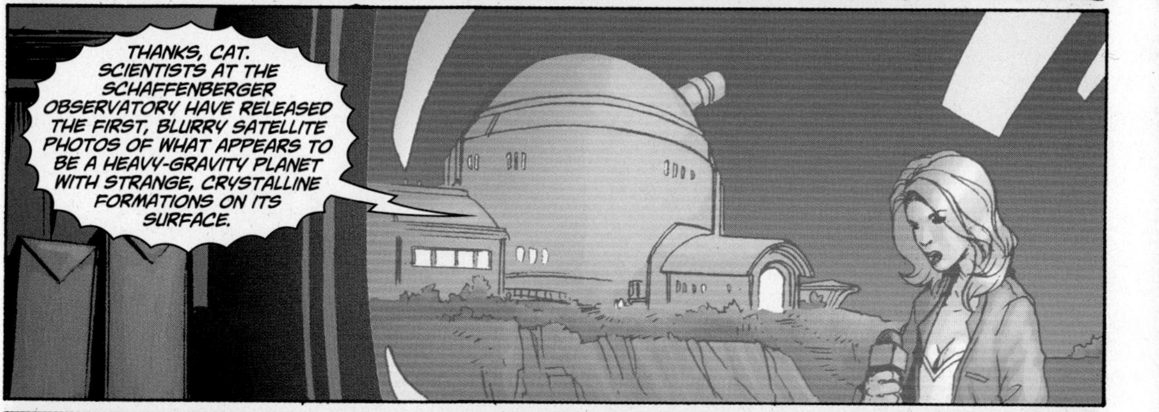
THANKS, CAT. SCIENTISTS AT THE SCHAFFENBERGER OBSERVATORY HAVE RELEASED THE FIRST, BLURRY SATELLITE PHOTOS OF WHAT APPEARS TO BE A HEAVY-GRAVITY PLANET WITH STRANGE, CRYSTALLINE FORMATIONS ON ITS SURFACE.

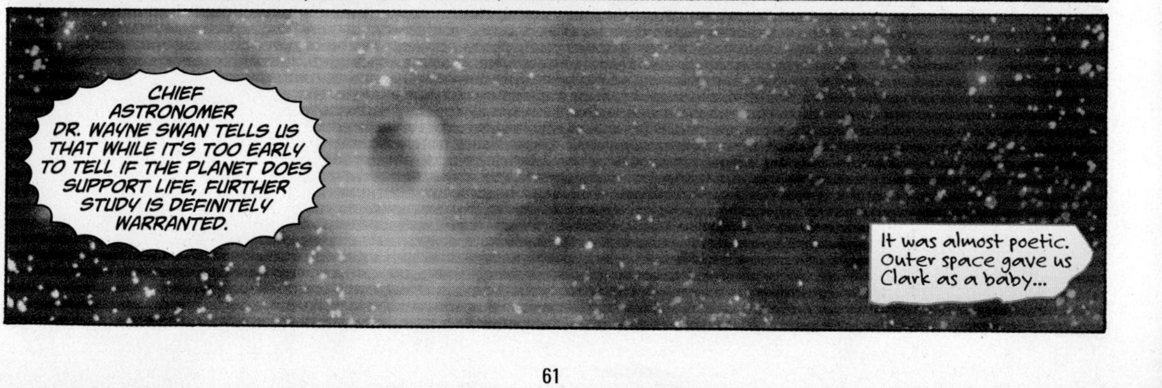
CHIEF ASTRONOMER DR. WAYNE SWAN TELLS US THAT WHILE IT'S TOO EARLY TO TELL IF THE PLANET DOES SUPPORT LIFE, FURTHER STUDY IS DEFINITELY WARRANTED.
It was almost poetic. Outer space gave us Clark as a baby...

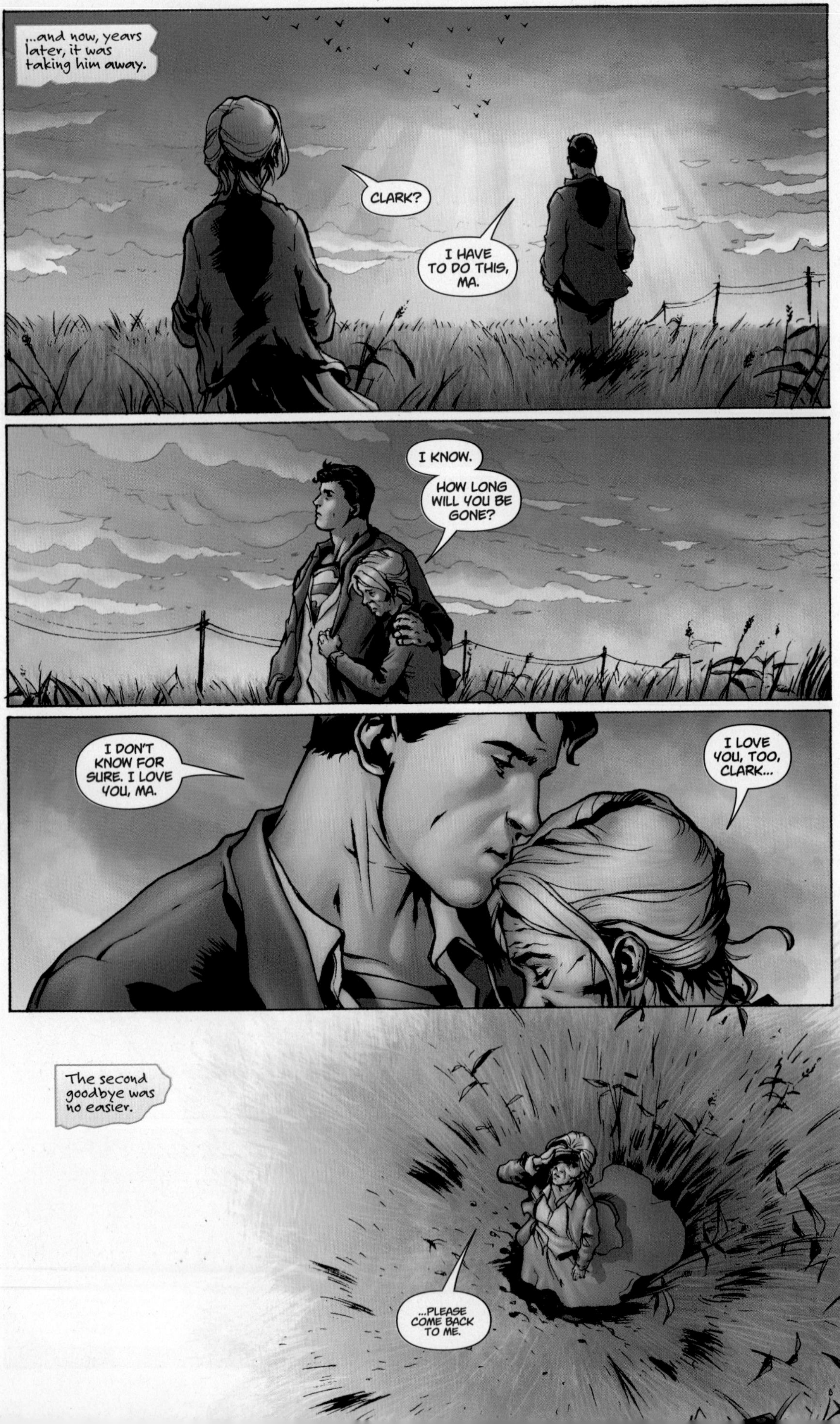
...and now, years later, it was taking him away.
CLARK?
I HAVE TO DO THIS, MA.
I KNOW.
HOW LONG WILL YOU BE GONE?
I DON'T KNOW FOR SURE. I LOVE YOU, MA.
I LOVE YOU, TOO, CLARK...
The second goodbye was no easier.
...PLEASE COME BACK TO ME.

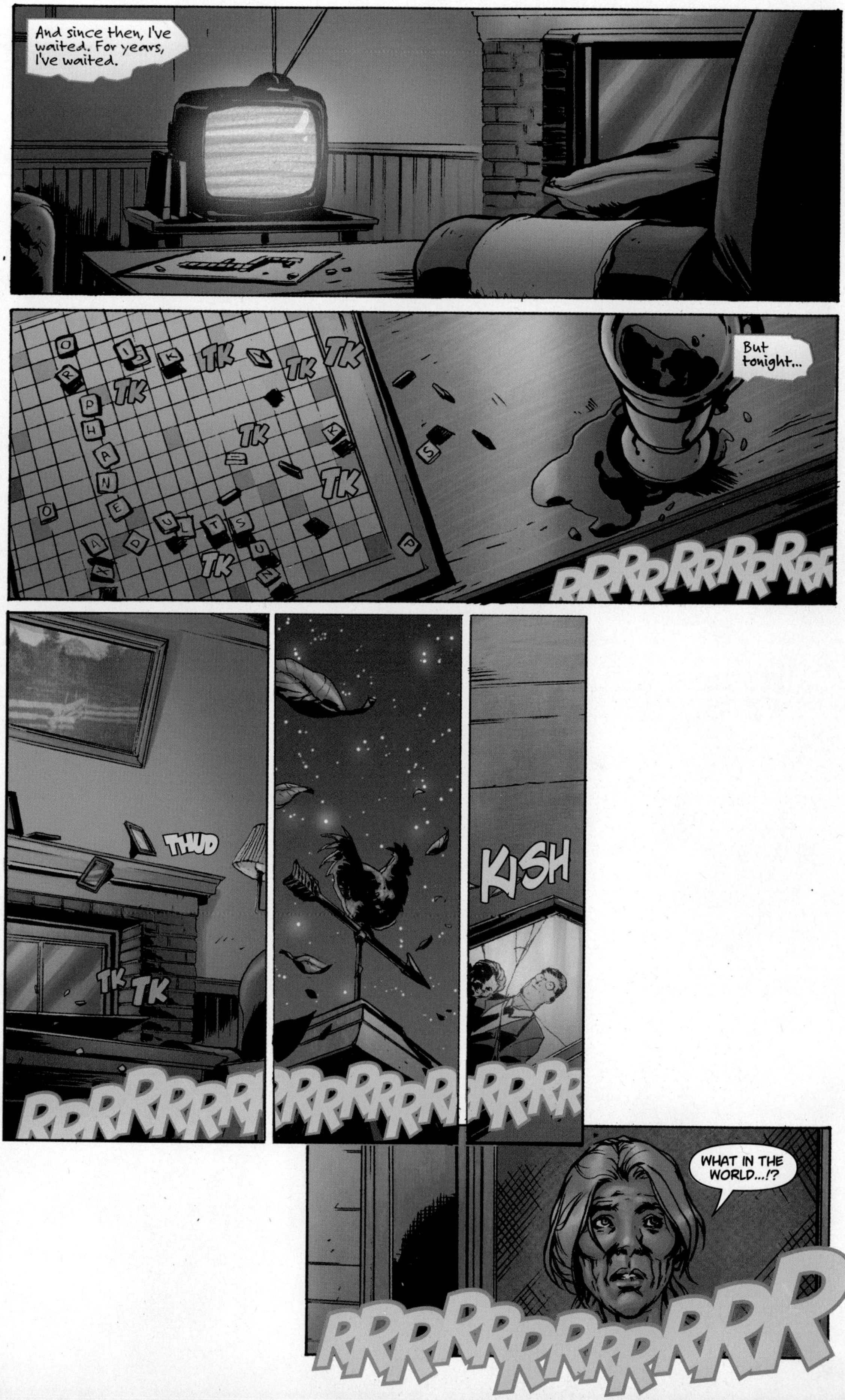

And since then, I've waited. For years, I've waited.
But tonight...
TK
RRRRRRRRRRR
THUD
TK TK
RRRRRRRR
RRRRRRRRR
KISH
RRRRR
WHAT IN THE WORLD...!?
RRRRRRRRRRRRRR

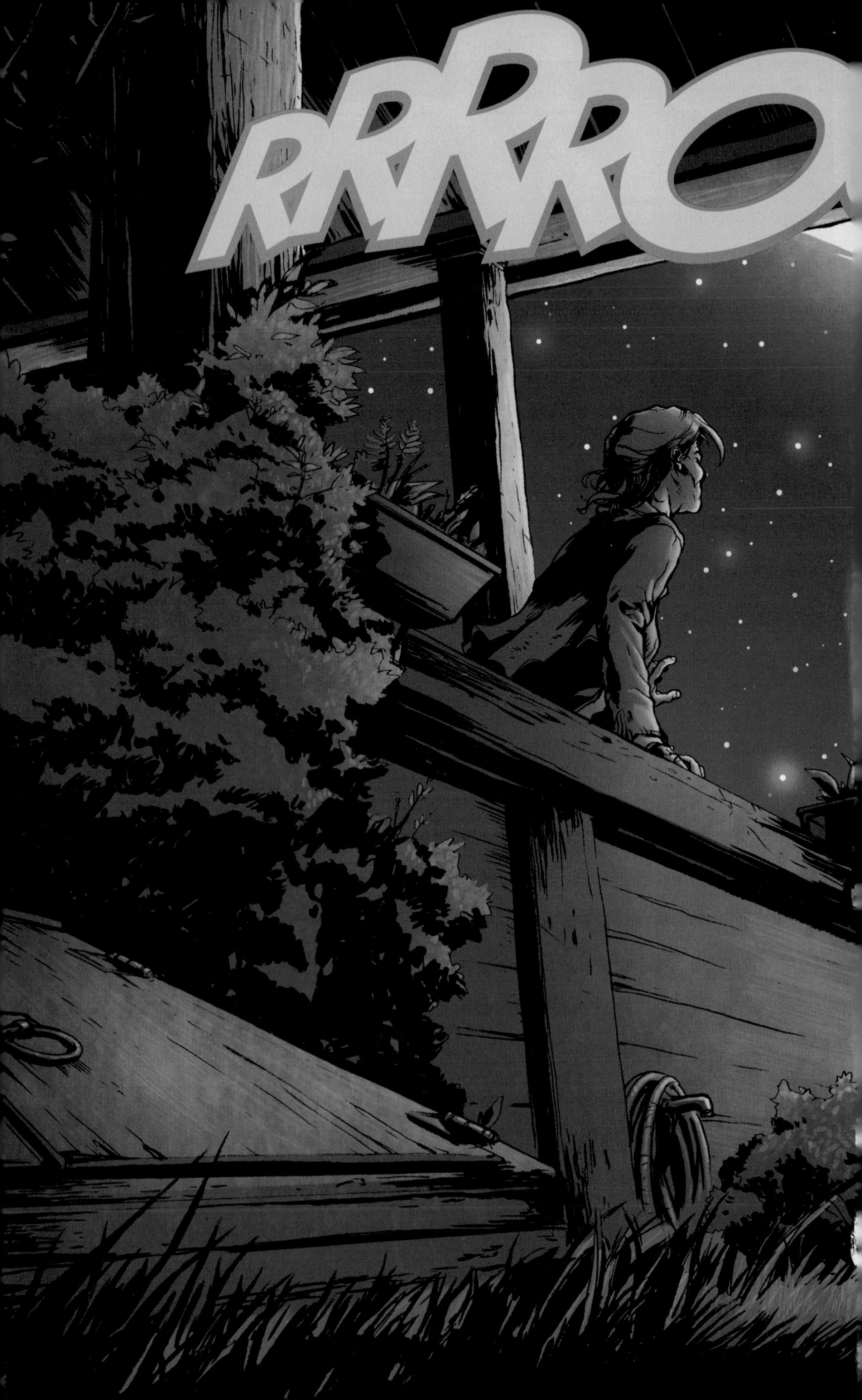
RRRRO

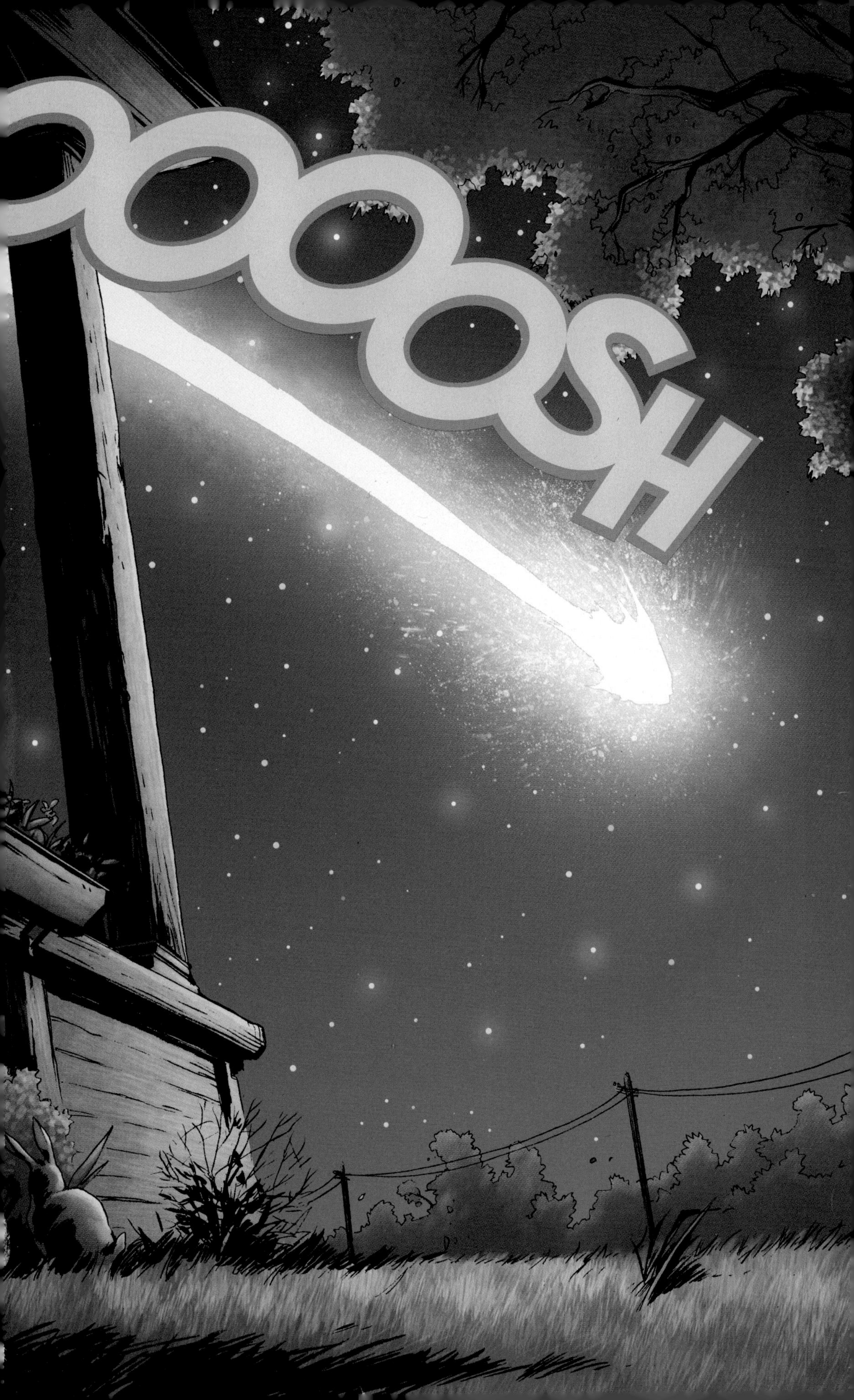
OOOOSH

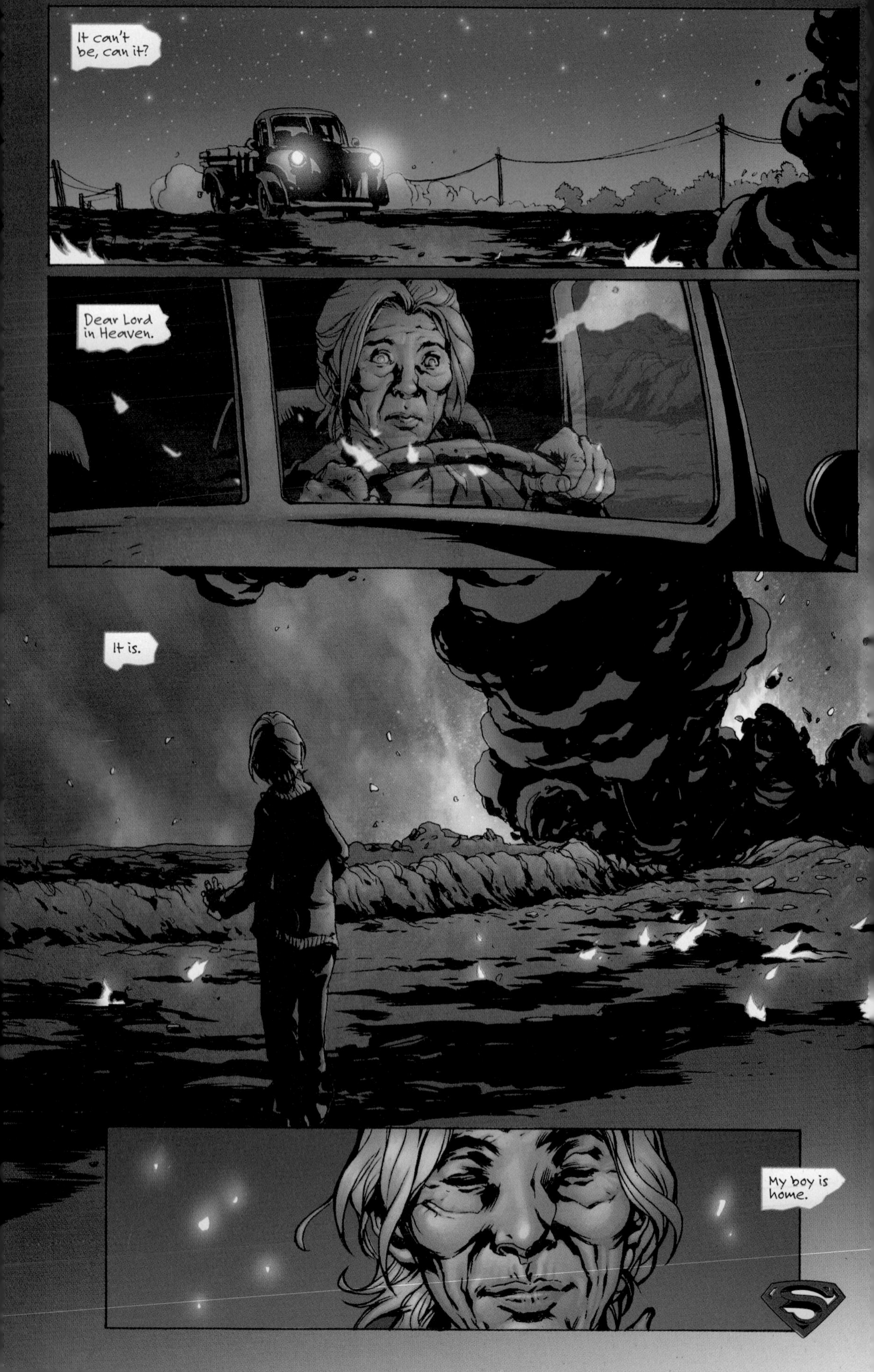
It can't be, can it?
Dear Lord in Heaven.
It is.
My boy is home.

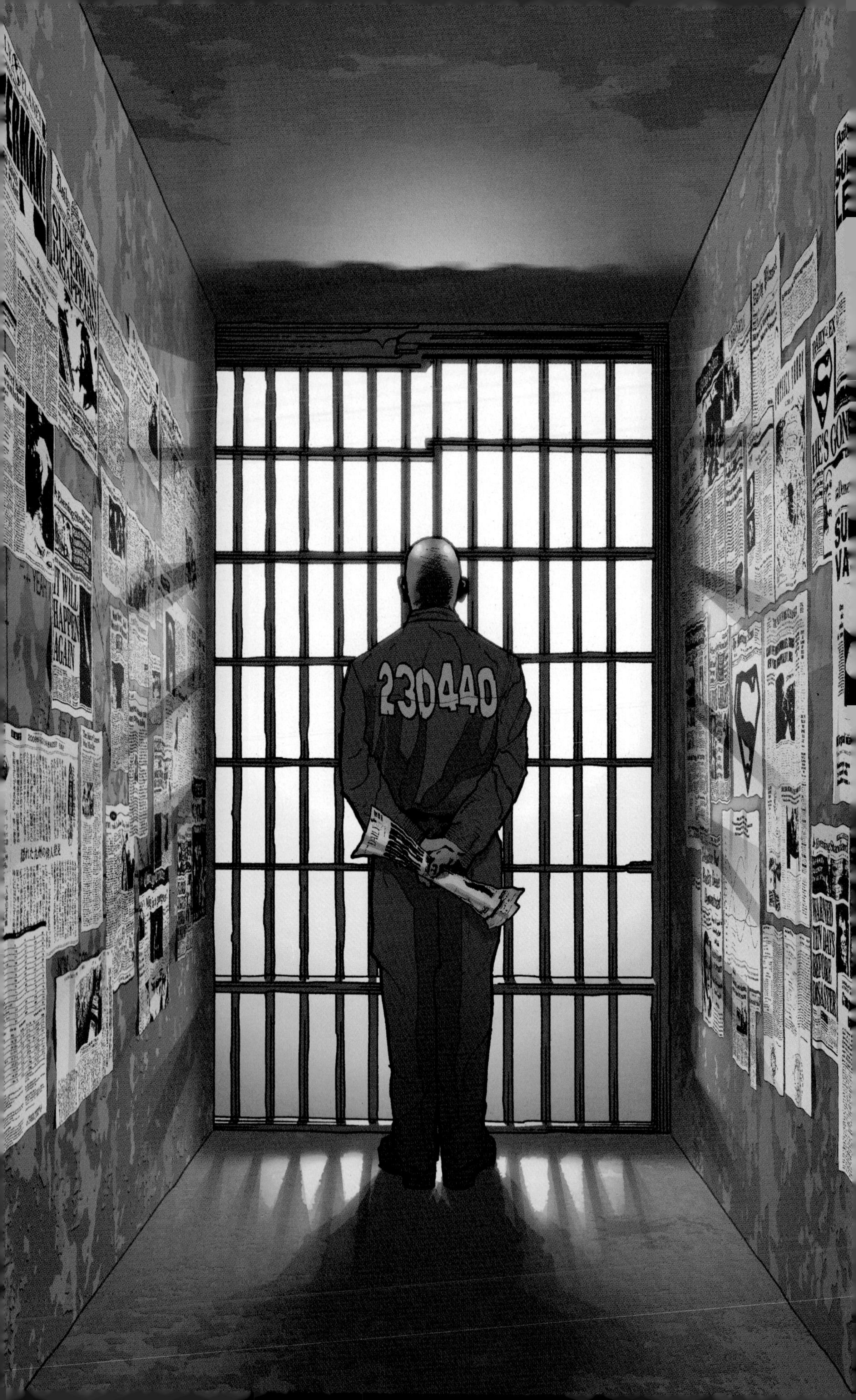
SUPERMAN DISAPPEARS
IT WILL HAPPEN AGAIN
230440
HE'S GONE
WARNED TEN DAYS BEFORE DISASTER

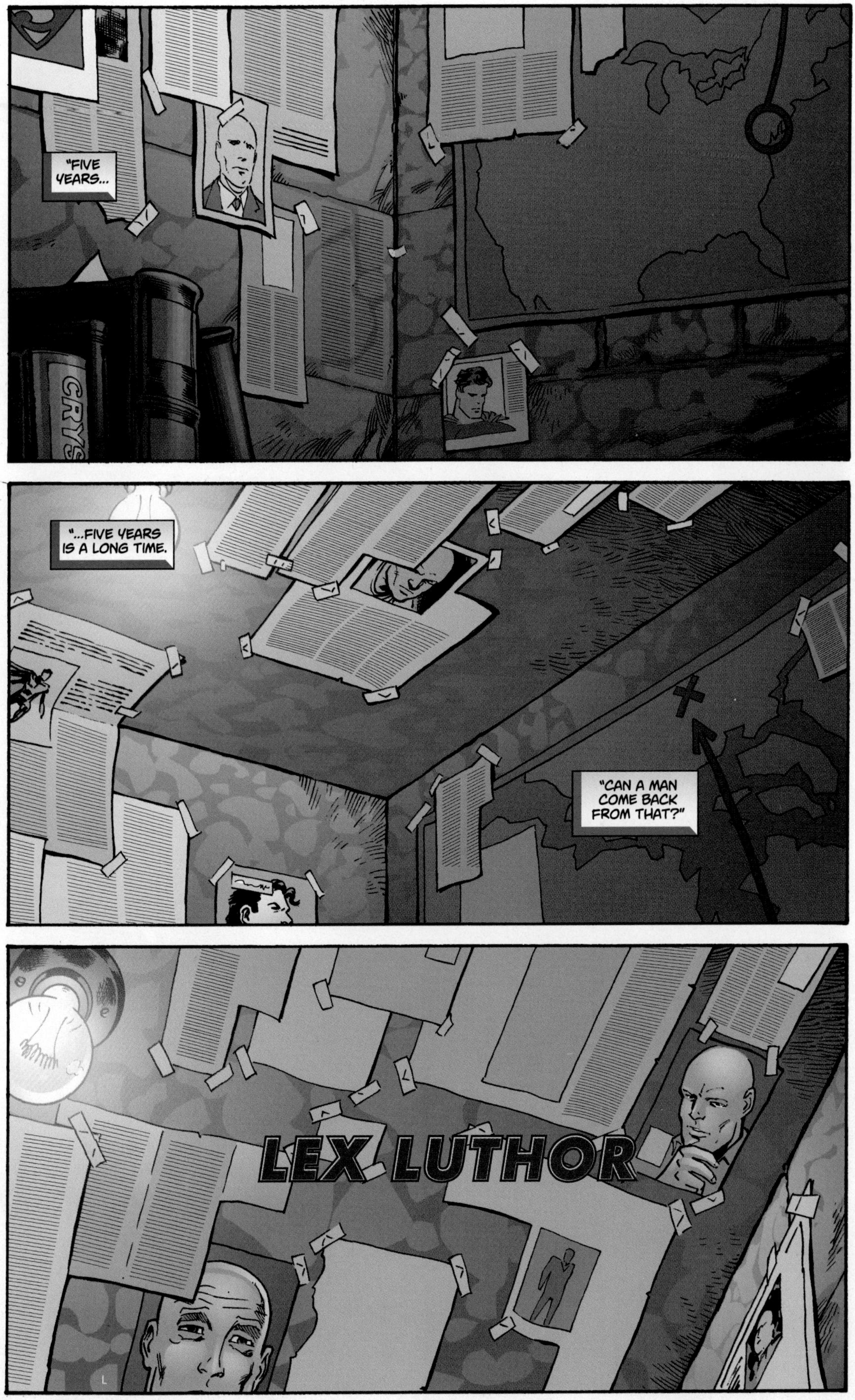
"FIVE YEARS...
CRYS
"...FIVE YEARS IS A LONG TIME.
"CAN A MAN COME BACK FROM THAT?"
LEX LUTHOR

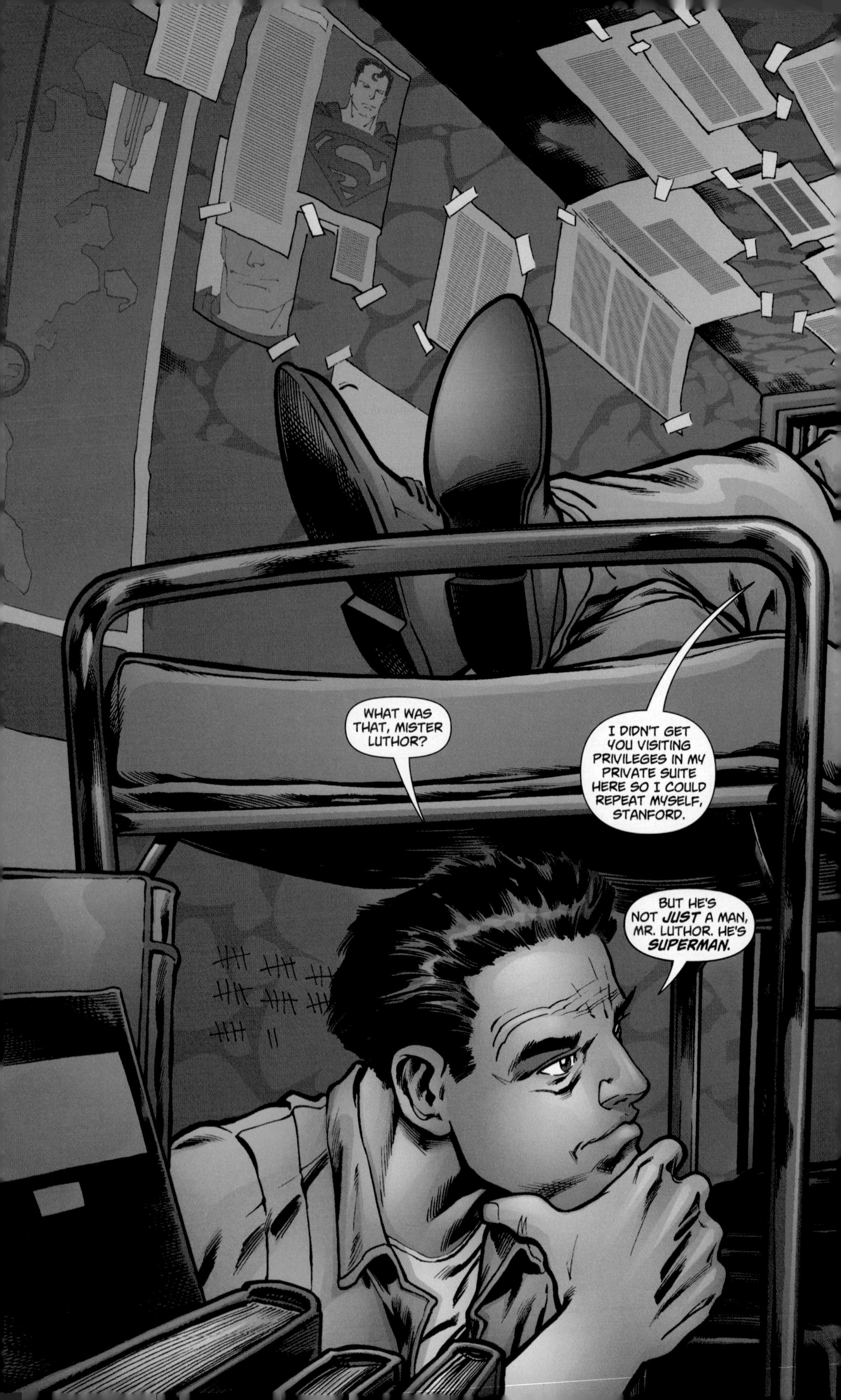
WHAT WAS THAT, MISTER LUTHOR?
I DIDN'T GET YOU VISITING PRIVILEGES IN MY PRIVATE SUITE HERE SO I COULD REPEAT MYSELF, STANFORD.
BUT HE'S NOT JUST A MAN, MR. LUTHOR. HE'S SUPERMAN.

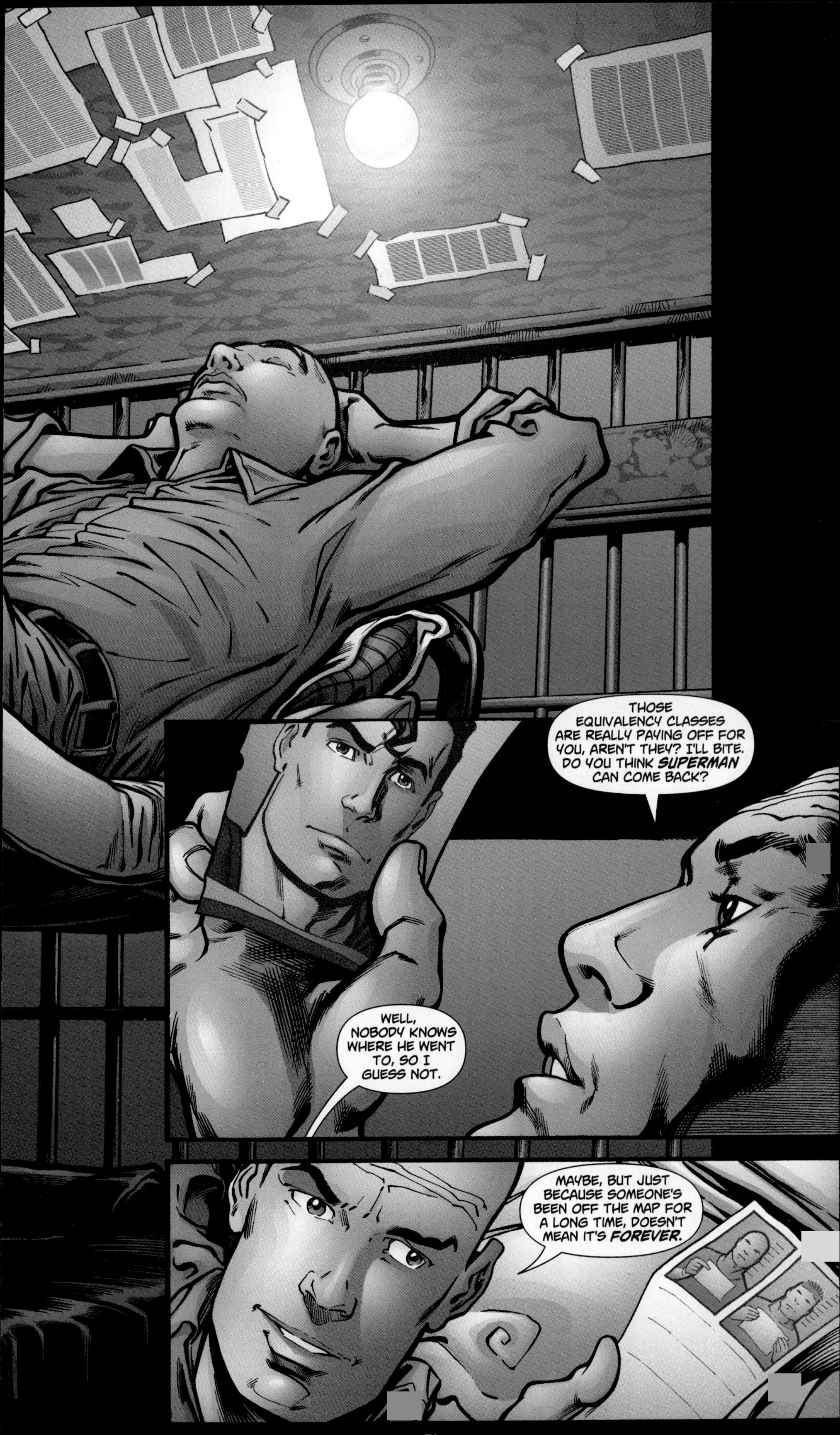
THOSE EQUIVALENCY CLASSES ARE REALLY PAYING OFF FOR YOU, AREN'T THEY? I'LL BITE. DO YOU THINK **SUPERMAN** CAN COME BACK?
WELL, NOBODY KNOWS WHERE HE WENT TO, SO I GUESS NOT.
MAYBE, BUT JUST BECAUSE SOMEONE'S BEEN OFF THE MAP FOR A LONG TIME, DOESN'T MEAN IT'S **FOREVER.**

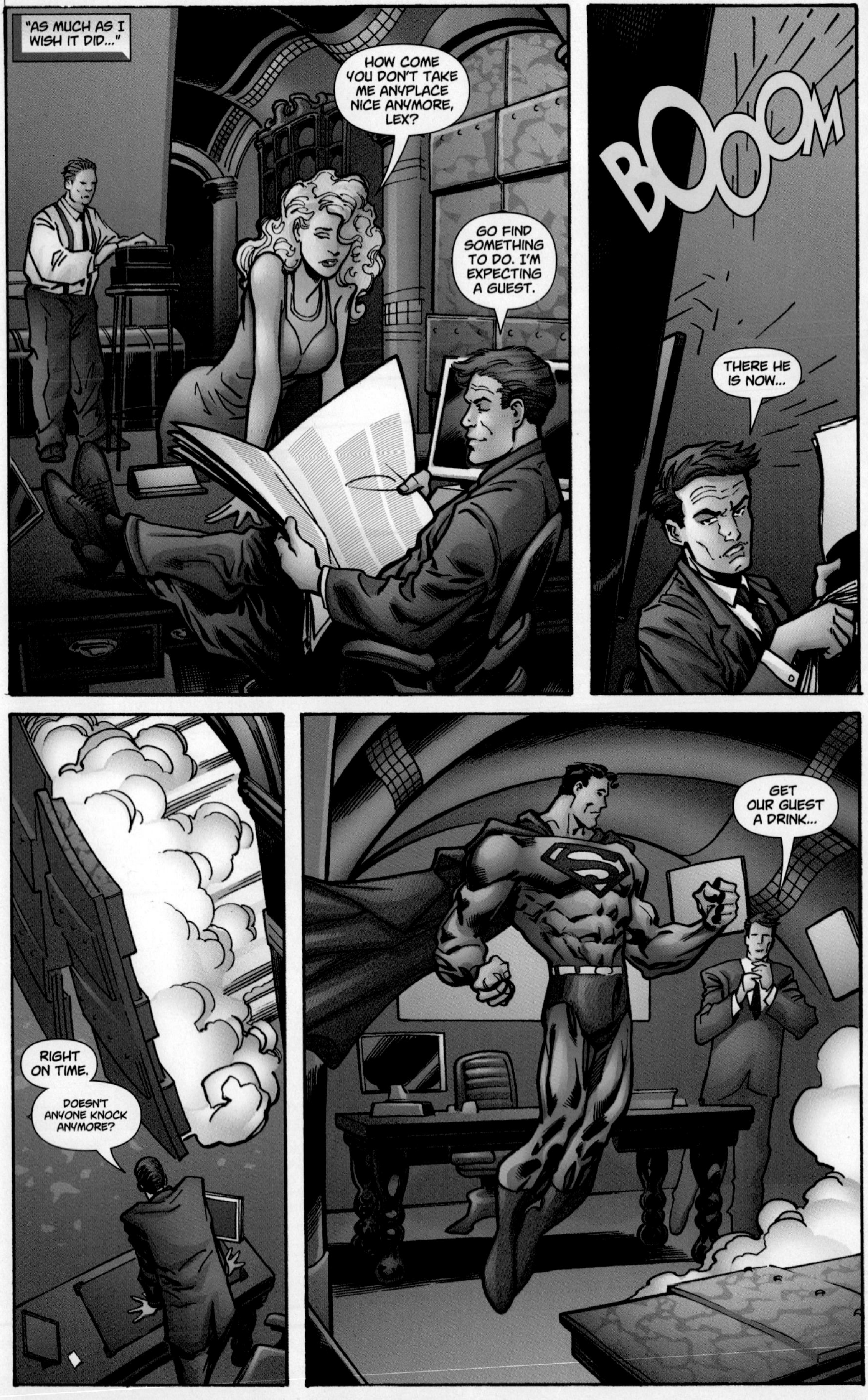
"AS MUCH AS I WISH IT DID..."
HOW COME YOU DON'T TAKE ME ANYPLACE NICE ANYMORE, LEX?
GO FIND SOMETHING TO DO. I'M EXPECTING A GUEST.
BOOOOM
THERE HE IS NOW...
RIGHT ON TIME.
DOESN'T ANYONE KNOCK ANYMORE?
GET OUR GUEST A DRINK...

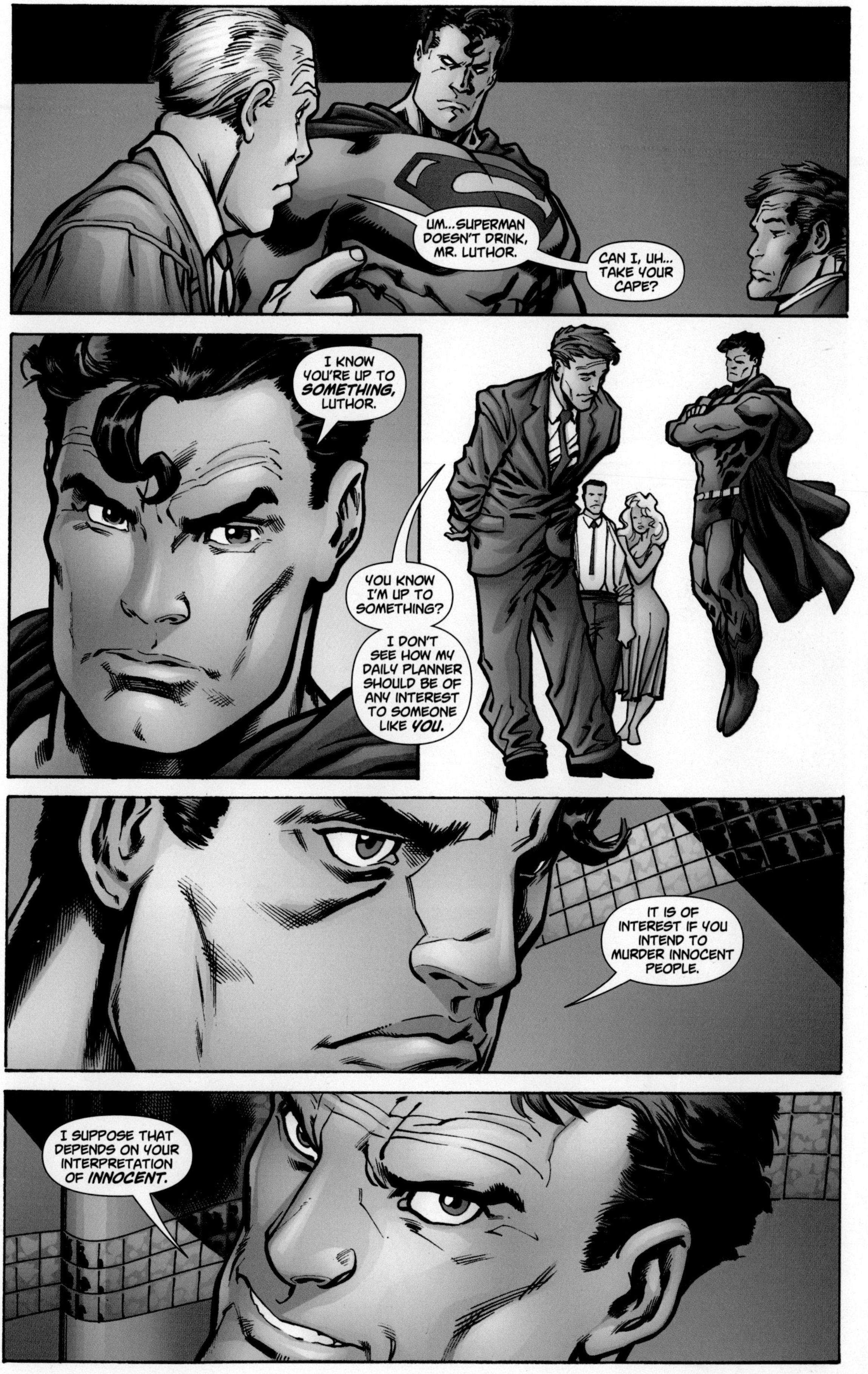

UM...SUPERMAN DOESN'T DRINK, MR. LUTHOR.
CAN I, UH... TAKE YOUR CAPE?
I KNOW YOU'RE UP TO SOMETHING, LUTHOR.
YOU KNOW I'M UP TO SOMETHING?
I DON'T SEE HOW MY DAILY PLANNER SHOULD BE OF ANY INTEREST TO SOMEONE LIKE YOU.
IT IS OF INTEREST IF YOU INTEND TO MURDER INNOCENT PEOPLE.
I SUPPOSE THAT DEPENDS ON YOUR INTERPRETATION OF INNOCENT.

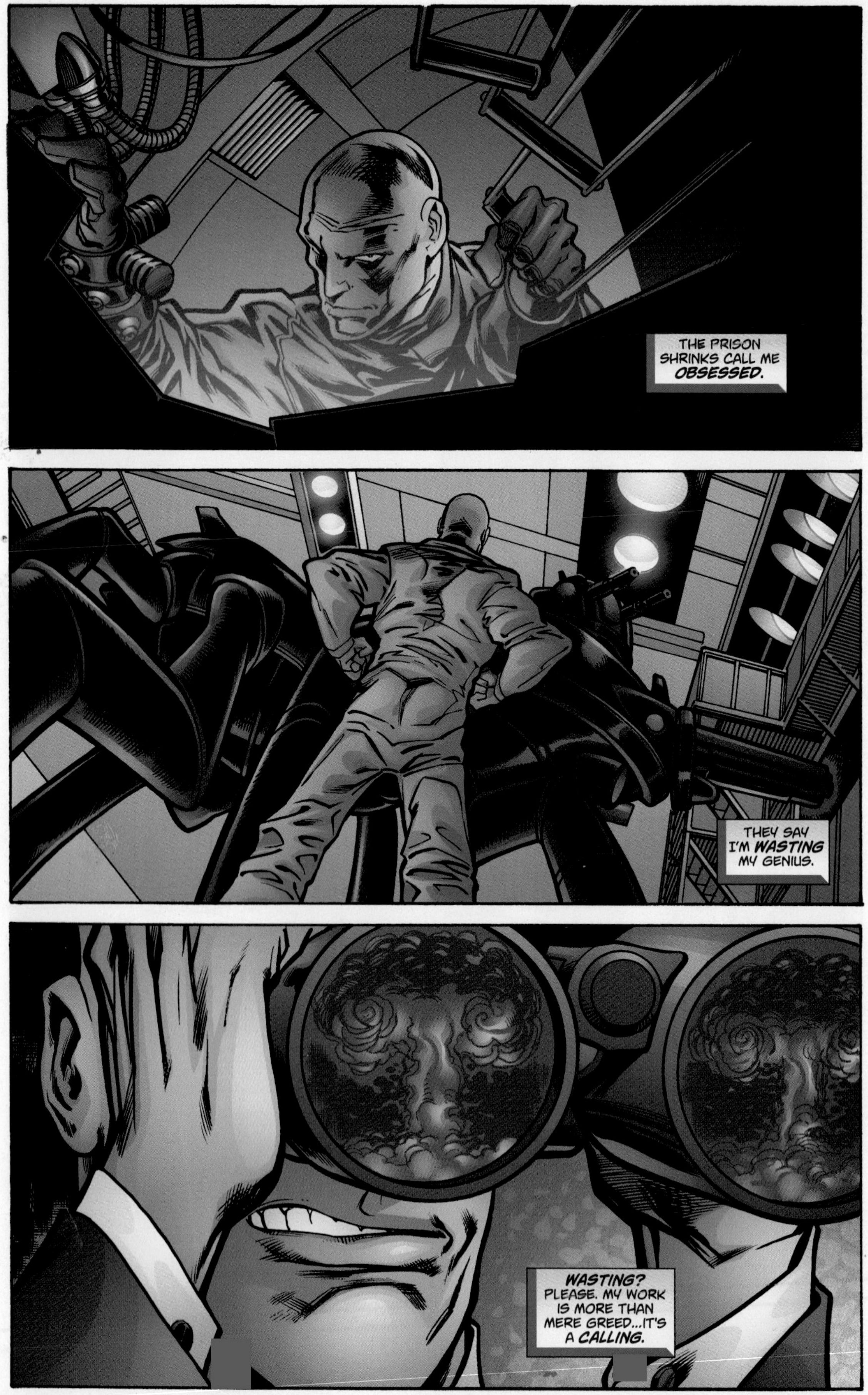
THE PRISON SHRINKS CALL ME OBSESSED.
THEY SAY I'M WASTING MY GENIUS.
WASTING? PLEASE. MY WORK IS MORE THAN MERE GREED...IT'S A CALLING.

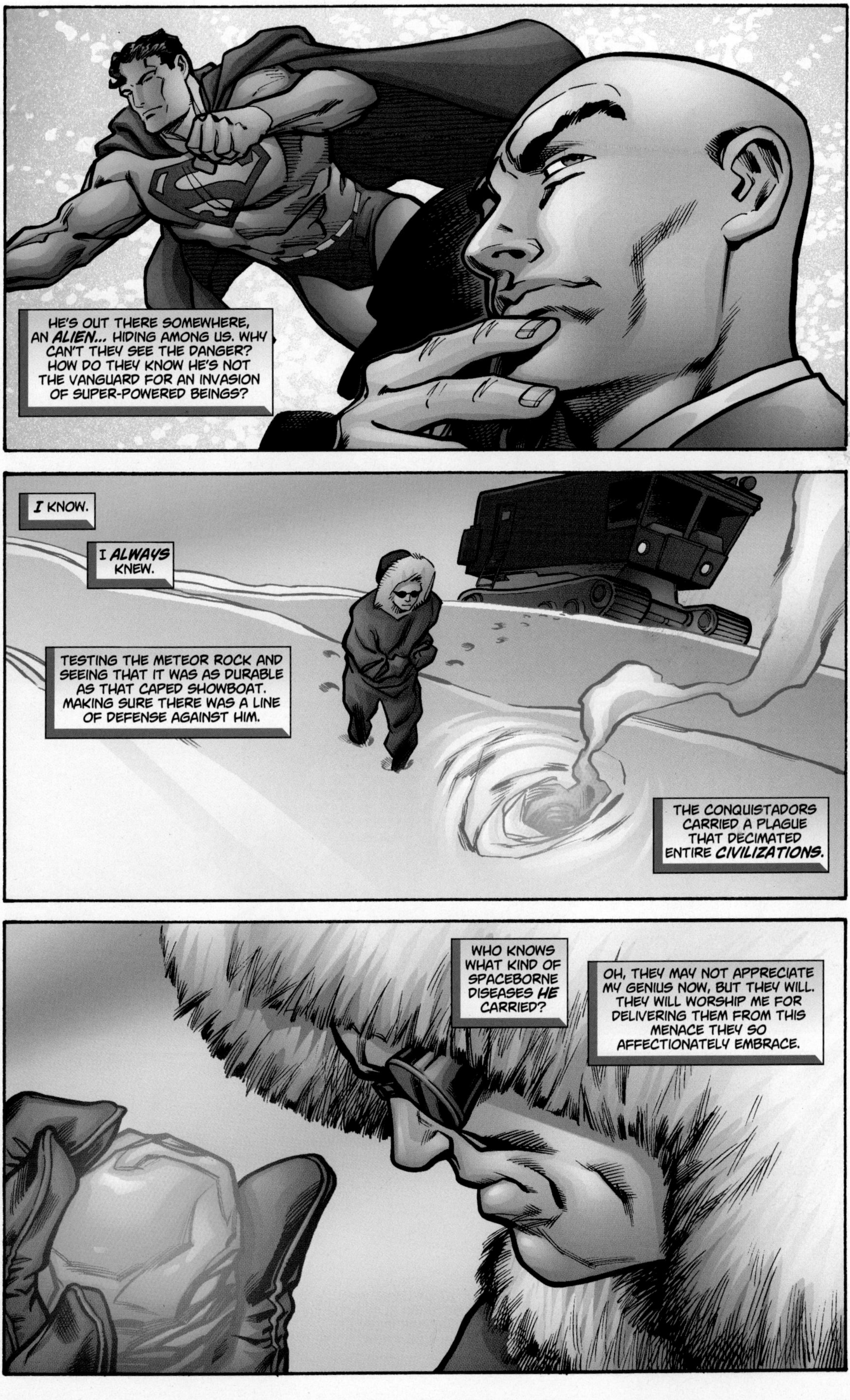
HE'S OUT THERE SOMEWHERE, AN ALIEN... HIDING AMONG US. WHY CAN'T THEY SEE THE DANGER? HOW DO THEY KNOW HE'S NOT THE VANGUARD FOR AN INVASION OF SUPER-POWERED BEINGS?
I KNOW.
I ALWAYS KNEW.
TESTING THE METEOR ROCK AND SEEING THAT IT WAS AS DURABLE AS THAT CAPED SHOWBOAT. MAKING SURE THERE WAS A LINE OF DEFENSE AGAINST HIM.
THE CONQUISTADORS CARRIED A PLAGUE THAT DECIMATED ENTIRE CIVILIZATIONS.
WHO KNOWS WHAT KIND OF SPACEBORNE DISEASES HE CARRIED?
OH, THEY MAY NOT APPRECIATE MY GENIUS NOW, BUT THEY WILL. THEY WILL WORSHIP ME FOR DELIVERING THEM FROM THIS MENACE THEY SO AFFECTIONATELY EMBRACE.

SURE, I'VE HAD A FEW... SETBACKS.

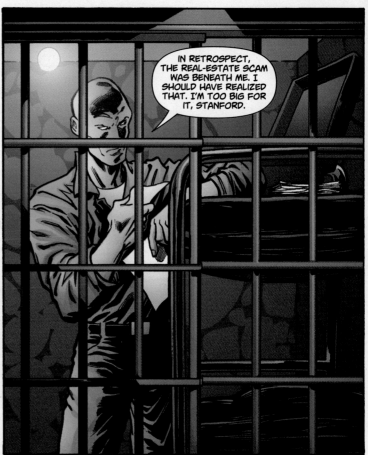

IN RETROSPECT, THE REAL-ESTATE SCAM WAS BENEATH ME. I SHOULD HAVE REALIZED THAT. I'M TOO BIG FOR IT, STANFORD.

STILL, MY PLAN WAS GENIUS... PURE GENIUS.

THERE'S NOTHING QUITE LIKE A MANMADE NATURAL DISASTER TO LINE ONE'S POCKETS.

IT'S NOT *EVERYONE* WHO GETS TO PLAY WITH NUCLEAR MISSILES, YOU KNOW.

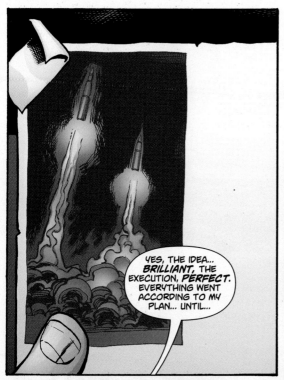

YES, THE IDEA... *BRILLIANT,* THE EXECUTION, *PERFECT.* EVERYTHING WENT ACCORDING TO MY PLAN... UNTIL...

UNTIL HE CAME ALONG AND RUINED EVERYTHING.

DO YOU BELIEVE IN *HATE* AT FIRST SIGHT, STANFORD?

YES, MISTER LUTHOR.

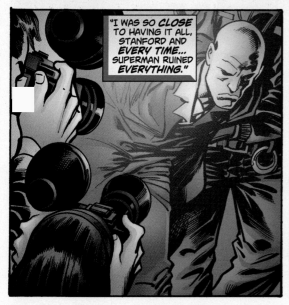

"I WAS SO *CLOSE* TO HAVING IT ALL, STANFORD AND *EVERY TIME...* SUPERMAN RUINED *EVERYTHING.*"

THAT WILL *NEVER* HAPPEN AGAIN. DID I TELL YOU ABOUT OUR FIRST MEETING?

WE COULD HAVE BEEN ALLIES, REALLY.

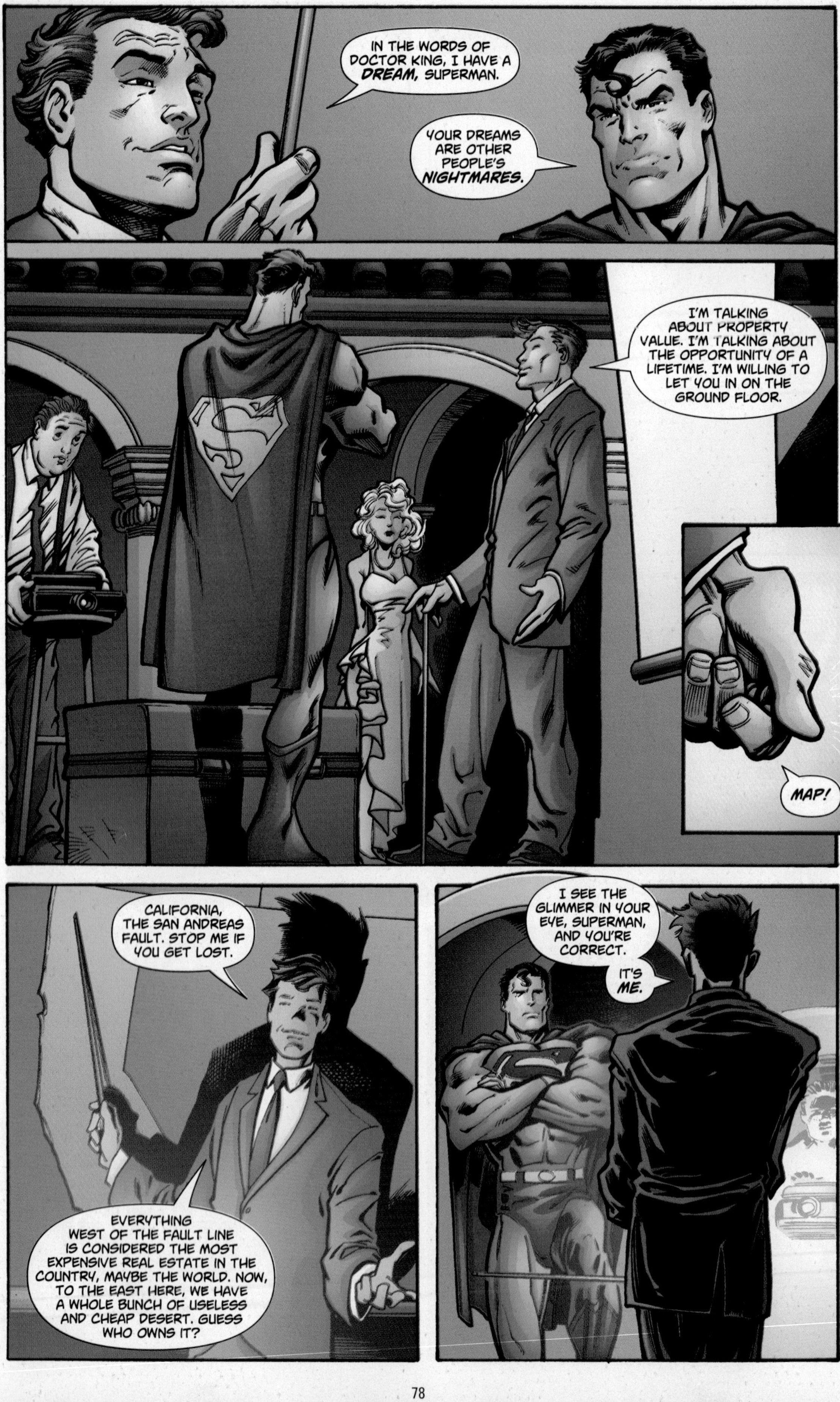

IN THE WORDS OF DOCTOR KING, I HAVE A DREAM, SUPERMAN.
YOUR DREAMS ARE OTHER PEOPLE'S NIGHTMARES.
I'M TALKING ABOUT PROPERTY VALUE. I'M TALKING ABOUT THE OPPORTUNITY OF A LIFETIME. I'M WILLING TO LET YOU IN ON THE GROUND FLOOR.
MAP!
CALIFORNIA, THE SAN ANDREAS FAULT. STOP ME IF YOU GET LOST.
EVERYTHING WEST OF THE FAULT LINE IS CONSIDERED THE MOST EXPENSIVE REAL ESTATE IN THE COUNTRY, MAYBE THE WORLD. NOW, TO THE EAST HERE, WE HAVE A WHOLE BUNCH OF USELESS AND CHEAP DESERT. GUESS WHO OWNS IT?
I SEE THE GLIMMER IN YOUR EYE, SUPERMAN, AND YOU'RE CORRECT.
IT'S ME.

"I WAS SO *SURE* OF MYSELF."

HERE!

BOOM! THIS SIDE SINKS.

THIS SIDE BECOMES A NEW WEST COAST WORTH *TRILLIONS.*

YOU'RE INSANE!

NAME CALLING? NOT VERY *SUPER* OF YOU, REALLY...

YOU ARE A DISTURBED MAN, LUTHOR. IT COULDN'T POSSIBLY WORK.

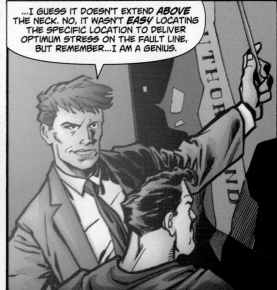

...I GUESS IT DOESN'T EXTEND *ABOVE* THE NECK. NO, IT WASN'T *EASY* LOCATING THE SPECIFIC LOCATION TO DELIVER OPTIMUM STRESS ON THE FAULT LINE, BUT REMEMBER...I AM A GENIUS.

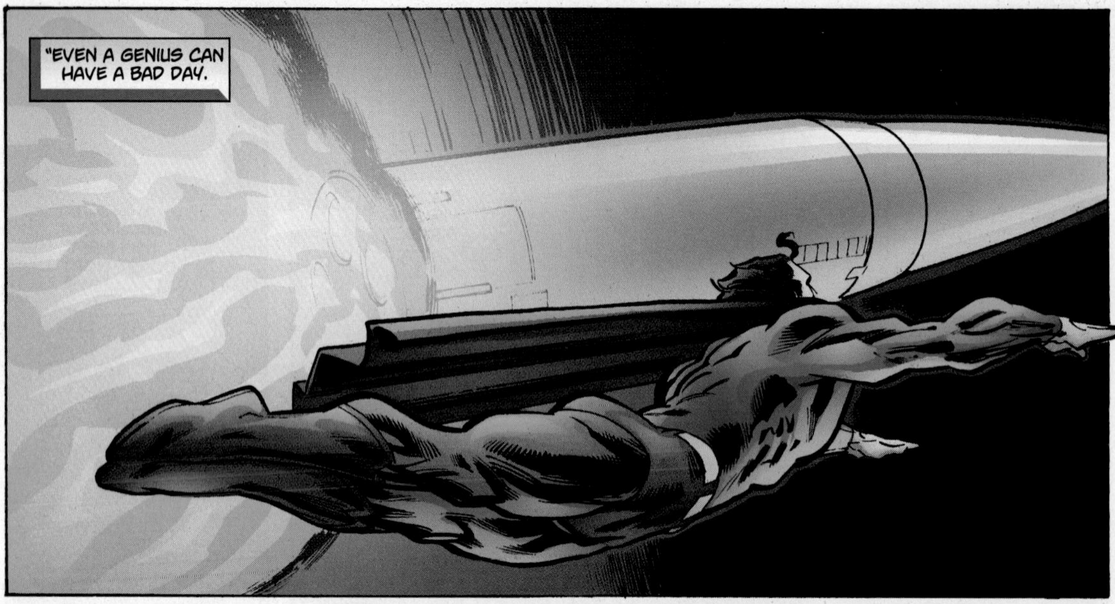
"EVEN A GENIUS CAN HAVE A BAD DAY.

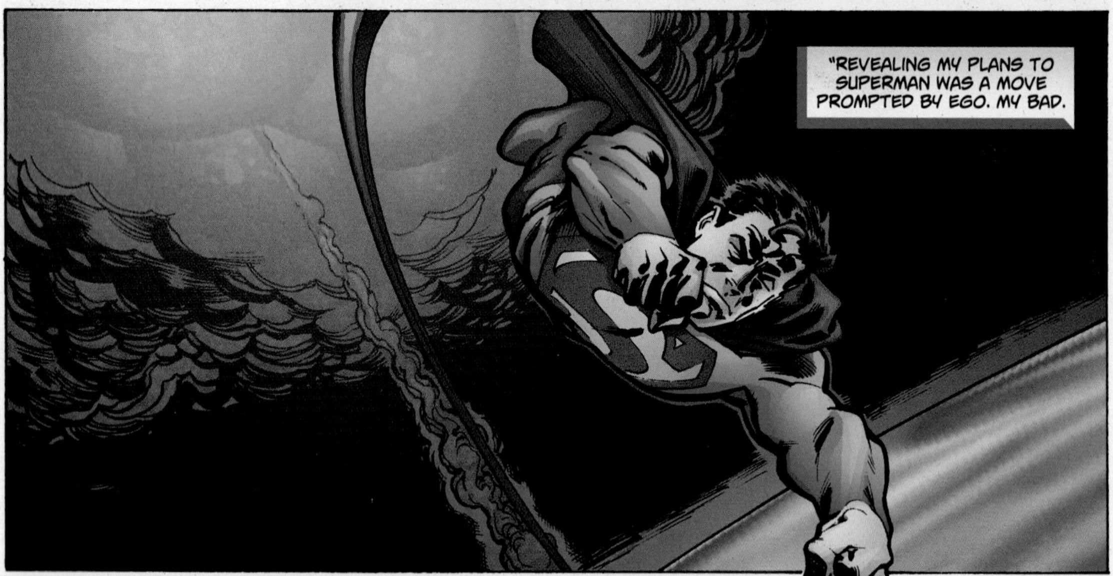
"REVEALING MY PLANS TO SUPERMAN WAS A MOVE PROMPTED BY EGO. MY BAD.

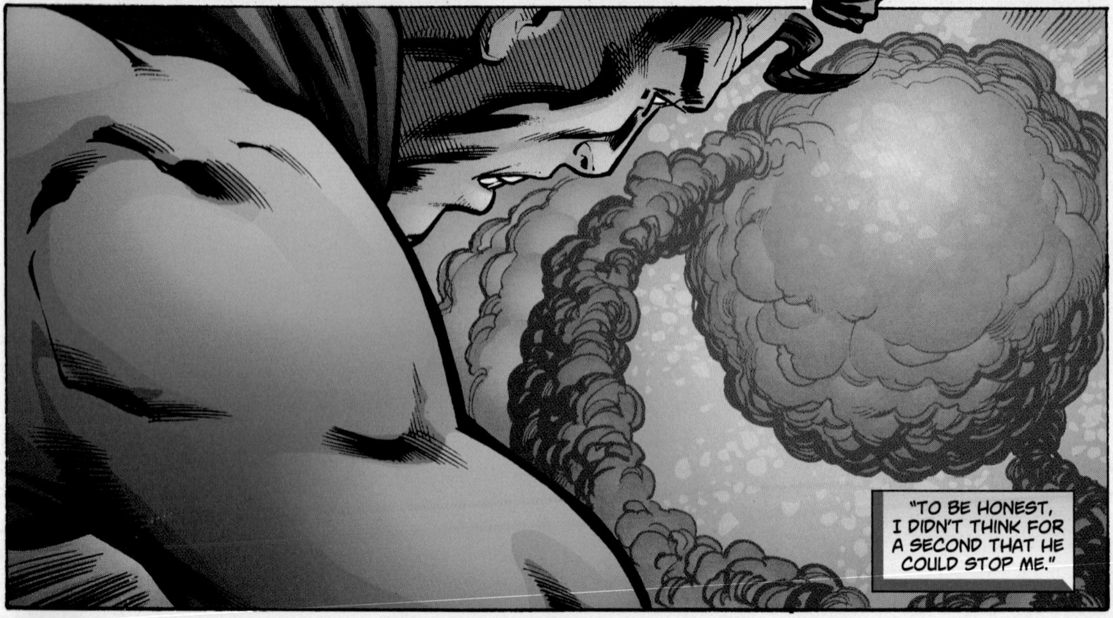
"TO BE HONEST, I DIDN'T THINK FOR A SECOND THAT HE COULD STOP ME."

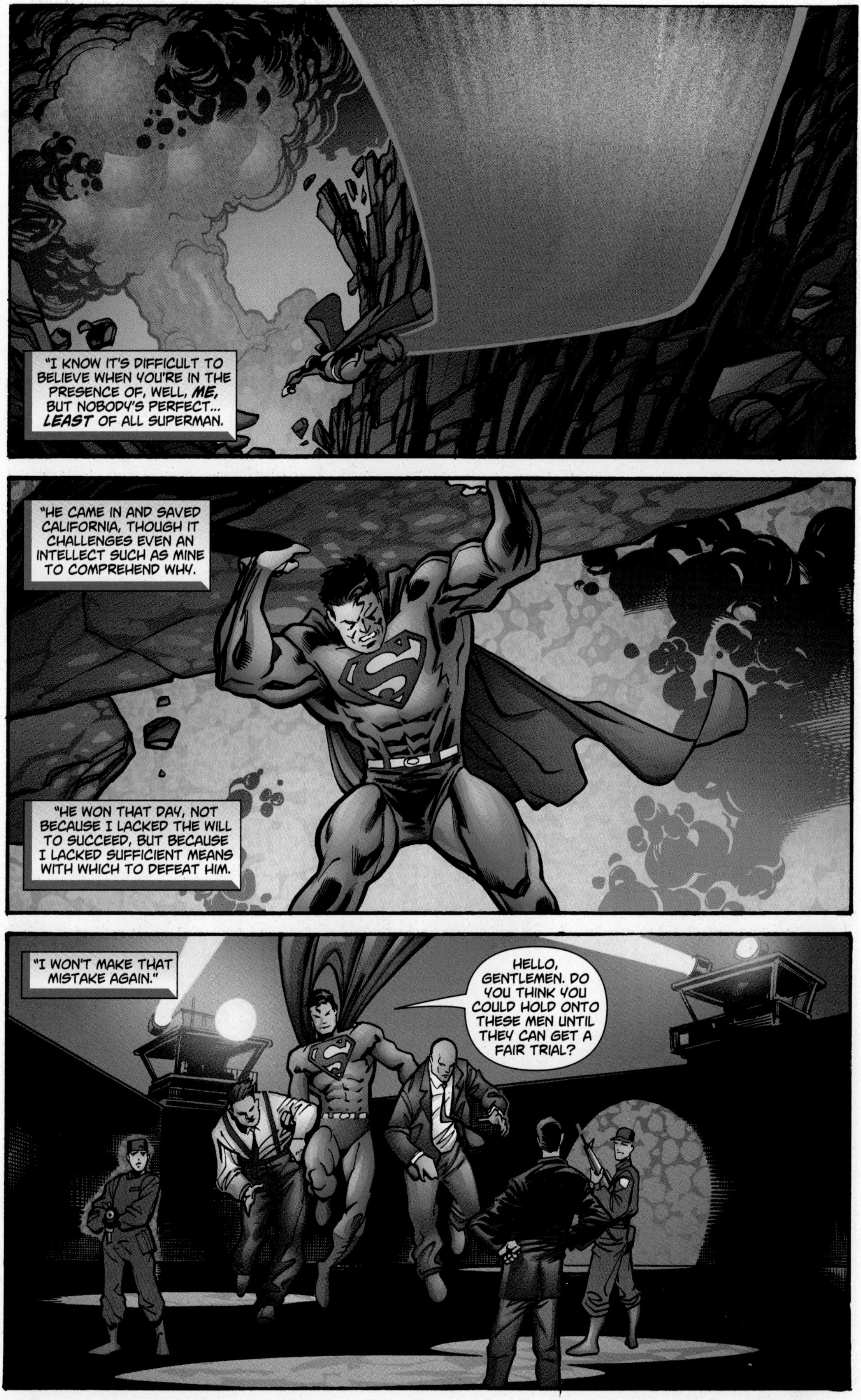
"I KNOW IT'S DIFFICULT TO BELIEVE WHEN YOU'RE IN THE PRESENCE OF, WELL, *ME,* BUT NOBODY'S PERFECT... *LEAST* OF ALL SUPERMAN.
"HE CAME IN AND SAVED CALIFORNIA, THOUGH IT CHALLENGES EVEN AN INTELLECT SUCH AS MINE TO COMPREHEND WHY.
"HE WON THAT DAY, NOT BECAUSE I LACKED THE WILL TO SUCCEED, BUT BECAUSE I LACKED SUFFICIENT MEANS WITH WHICH TO DEFEAT HIM.
"I WON'T MAKE THAT MISTAKE AGAIN."
HELLO, GENTLEMEN. DO YOU THINK YOU COULD HOLD ONTO THESE MEN UNTIL THEY CAN GET A FAIR TRIAL?

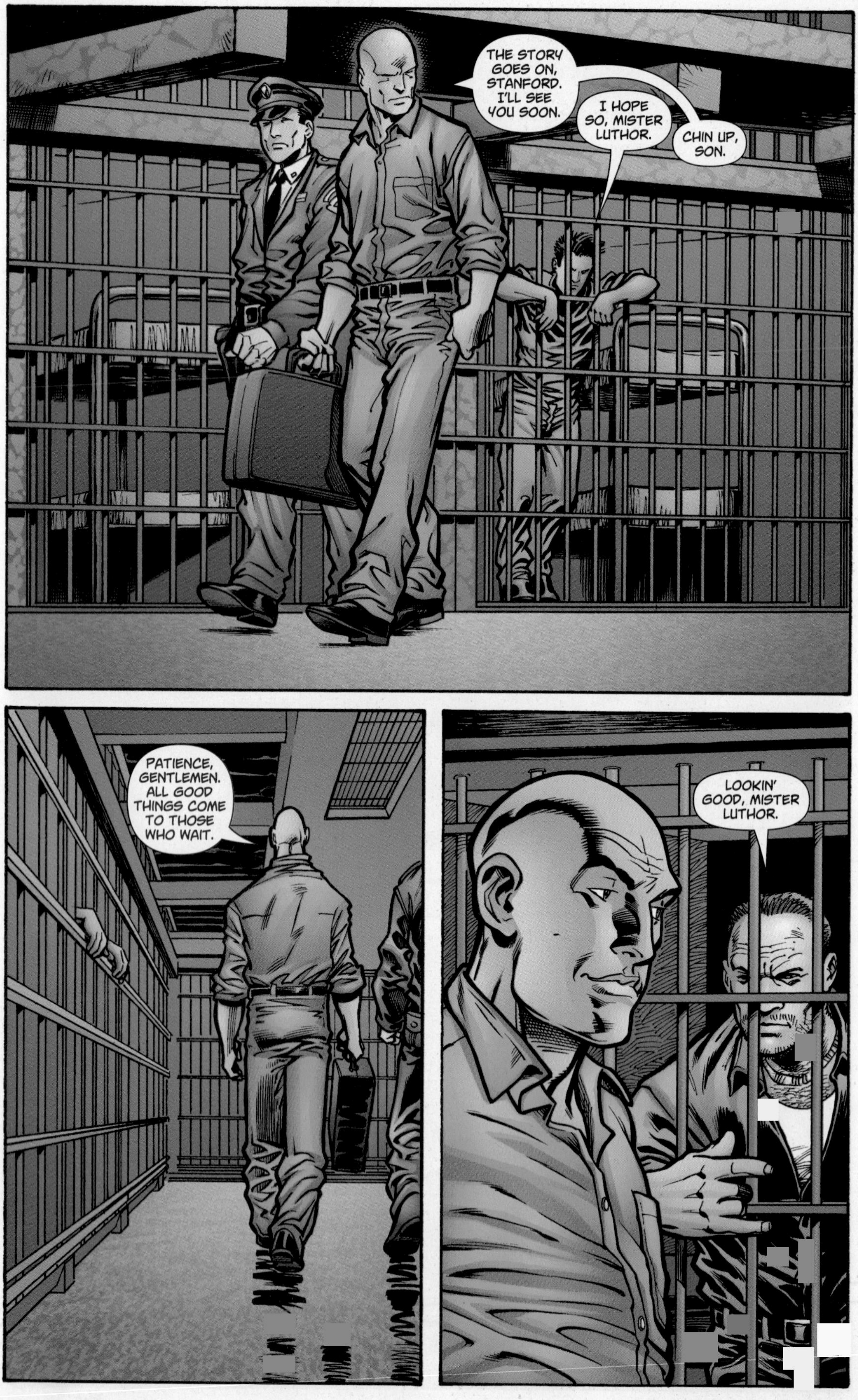
THE STORY GOES ON, STANFORD. I'LL SEE YOU SOON.
I HOPE SO, MISTER LUTHOR.
CHIN UP, SON.
PATIENCE, GENTLEMEN. ALL GOOD THINGS COME TO THOSE WHO WAIT.
LOOKIN' GOOD, MISTER LUTHOR.

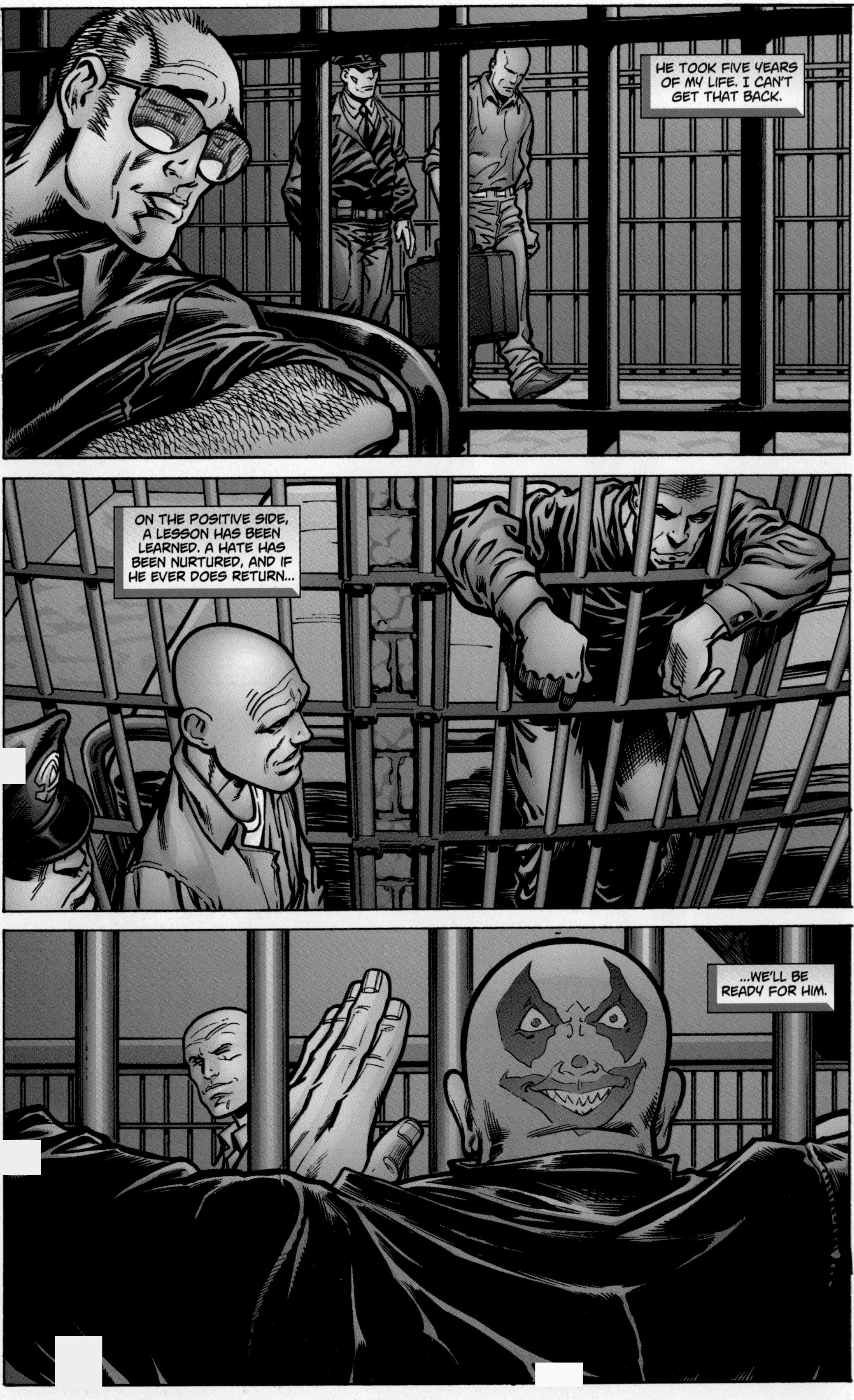
HE TOOK FIVE YEARS OF MY LIFE. I CAN'T GET THAT BACK.
ON THE POSITIVE SIDE, A LESSON HAS BEEN LEARNED. A HATE HAS BEEN NURTURED, AND IF HE EVER DOES RETURN...
...WE'LL BE READY FOR HIM.

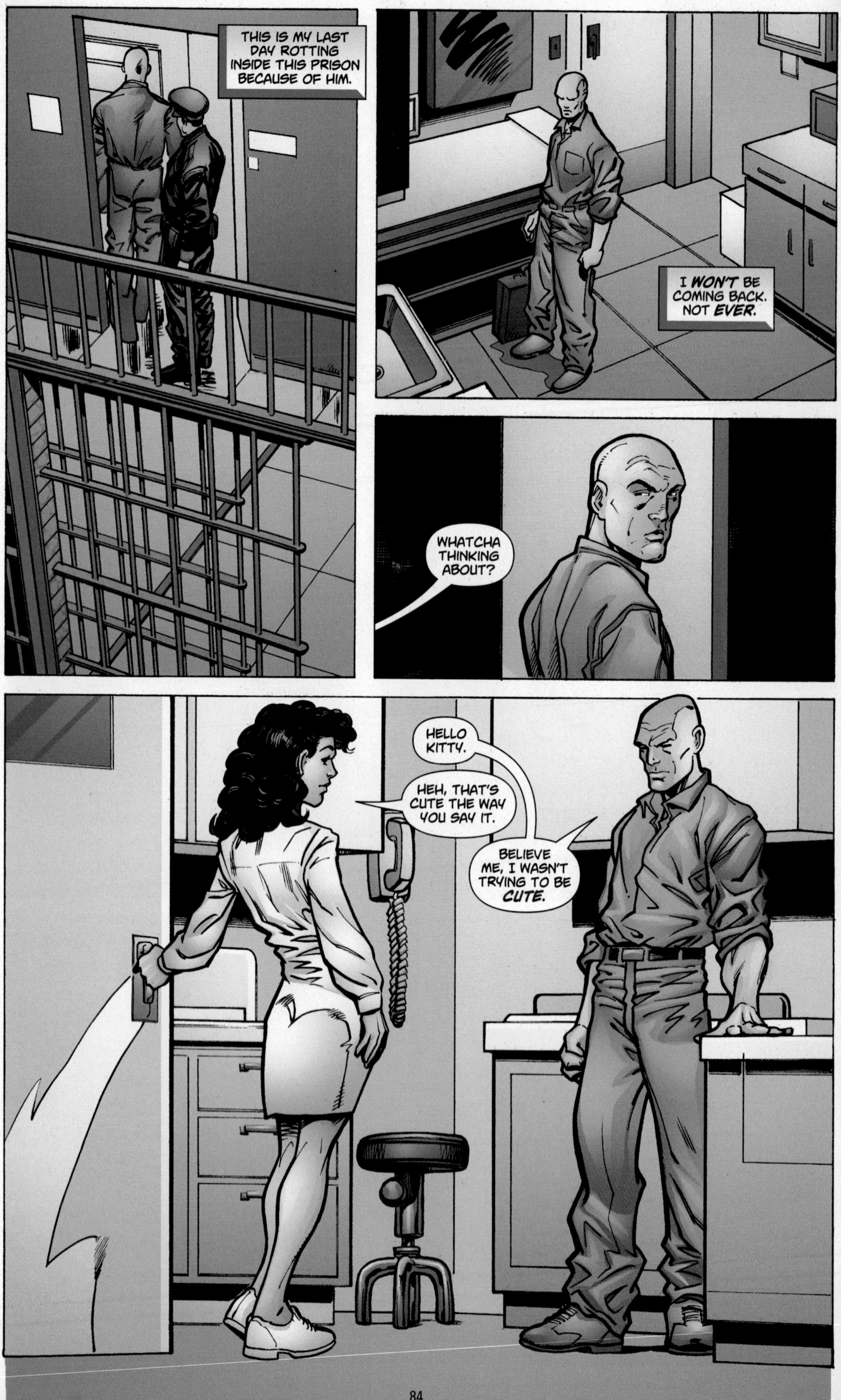
THIS IS MY LAST DAY ROTTING INSIDE THIS PRISON BECAUSE OF HIM.
I WON'T BE COMING BACK. NOT EVER.
WHATCHA THINKING ABOUT?
HELLO KITTY.
HEH, THAT'S CUTE THE WAY YOU SAY IT.
BELIEVE ME, I WASN'T TRYING TO BE CUTE.

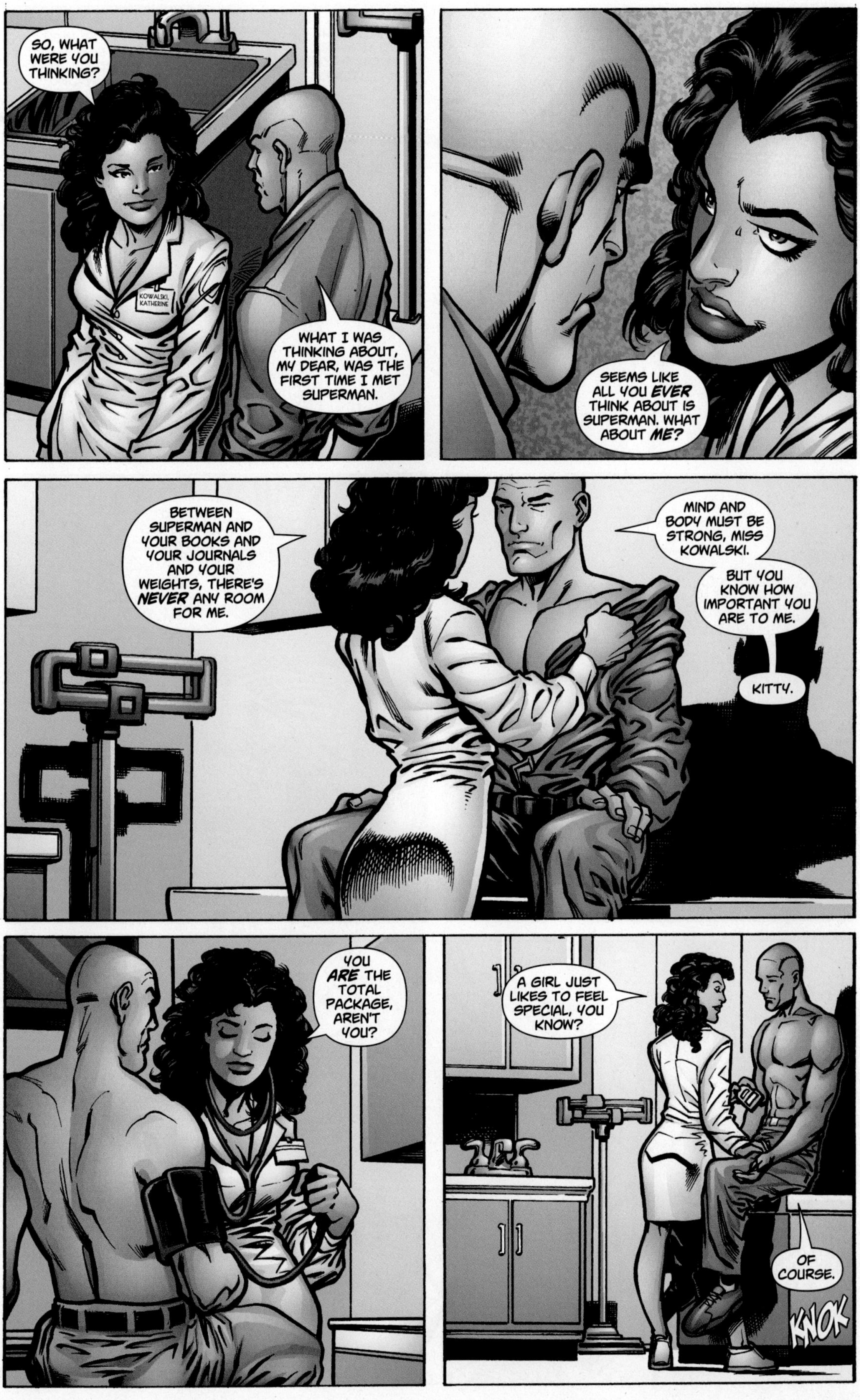
SO, WHAT WERE YOU THINKING?
KOWALSKI, KATHERINE
WHAT I WAS THINKING ABOUT, MY DEAR, WAS THE FIRST TIME I MET SUPERMAN.
SEEMS LIKE ALL YOU EVER THINK ABOUT IS SUPERMAN. WHAT ABOUT ME?
BETWEEN SUPERMAN AND YOUR BOOKS AND YOUR JOURNALS AND YOUR WEIGHTS, THERE'S NEVER ANY ROOM FOR ME.
MIND AND BODY MUST BE STRONG, MISS KOWALSKI.
BUT YOU KNOW HOW IMPORTANT YOU ARE TO ME.
KITTY.
YOU ARE THE TOTAL PACKAGE, AREN'T YOU?
A GIRL JUST LIKES TO FEEL SPECIAL, YOU KNOW?
OF COURSE.
KNOK

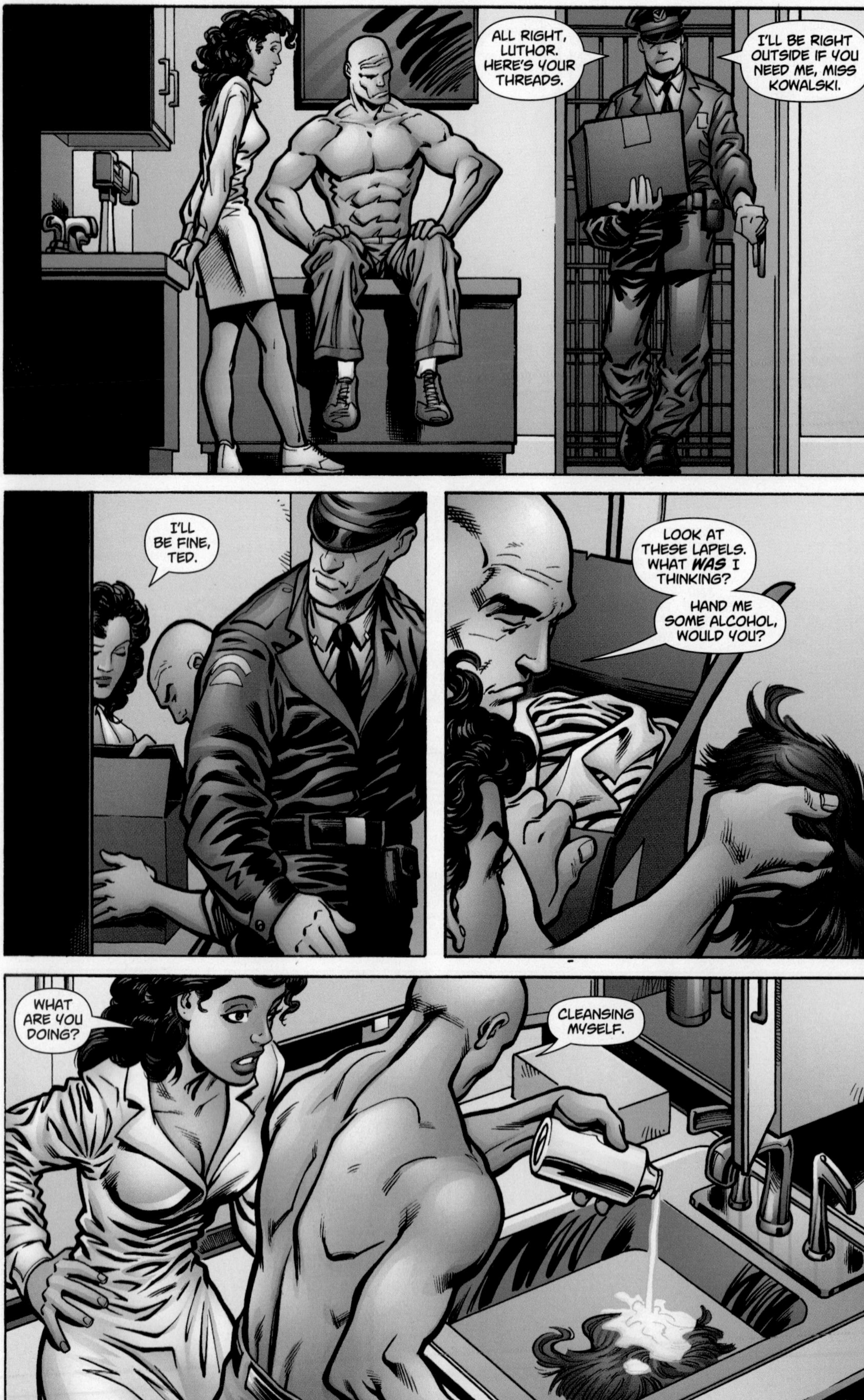
ALL RIGHT, LUTHOR. HERE'S YOUR THREADS.
I'LL BE RIGHT OUTSIDE IF YOU NEED ME, MISS KOWALSKI.
I'LL BE FINE, TED.
LOOK AT THESE LAPELS. WHAT *WAS* I THINKING?
HAND ME SOME ALCOHOL, WOULD YOU?
WHAT ARE YOU DOING?
CLEANSING MYSELF.

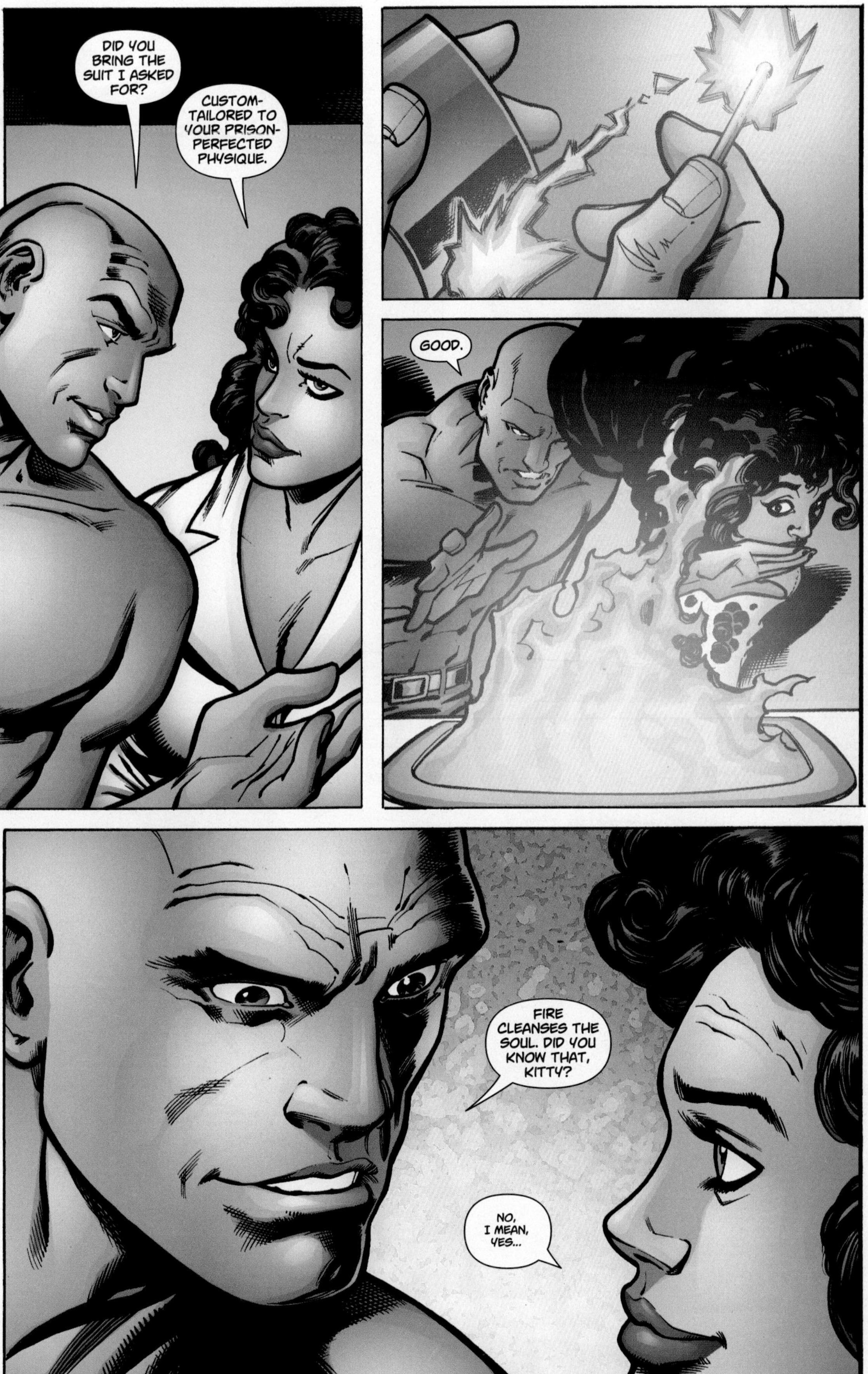
DID YOU BRING THE SUIT I ASKED FOR?
CUSTOM-TAILORED TO YOUR PRISON-PERFECTED PHYSIQUE.
GOOD.
FIRE CLEANSES THE SOUL. DID YOU KNOW THAT, KITTY?
NO, I MEAN, YES...

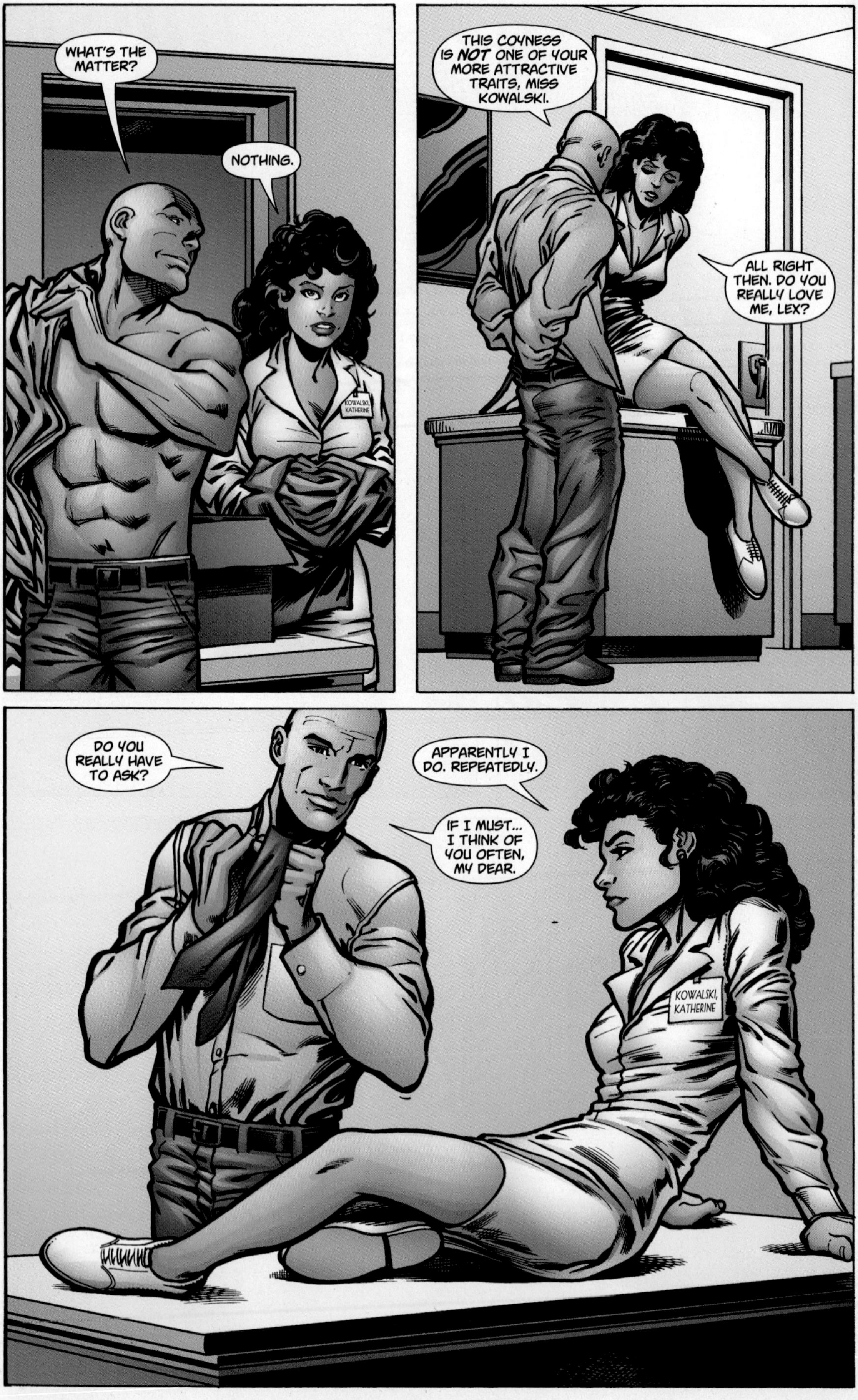
WHAT'S THE MATTER?
NOTHING.
KOWALSKI, KATHERINE
THIS COYNESS IS NOT ONE OF YOUR MORE ATTRACTIVE TRAITS, MISS KOWALSKI.
ALL RIGHT THEN. DO YOU REALLY LOVE ME, LEX?
DO YOU REALLY HAVE TO ASK?
APPARENTLY I DO. REPEATEDLY.
IF I MUST... I THINK OF YOU OFTEN, MY DEAR.
KOWALSKI, KATHERINE

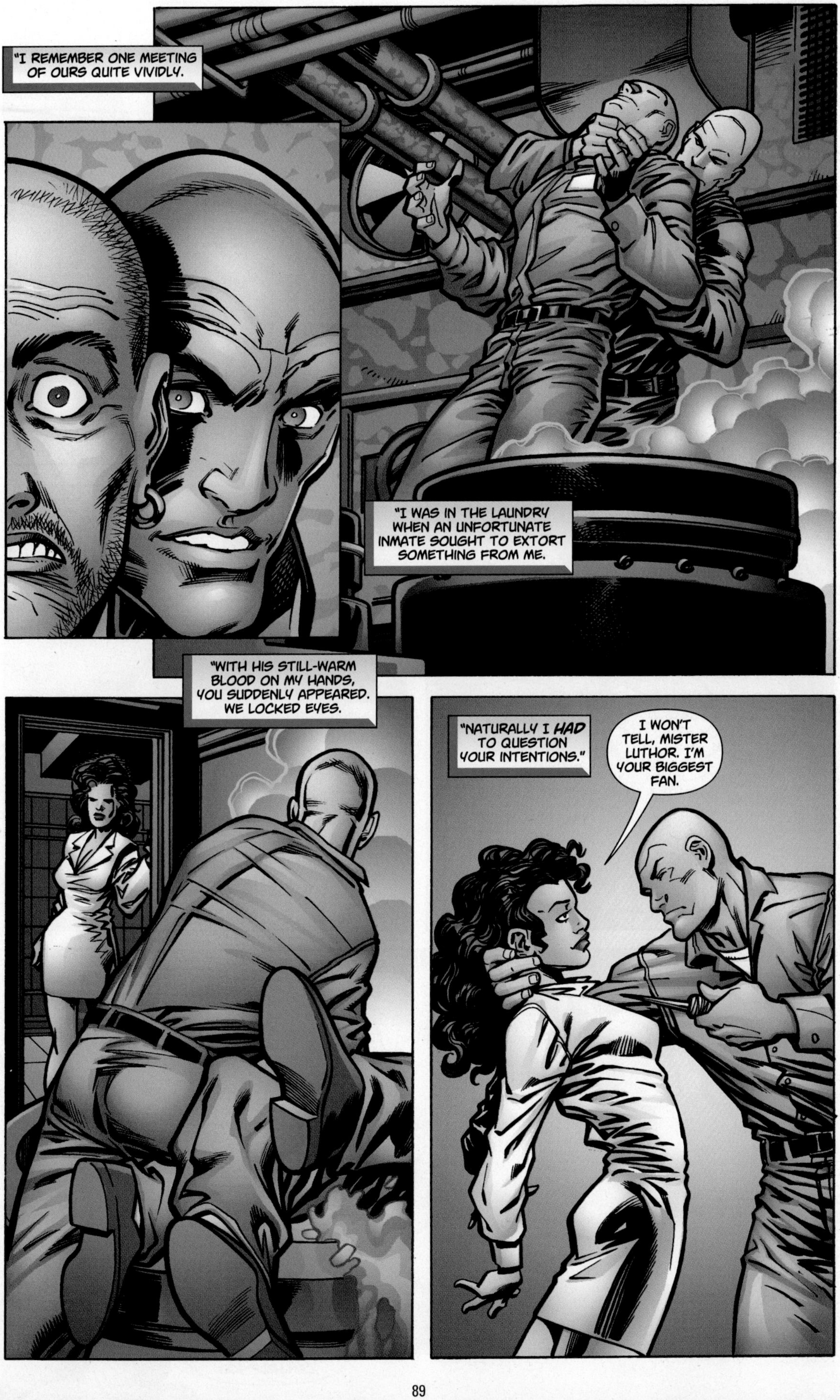

"I REMEMBER ONE MEETING OF OURS QUITE VIVIDLY.
"I WAS IN THE LAUNDRY WHEN AN UNFORTUNATE INMATE SOUGHT TO EXTORT SOMETHING FROM ME.
"WITH HIS STILL-WARM BLOOD ON MY HANDS, YOU SUDDENLY APPEARED. WE LOCKED EYES.
"NATURALLY I HAD TO QUESTION YOUR INTENTIONS."
I WON'T TELL, MISTER LUTHOR. I'M YOUR BIGGEST FAN.

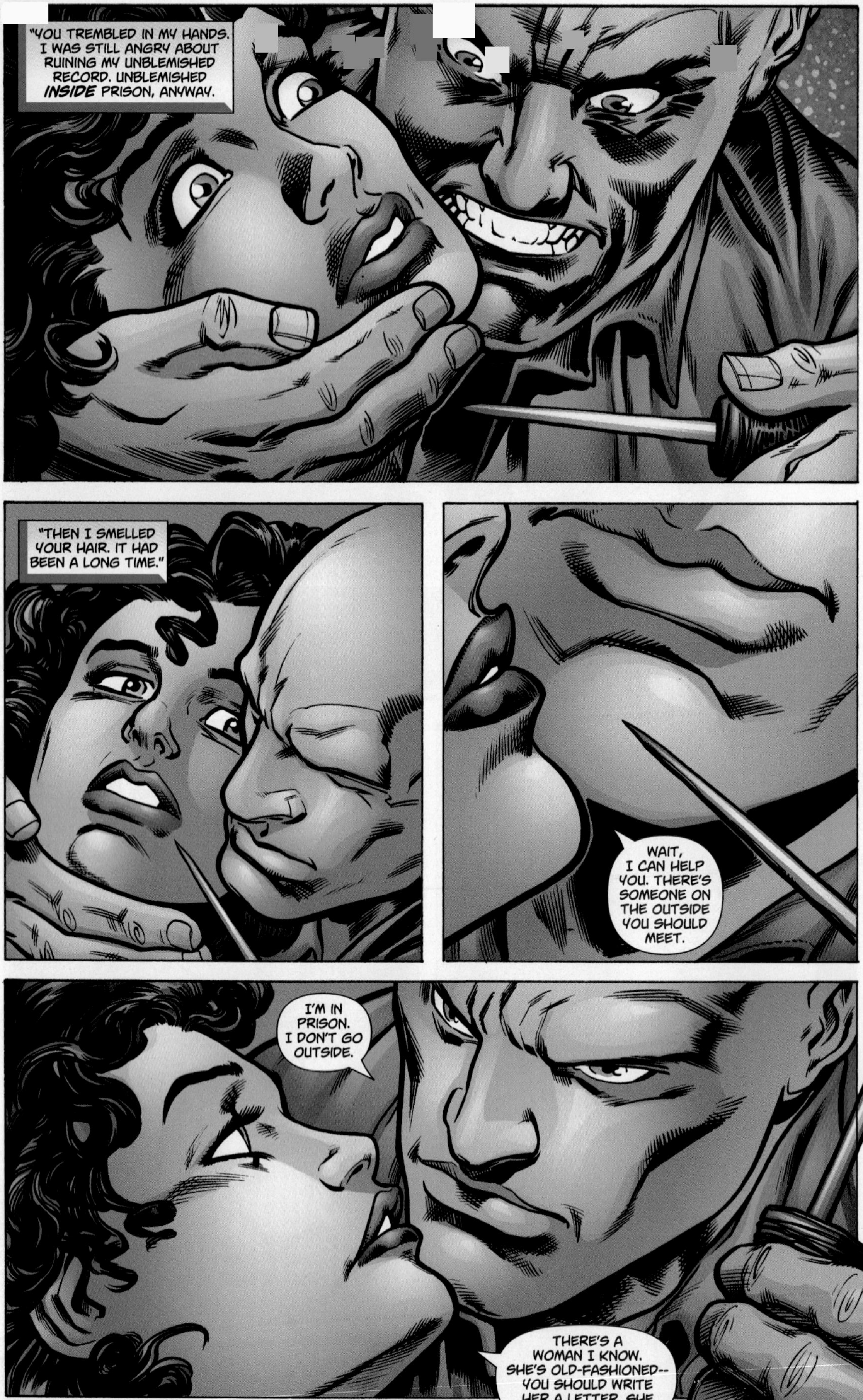
"YOU TREMBLED IN MY HANDS. I WAS STILL ANGRY ABOUT RUINING MY UNBLEMISHED RECORD. UNBLEMISHED *INSIDE* PRISON, ANYWAY.
"THEN I SMELLED YOUR HAIR. IT HAD BEEN A LONG TIME."
WAIT, I CAN HELP YOU. THERE'S SOMEONE ON THE OUTSIDE YOU SHOULD MEET.
I'M IN PRISON. I DON'T GO OUTSIDE.
THERE'S A WOMAN I KNOW. SHE'S OLD-FASHIONED-- YOU SHOULD WRITE HER A LETTER. SHE CAN HELP YOU.

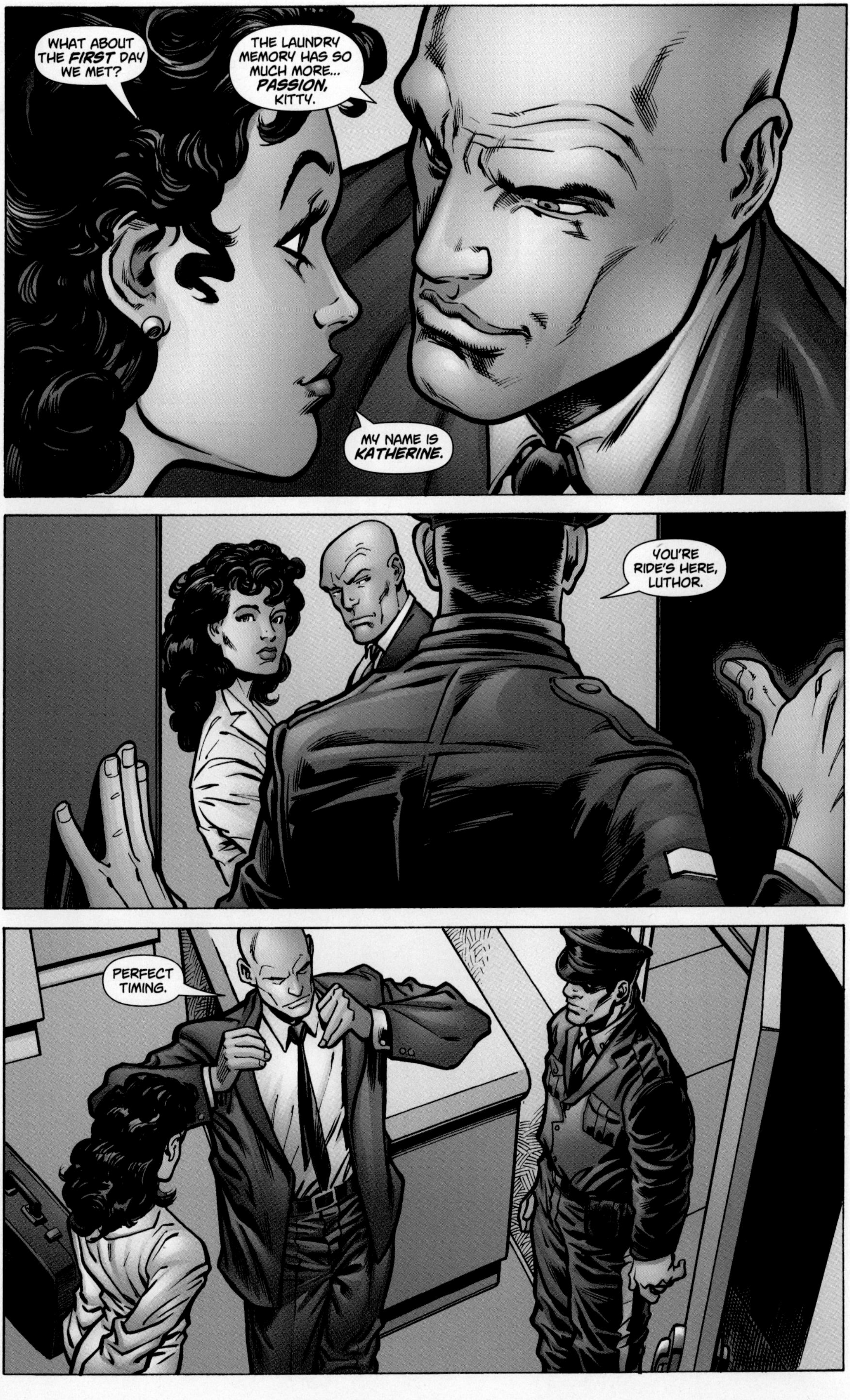
WHAT ABOUT THE FIRST DAY WE MET?
THE LAUNDRY MEMORY HAS SO MUCH MORE... PASSION, KITTY.
MY NAME IS KATHERINE.
YOU'RE RIDE'S HERE, LUTHOR.
PERFECT TIMING.

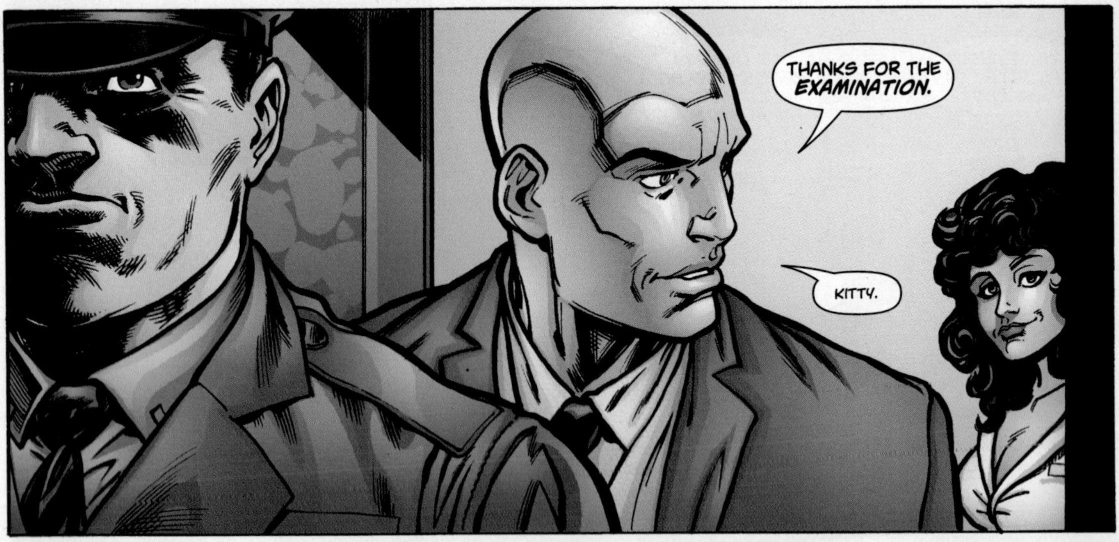
THANKS FOR THE EXAMINATION.
KITTY.

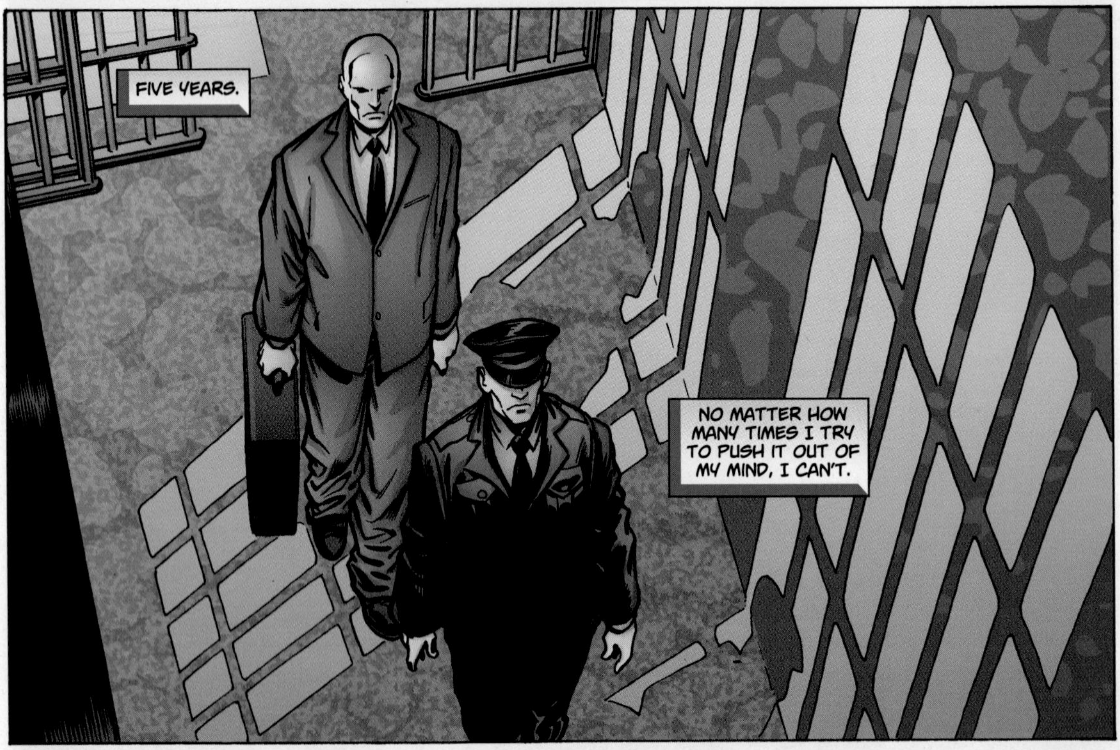
FIVE YEARS.
NO MATTER HOW MANY TIMES I TRY TO PUSH IT OUT OF MY MIND, I CAN'T.

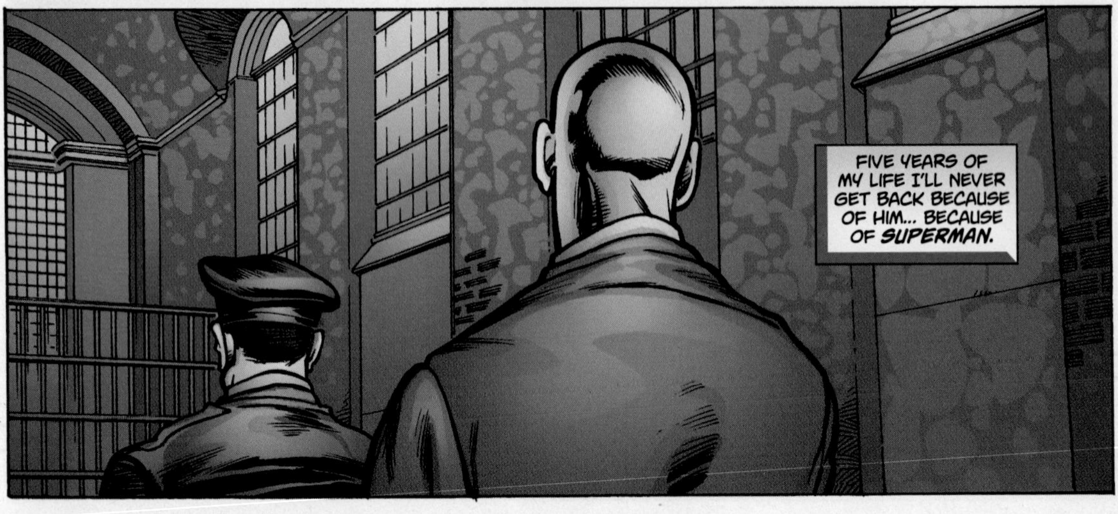
FIVE YEARS OF MY LIFE I'LL NEVER GET BACK BECAUSE OF HIM... BECAUSE OF SUPERMAN.

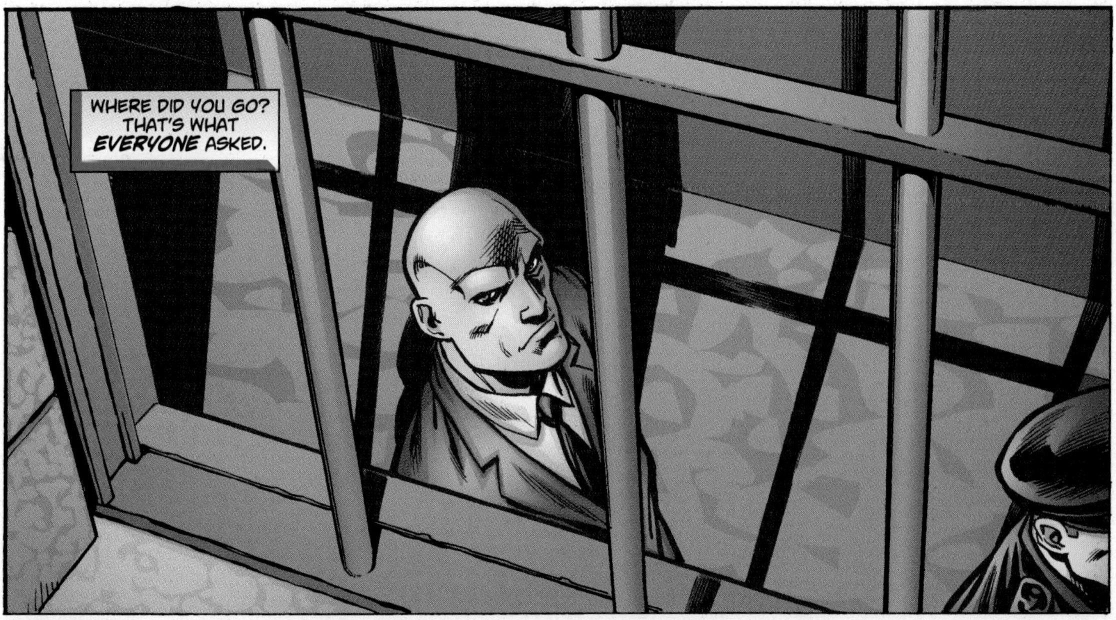
WHERE DID YOU GO? THAT'S WHAT EVERYONE ASKED.

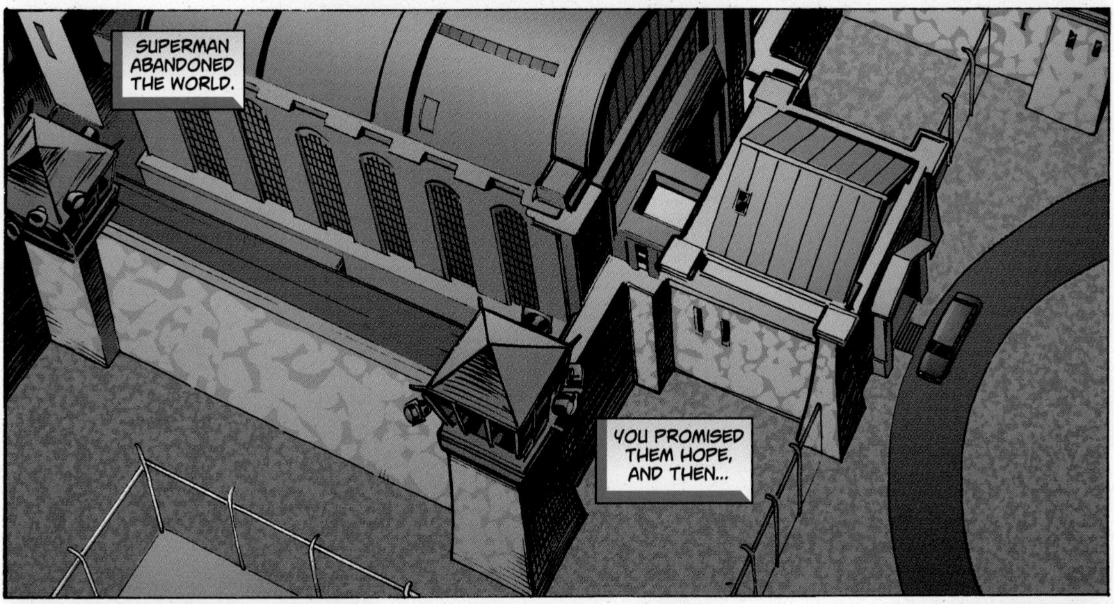
SUPERMAN ABANDONED THE WORLD.
YOU PROMISED THEM HOPE, AND THEN...

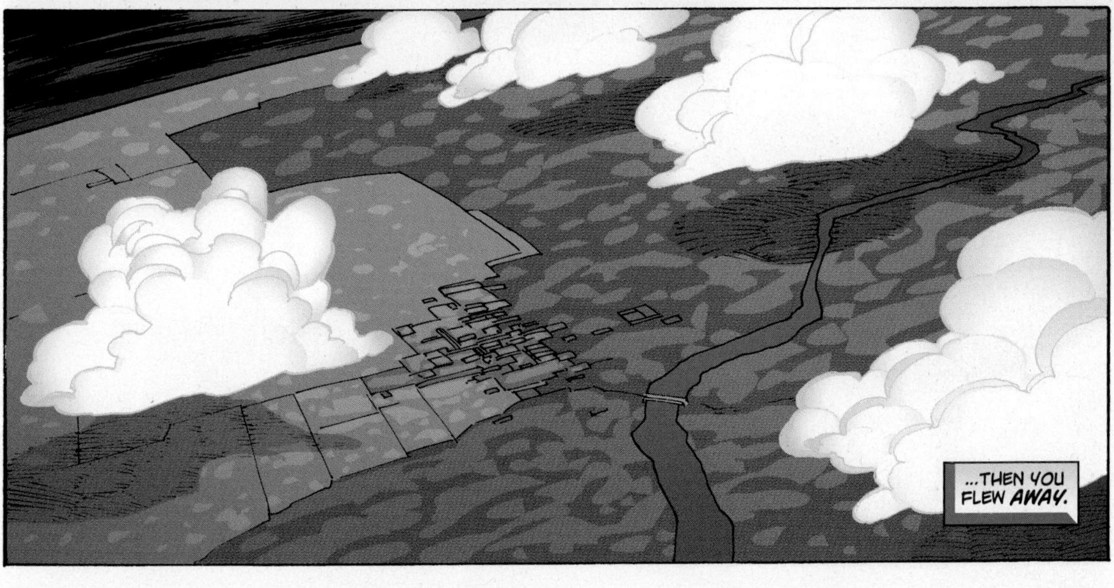
...THEN YOU FLEW AWAY.

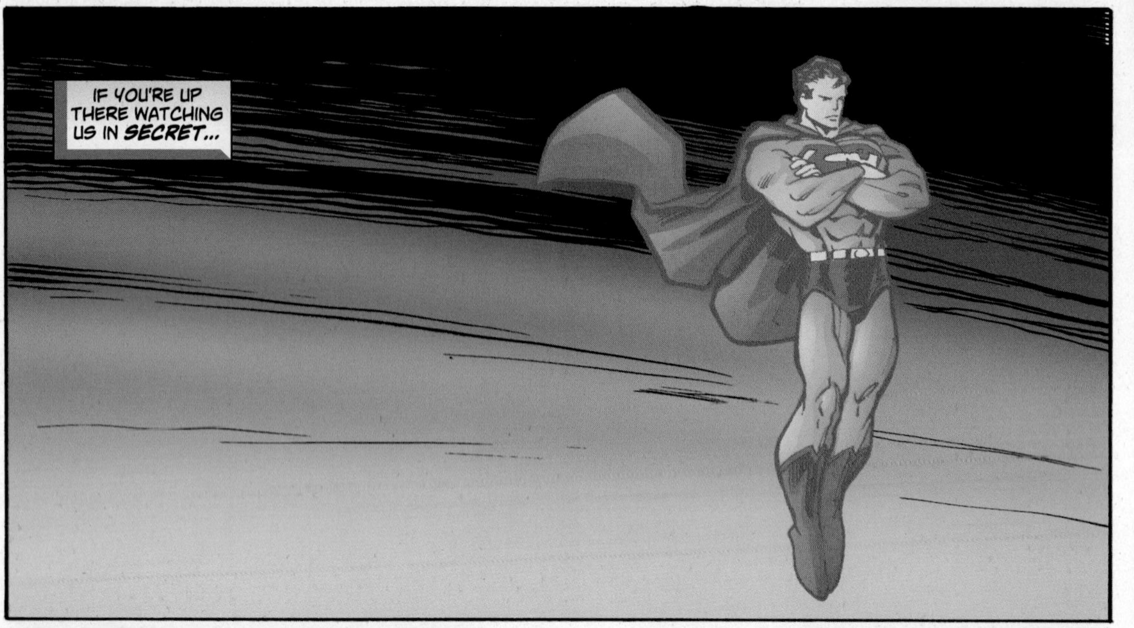
IF YOU'RE UP THERE WATCHING US IN SECRET...

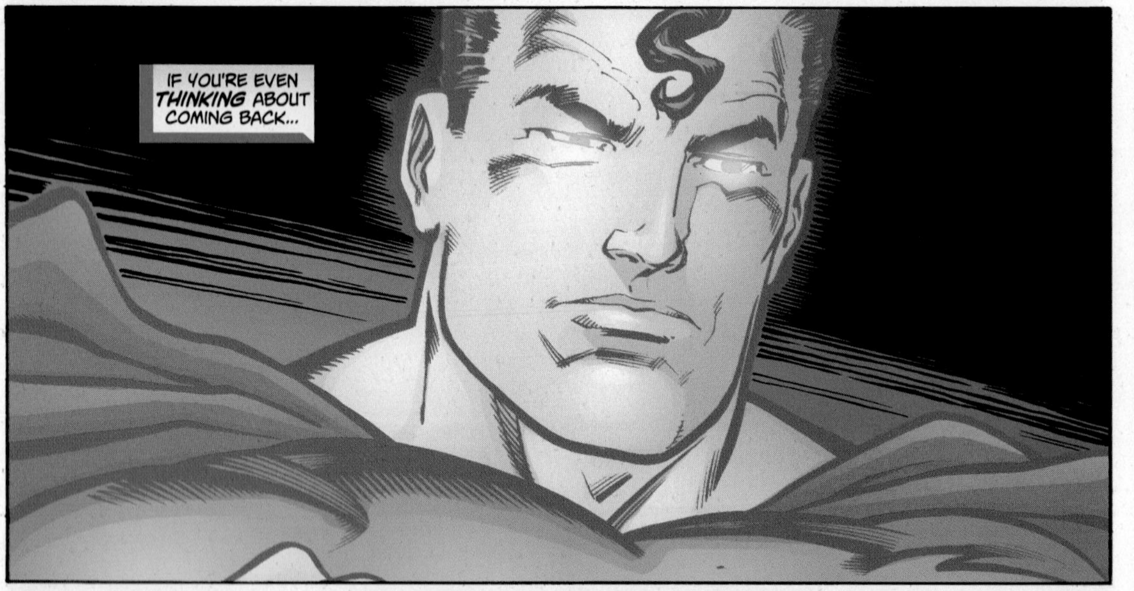
IF YOU'RE EVEN THINKING ABOUT COMING BACK...

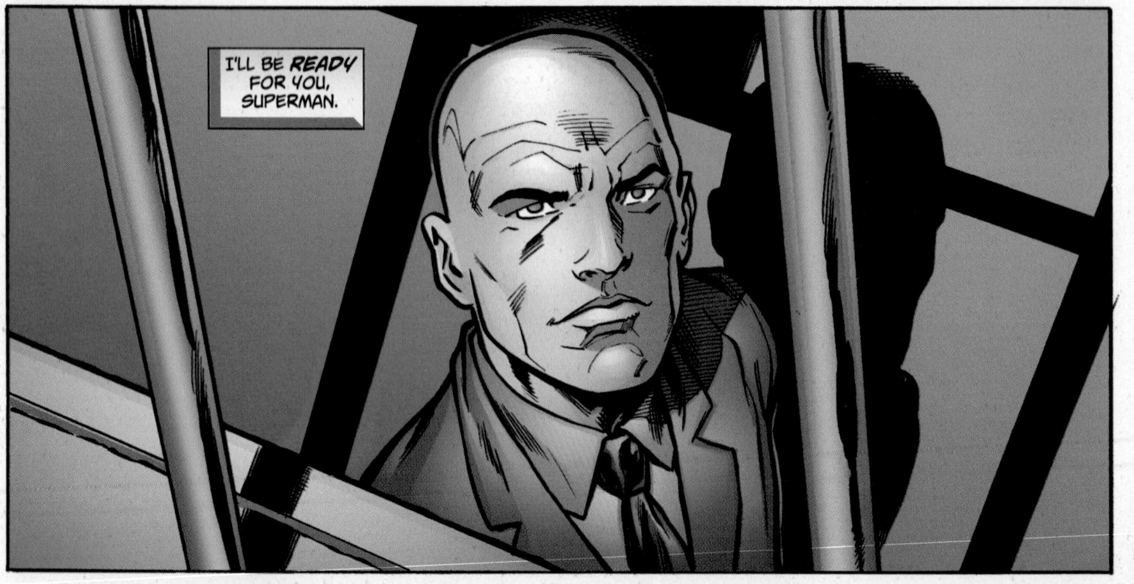
I'LL BE READY FOR YOU, SUPERMAN.

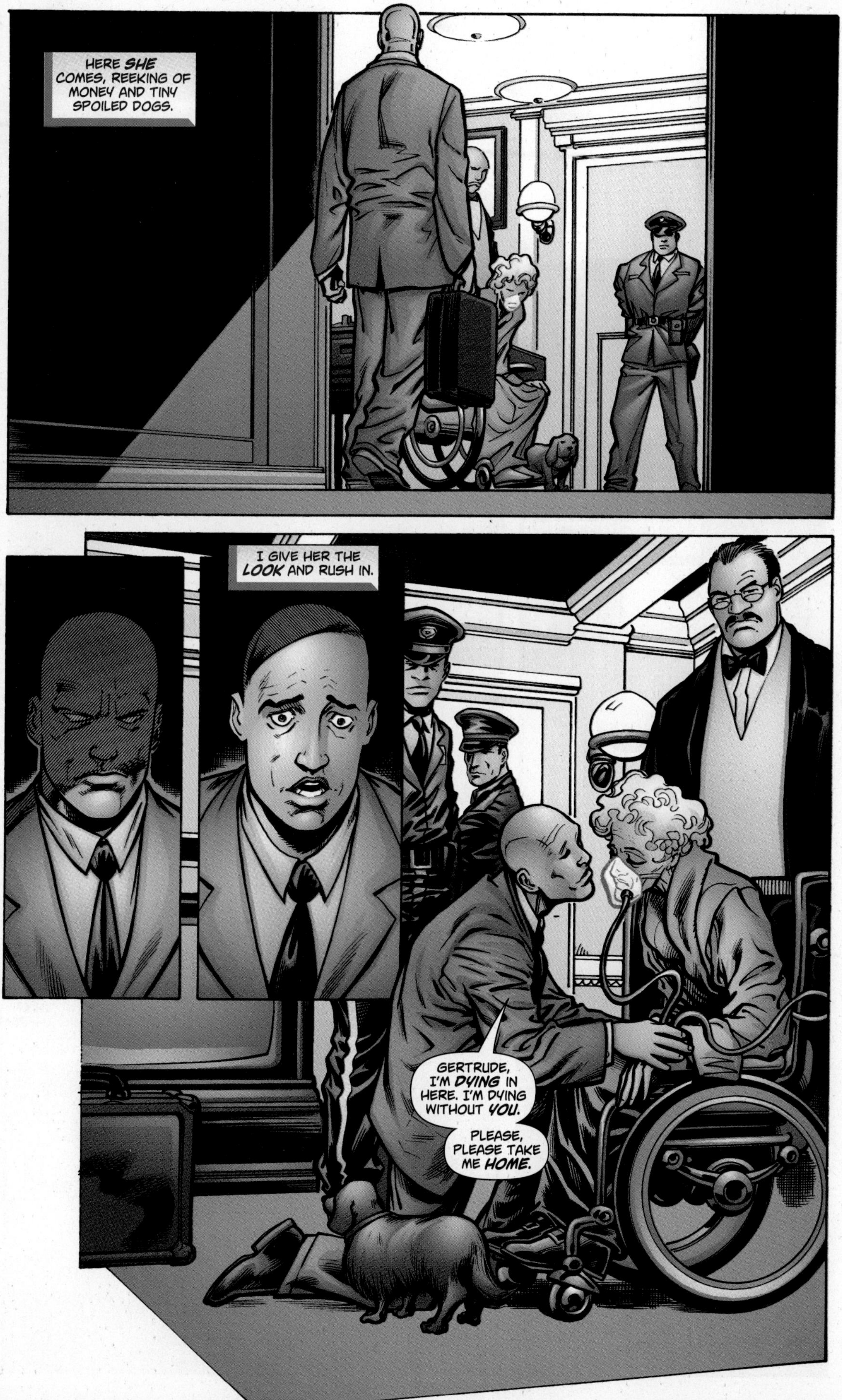
HERE SHE COMES, REEKING OF MONEY AND TINY SPOILED DOGS.
I GIVE HER THE LOOK AND RUSH IN.
GERTRUDE, I'M DYING IN HERE. I'M DYING WITHOUT YOU.
PLEASE, PLEASE TAKE ME HOME.

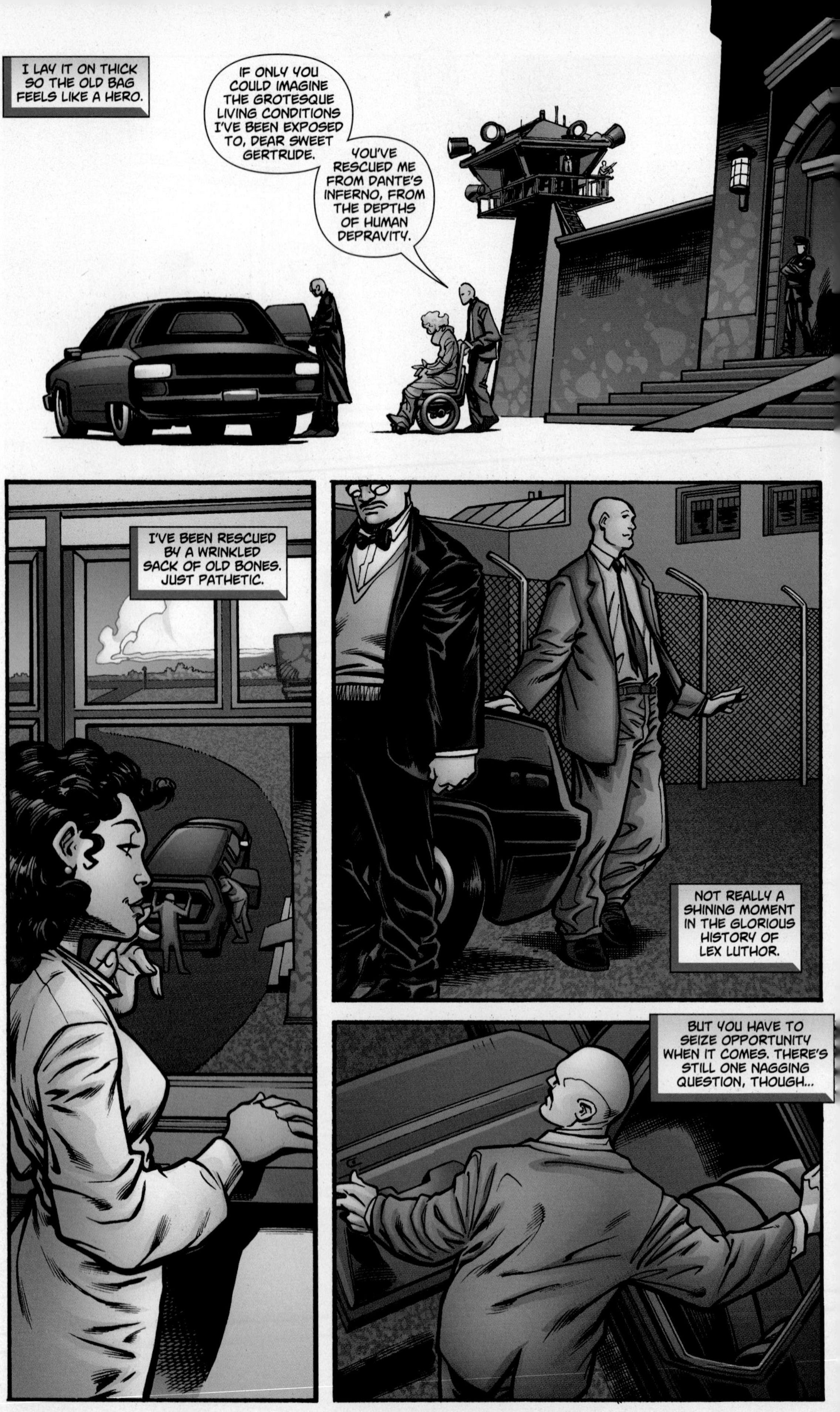
I LAY IT ON THICK SO THE OLD BAG FEELS LIKE A HERO.
IF ONLY YOU COULD IMAGINE THE GROTESQUE LIVING CONDITIONS I'VE BEEN EXPOSED TO, DEAR SWEET GERTRUDE.
YOU'VE RESCUED ME FROM DANTE'S INFERNO, FROM THE DEPTHS OF HUMAN DEPRAVITY.
I'VE BEEN RESCUED BY A WRINKLED SACK OF OLD BONES. JUST PATHETIC.
NOT REALLY A SHINING MOMENT IN THE GLORIOUS HISTORY OF LEX LUTHOR.
BUT YOU HAVE TO SEIZE OPPORTUNITY WHEN IT COMES. THERE'S STILL ONE NAGGING QUESTION, THOUGH...

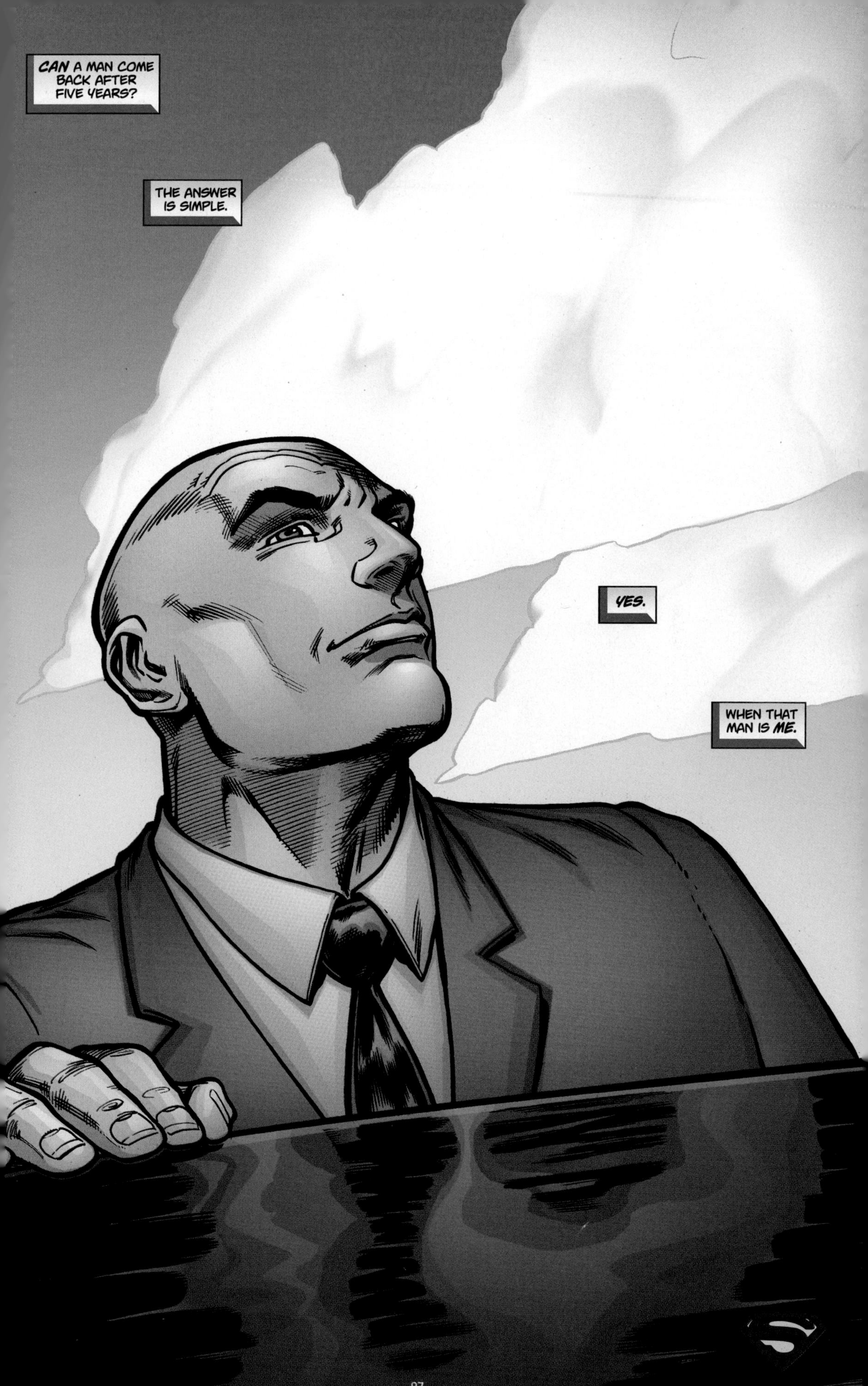
CAN A MAN COME BACK AFTER FIVE YEARS?
THE ANSWER IS SIMPLE.
YES.
WHEN THAT MAN IS ME.

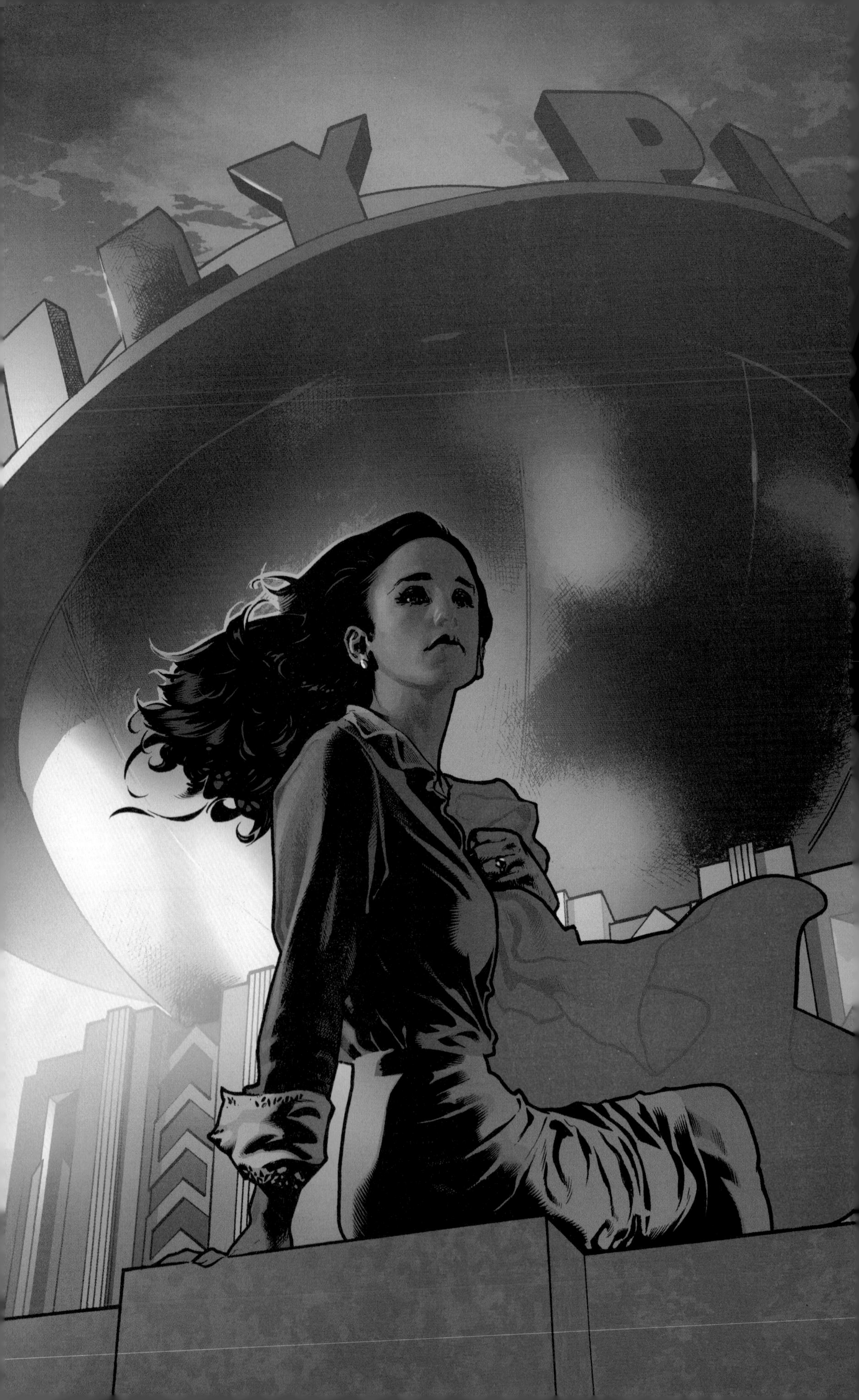

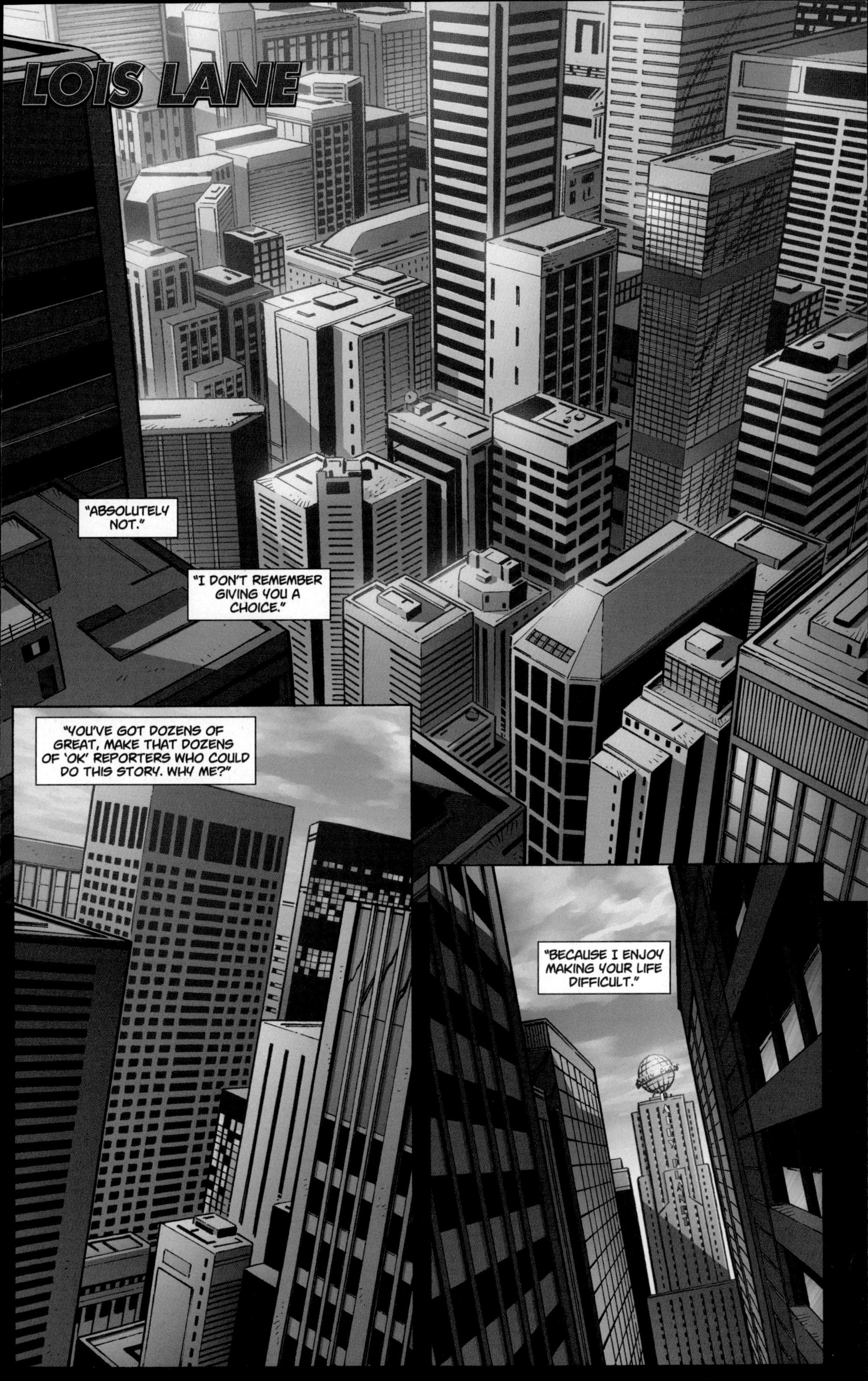
LOIS LANE
"ABSOLUTELY NOT."
"I DON'T REMEMBER GIVING YOU A CHOICE."
"YOU'VE GOT DOZENS OF GREAT, MAKE THAT DOZENS OF 'OK' REPORTERS WHO COULD DO THIS STORY. WHY ME?"
"BECAUSE I ENJOY MAKING YOUR LIFE DIFFICULT."

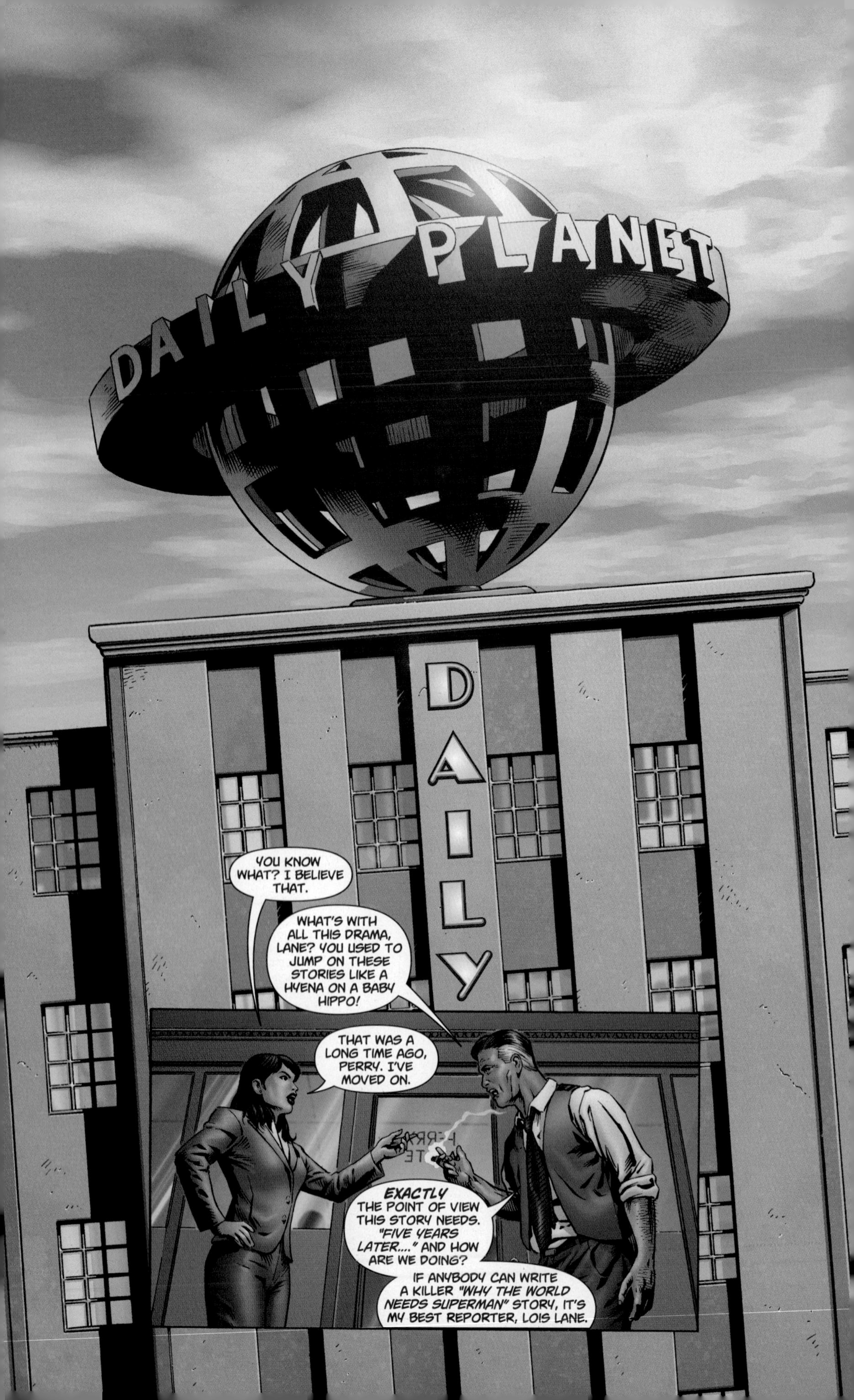
DAILY PLANET
DAILY
YOU KNOW WHAT? I BELIEVE THAT.
WHAT'S WITH ALL THIS DRAMA, LANE? YOU USED TO JUMP ON THESE STORIES LIKE A HYENA ON A BABY HIPPO!
THAT WAS A LONG TIME AGO, PERRY. I'VE MOVED ON.
EXACTLY THE POINT OF VIEW THIS STORY NEEDS. "FIVE YEARS LATER...." AND HOW ARE WE DOING?
IF ANYBODY CAN WRITE A KILLER "WHY THE WORLD NEEDS SUPERMAN" STORY, IT'S MY BEST REPORTER, LOIS LANE.

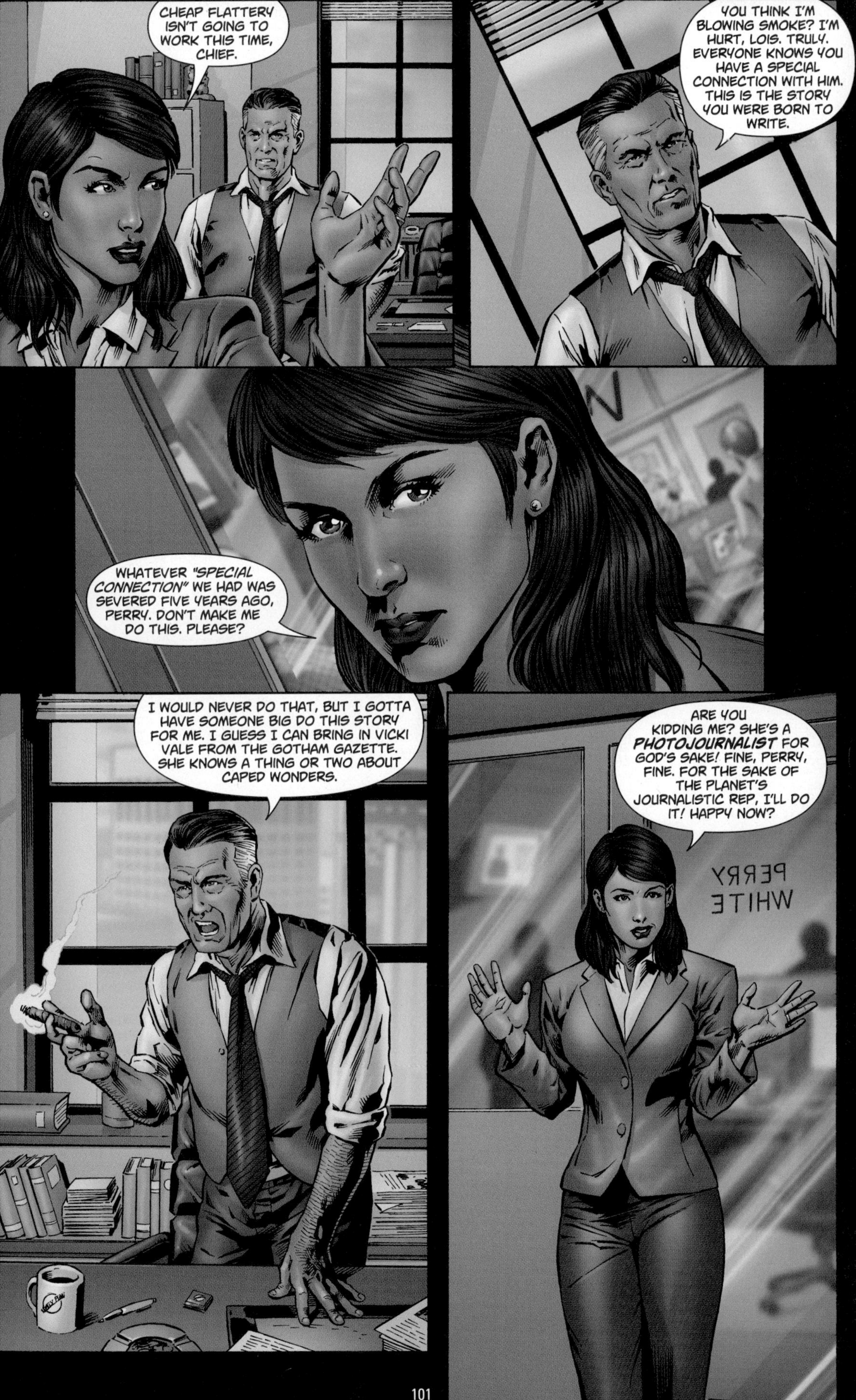
CHEAP FLATTERY ISN'T GOING TO WORK THIS TIME, CHIEF.
YOU THINK I'M BLOWING SMOKE? I'M HURT, LOIS. TRULY. EVERYONE KNOWS YOU HAVE A SPECIAL CONNECTION WITH HIM. THIS IS THE STORY YOU WERE BORN TO WRITE.
WHATEVER *"SPECIAL CONNECTION"* WE HAD WAS SEVERED FIVE YEARS AGO, PERRY. DON'T MAKE ME DO THIS. PLEASE?
I WOULD NEVER DO THAT, BUT I GOTTA HAVE SOMEONE BIG DO THIS STORY FOR ME. I GUESS I CAN BRING IN VICKI VALE FROM THE GOTHAM GAZETTE. SHE KNOWS A THING OR TWO ABOUT CAPED WONDERS.
ARE YOU KIDDING ME? SHE'S A ***PHOTOJOURNALIST*** FOR GOD'S SAKE! FINE, PERRY, FINE. FOR THE SAKE OF THE PLANET'S JOURNALISTIC REP, I'LL DO IT! HAPPY NOW?

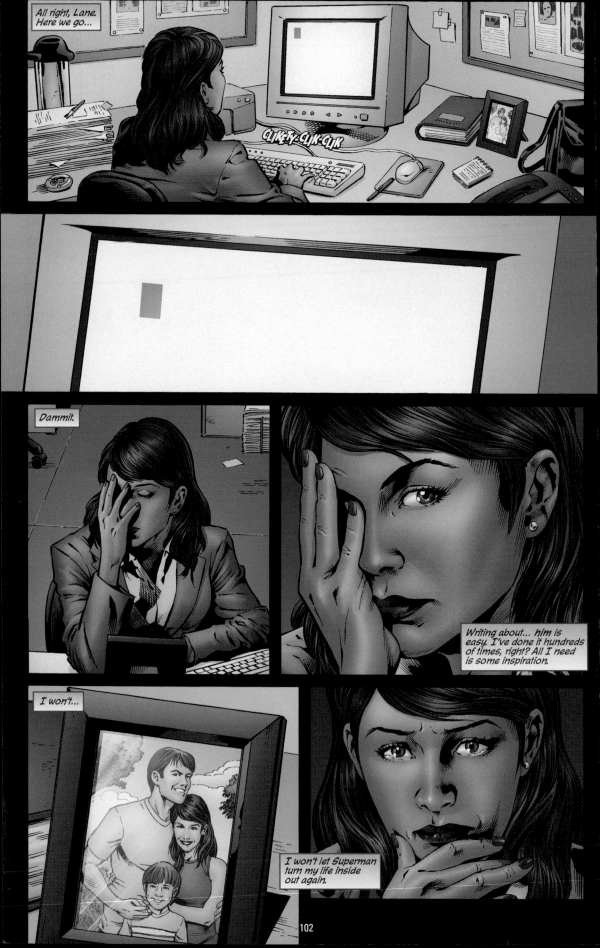

All right, Lane. Here we go...

CLIKETY-CLIK-CLIK

Dammit.

Writing about... *him* is easy. I've done it hundreds of times, right? All I need is some inspiration.

I won't...

I won't let Superman turn my life inside out again.

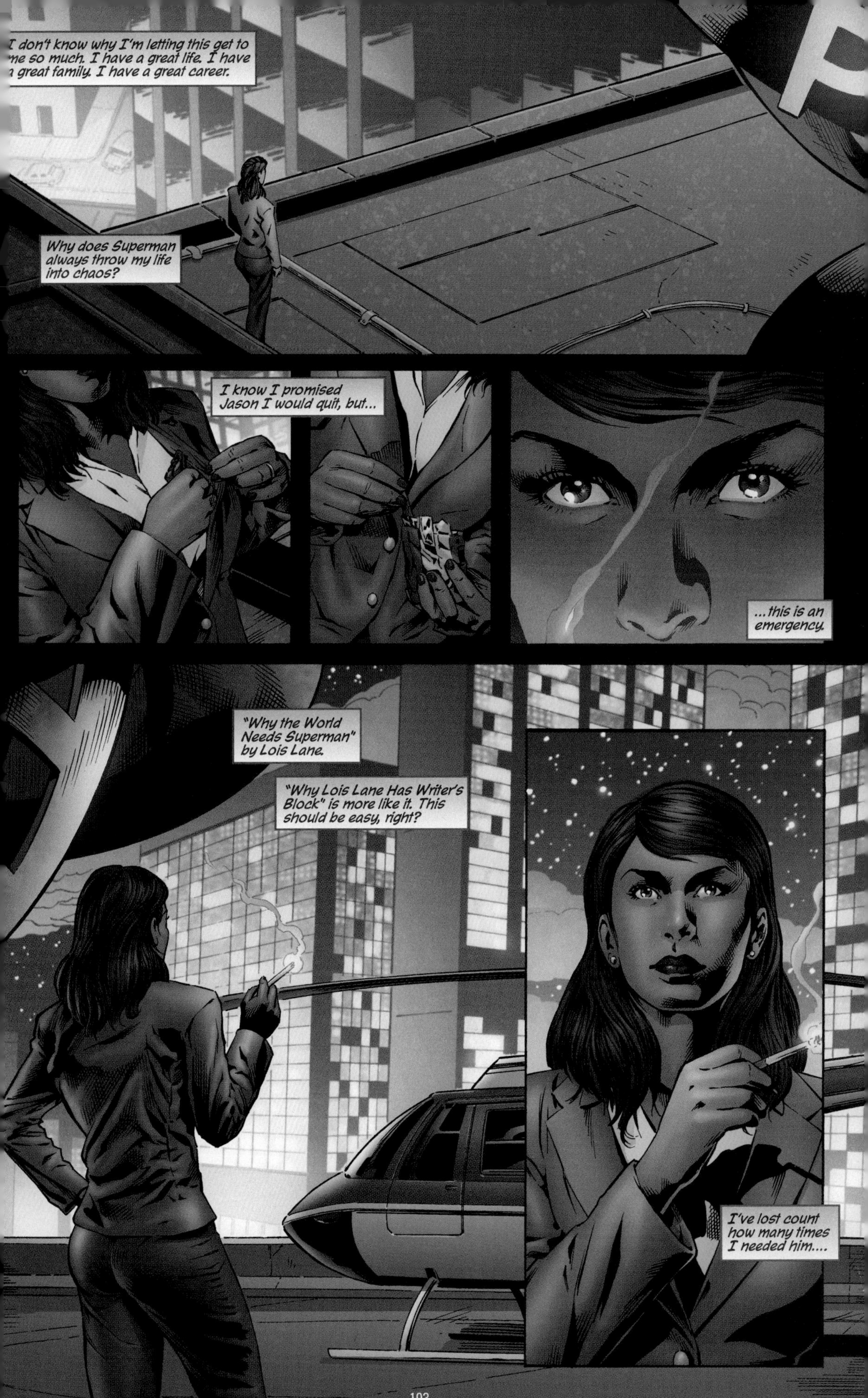
I don't know why I'm letting this get to me so much. I have a great life. I have a great family. I have a great career.
Why does Superman always throw my life into chaos?
I know I promised Jason I would quit, but...
...this is an emergency.
"Why the World Needs Superman" by Lois Lane.
"Why Lois Lane Has Writer's Block" is more like it. This should be easy, right?
I've lost count how many times I needed him....

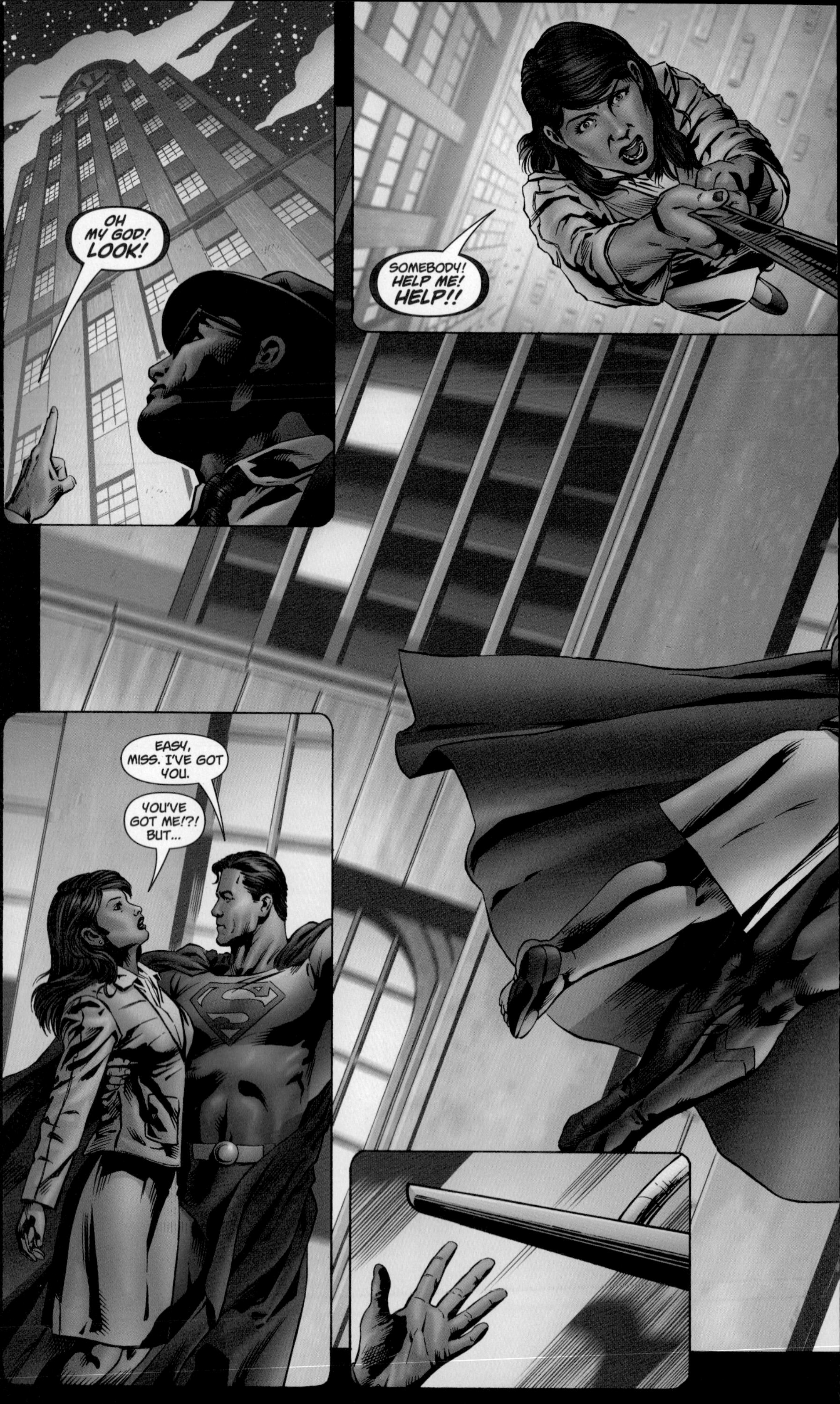
OH MY GOD! LOOK!
SOMEBODY! HELP ME! HELP!!
EASY, MISS. I'VE GOT YOU.
YOU'VE GOT ME!?! BUT...

AAAAAAAAAAAAAH!!

...WHO'S GOT YOU?!?

...but I stopped needing him long ago.

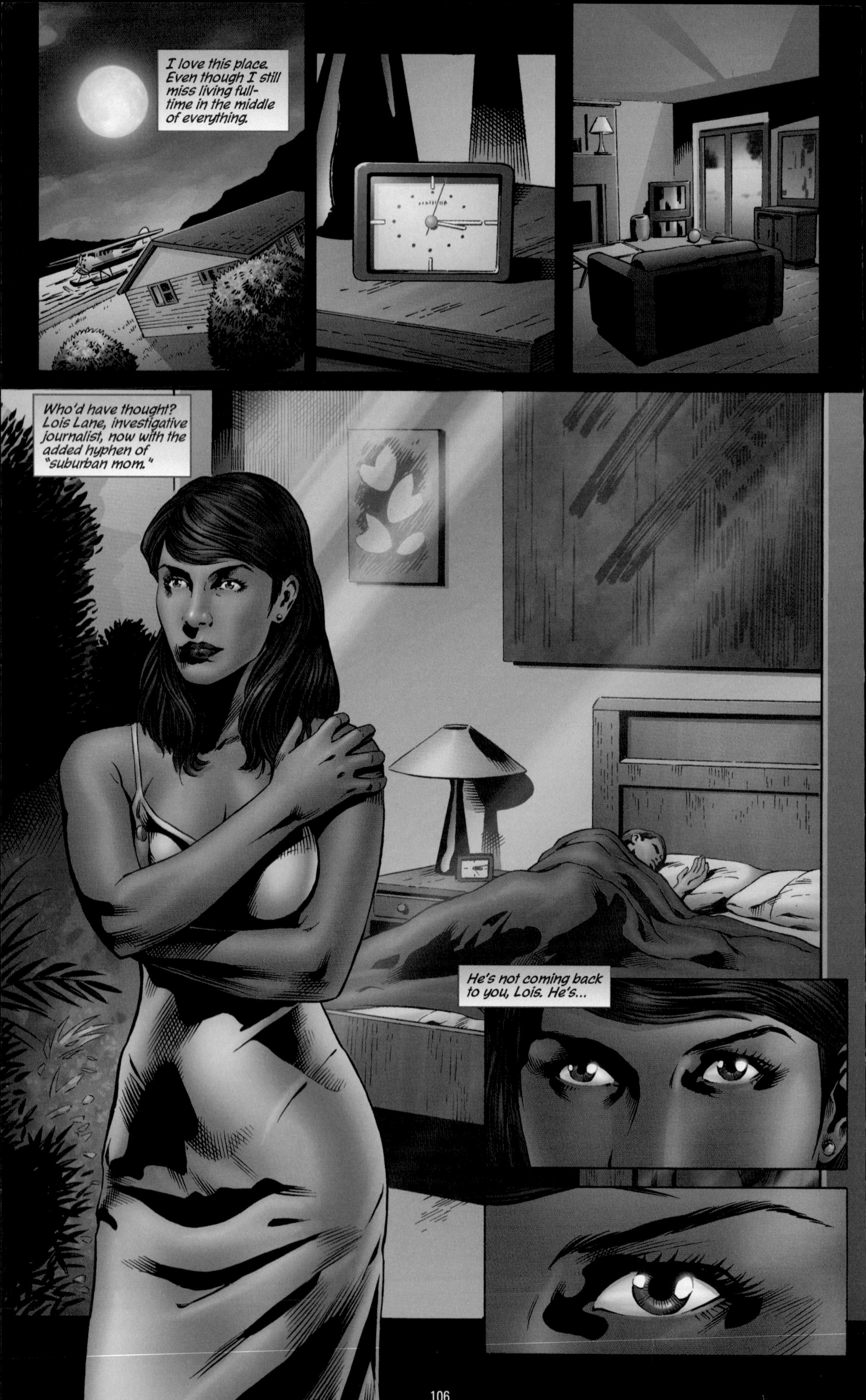
I love this place. Even though I still miss living full-time in the middle of everything.
Who'd have thought? Lois Lane, investigative journalist, now with the added hyphen of "suburban mom."
He's not coming back to you, Lois. He's...

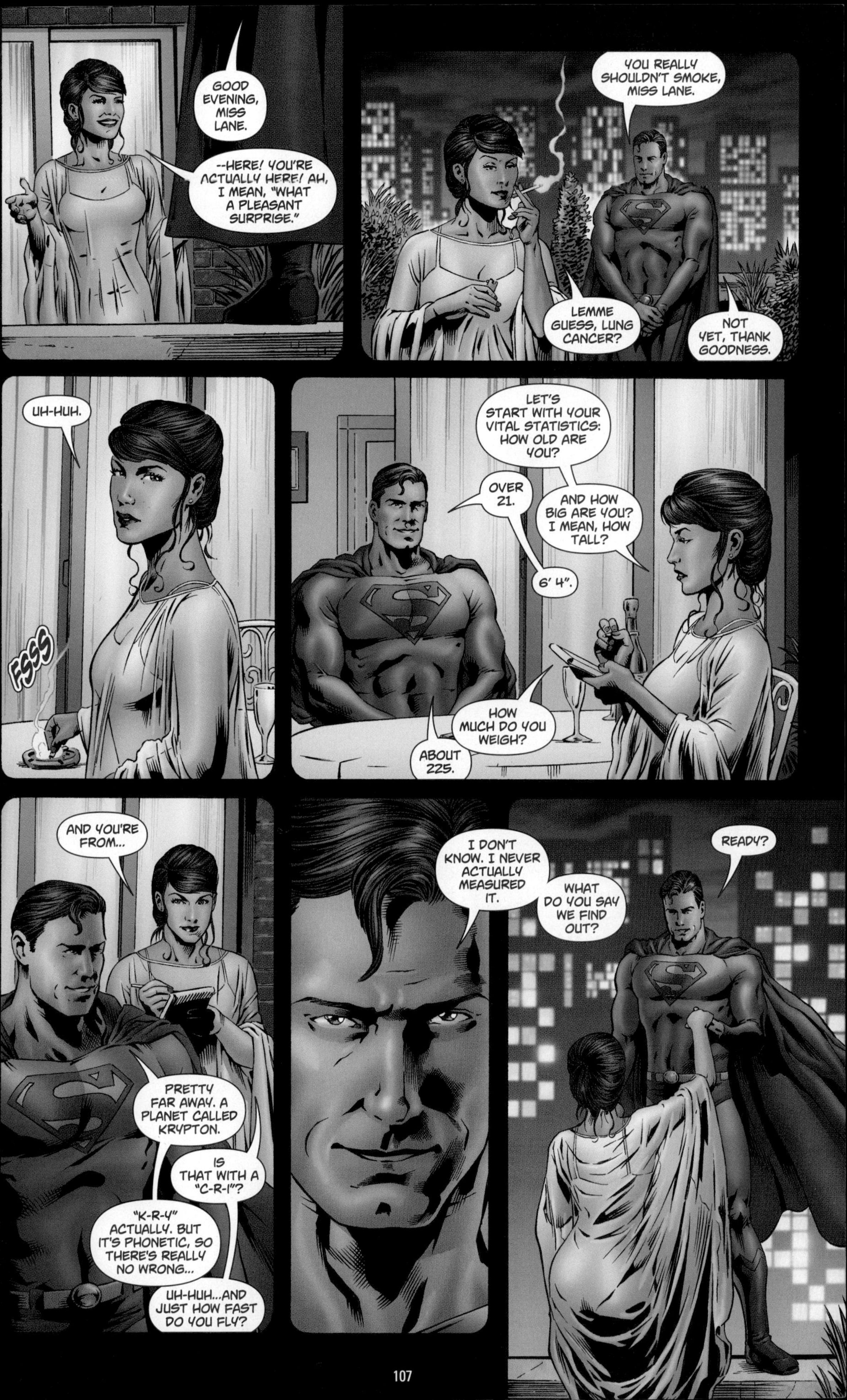
GOOD EVENING, MISS LANE.
--HERE! YOU'RE ACTUALLY HERE! AH, I MEAN, "WHAT A PLEASANT SURPRISE."
YOU REALLY SHOULDN'T SMOKE, MISS LANE.
LEMME GUESS, LUNG CANCER?
NOT YET, THANK GOODNESS.
UH-HUH.
FSSS
LET'S START WITH YOUR VITAL STATISTICS: HOW OLD ARE YOU?
OVER 21.
AND HOW BIG ARE YOU? I MEAN, HOW TALL?
6' 4".
HOW MUCH DO YOU WEIGH?
ABOUT 225.
AND YOU'RE FROM...
PRETTY FAR AWAY. A PLANET CALLED KRYPTON.
IS THAT WITH A "C-R-I"?
"K-R-Y" ACTUALLY. BUT IT'S PHONETIC, SO THERE'S REALLY NO WRONG...
UH-HUH...AND JUST HOW FAST DO YOU FLY?
I DON'T KNOW. I NEVER ACTUALLY MEASURED IT.
WHAT DO YOU SAY WE FIND OUT?
READY?

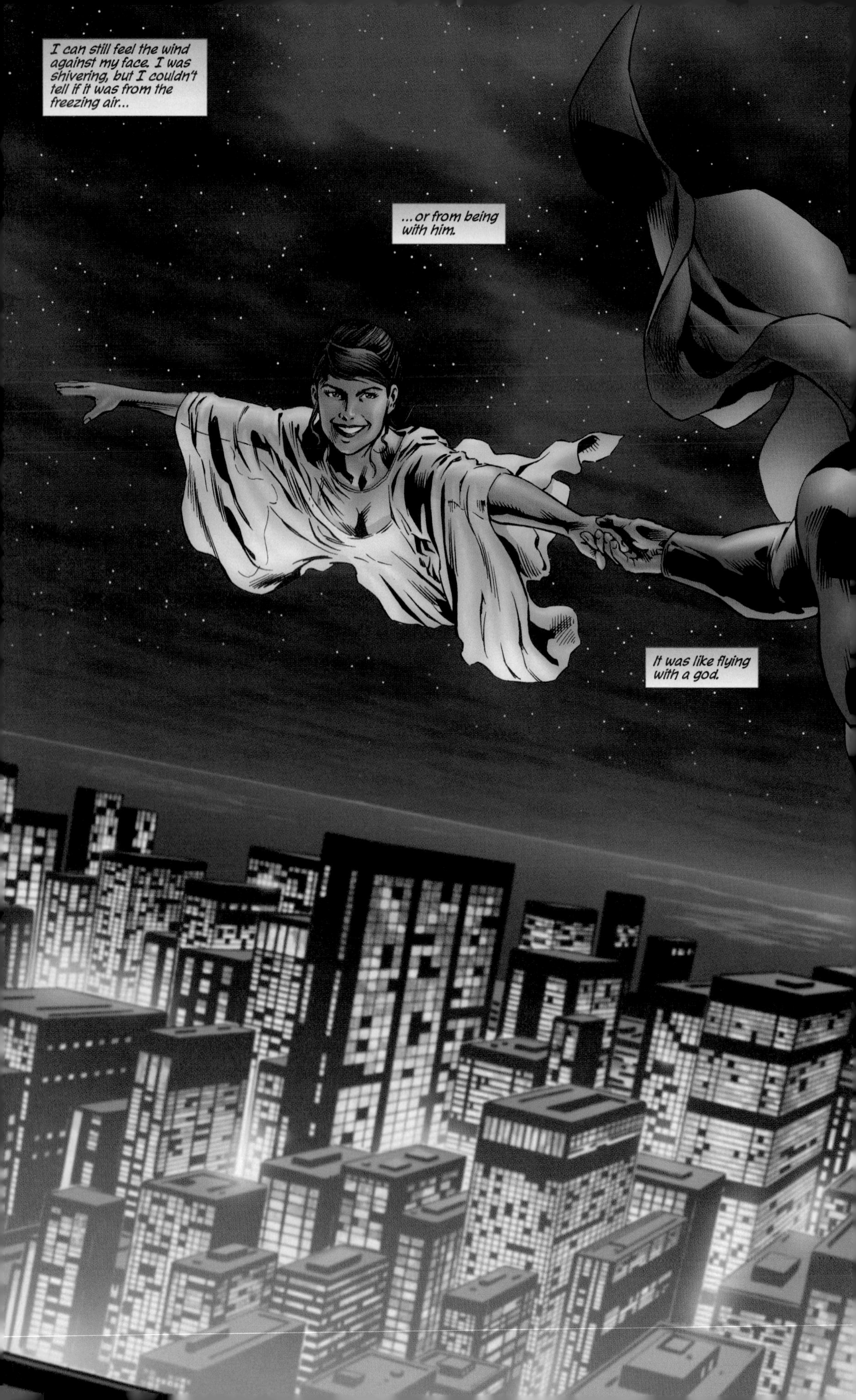
I can still feel the wind against my face. I was shivering, but I couldn't tell if it was from the freezing air...
...or from being with him.
It was like flying with a god.

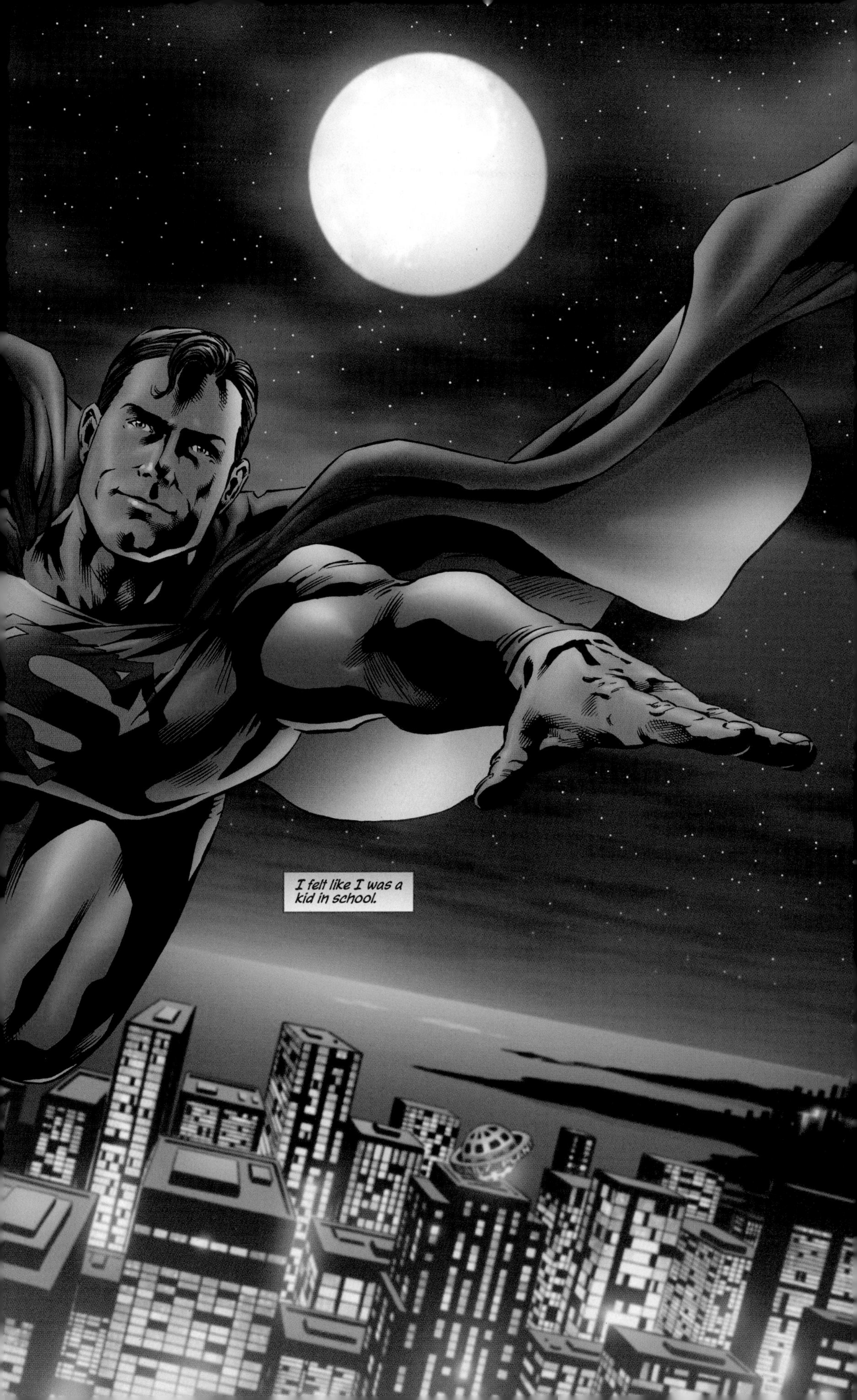
I felt like I was a kid in school.

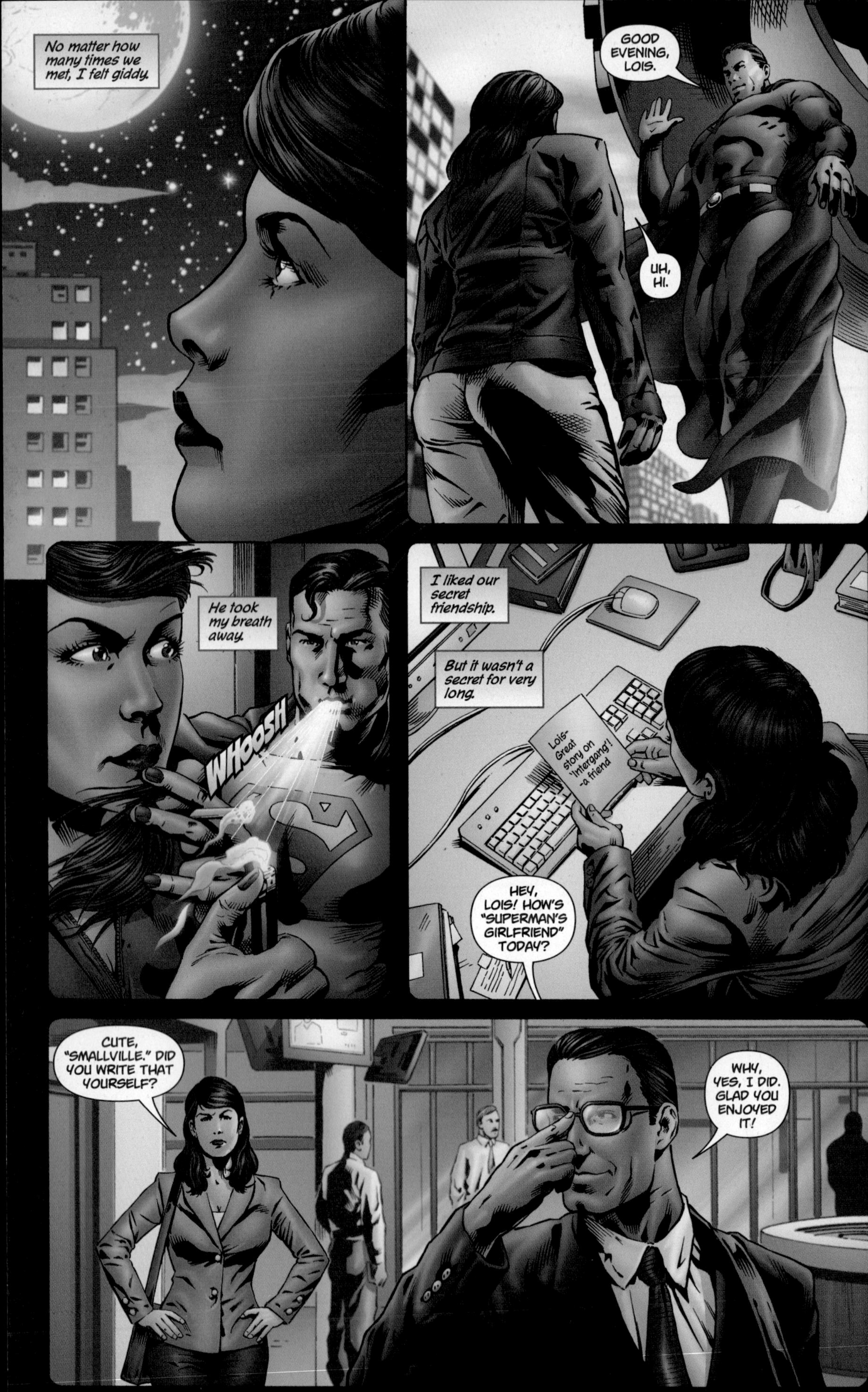
No matter how many times we met, I felt giddy.
GOOD EVENING, LOIS.
UH, HI.
He took my breath away.
WHOOSH
I liked our secret friendship.
But it wasn't a secret for very long.
Lois- Great story on "Intergang"! -a friend
HEY, LOIS! HOW'S "SUPERMAN'S GIRLFRIEND" TODAY?
CUTE, "SMALLVILLE." DID YOU WRITE THAT YOURSELF?
WHY, YES, I DID. GLAD YOU ENJOYED IT!

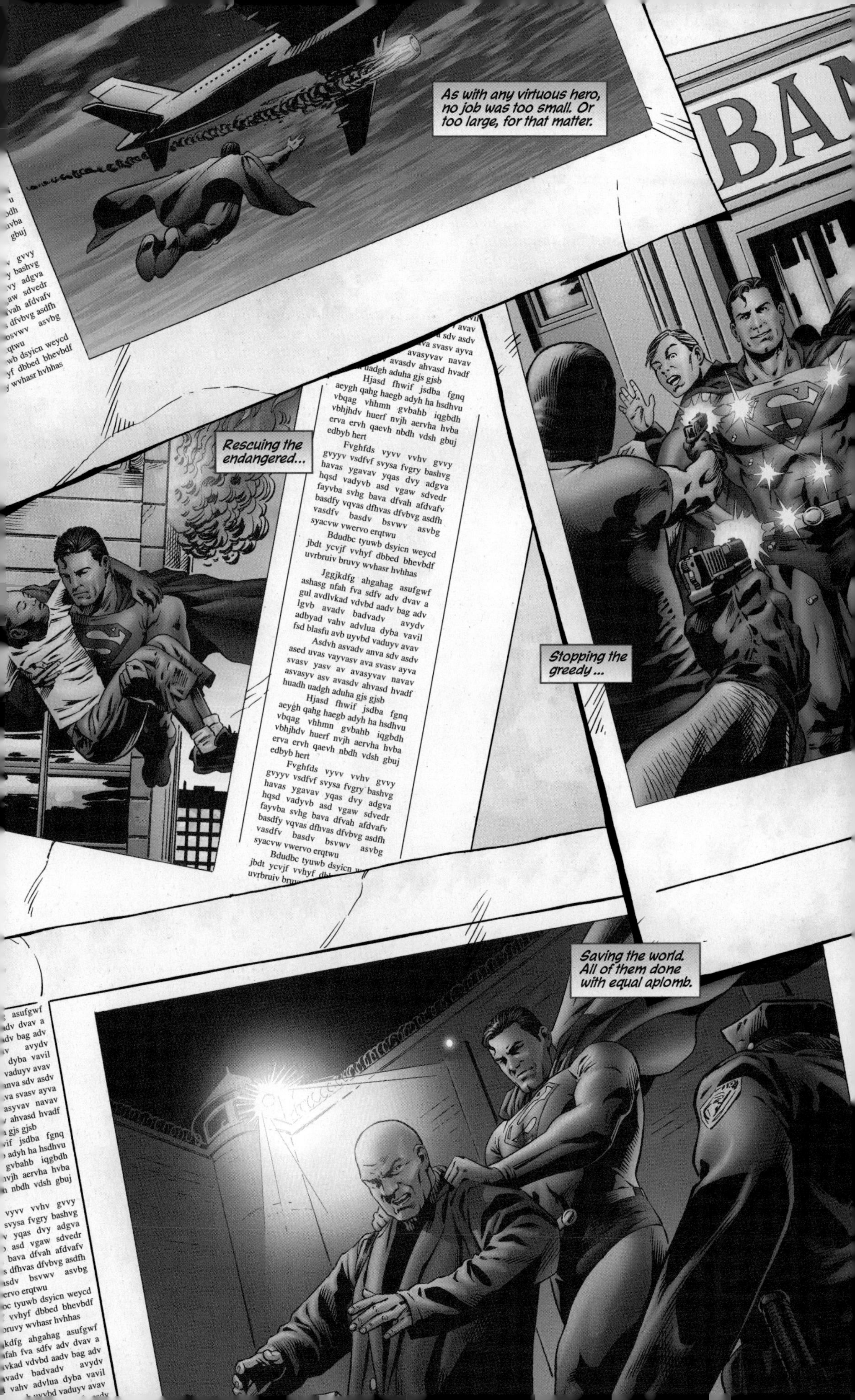
As with any virtuous hero, no job was too small. Or too large, for that matter.
Rescuing the endangered...
Stopping the greedy ...
Saving the world. All of them done with equal aplomb.

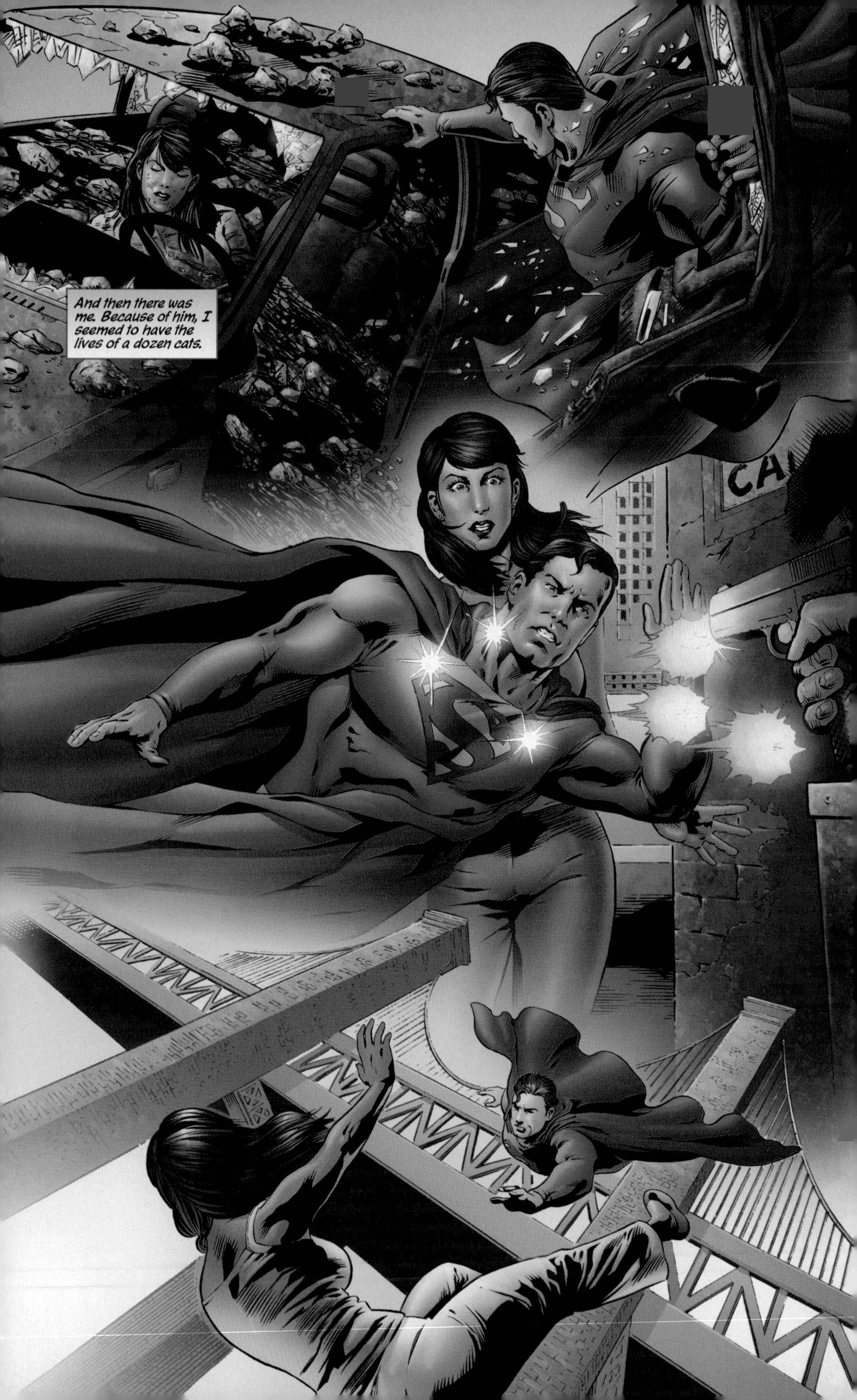
And then there was me. Because of him, I seemed to have the lives of a dozen cats.

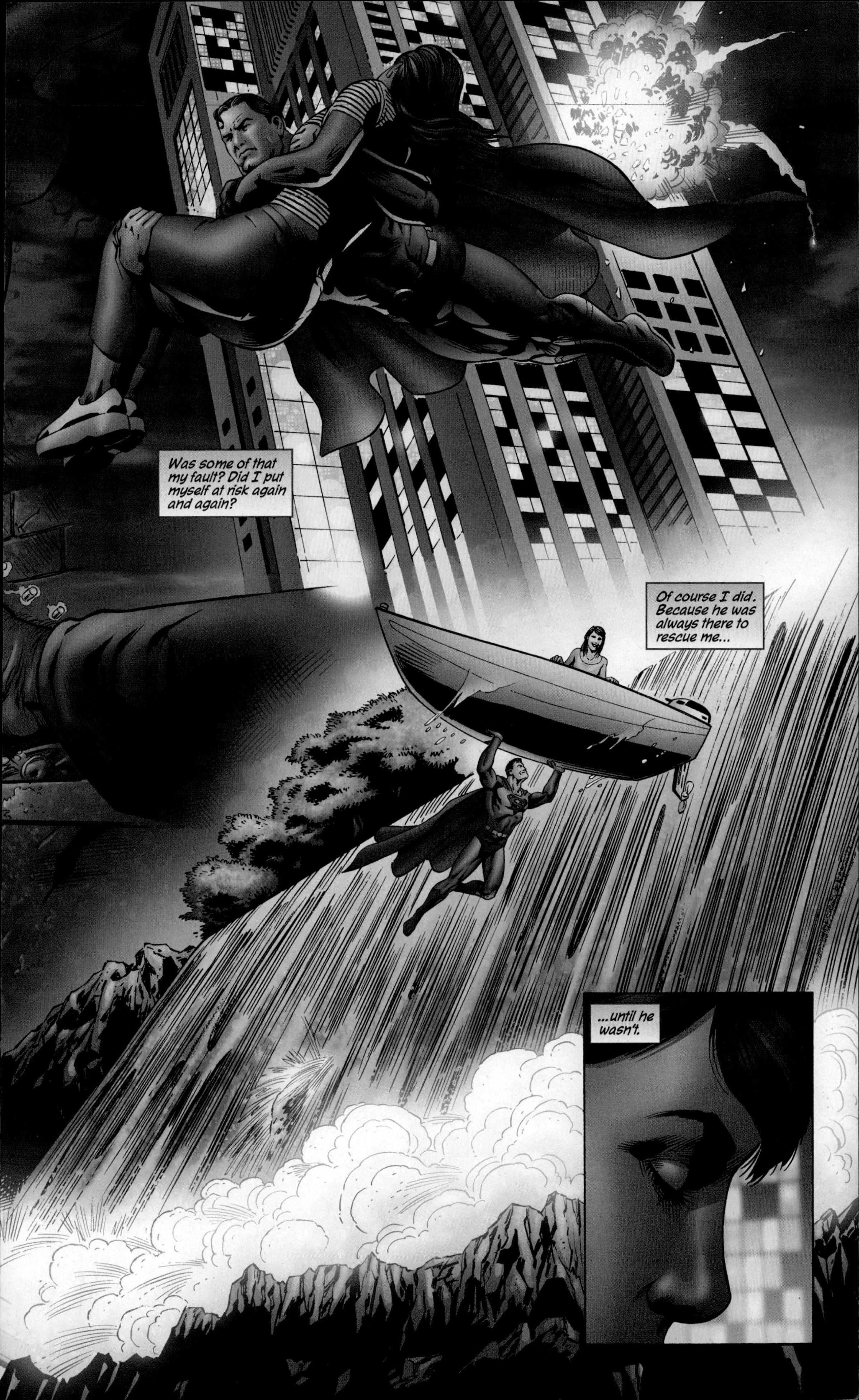
Was some of that my fault? Did I put myself at risk again and again?
Of course I did. Because he was always there to rescue me...
...until he wasn't.

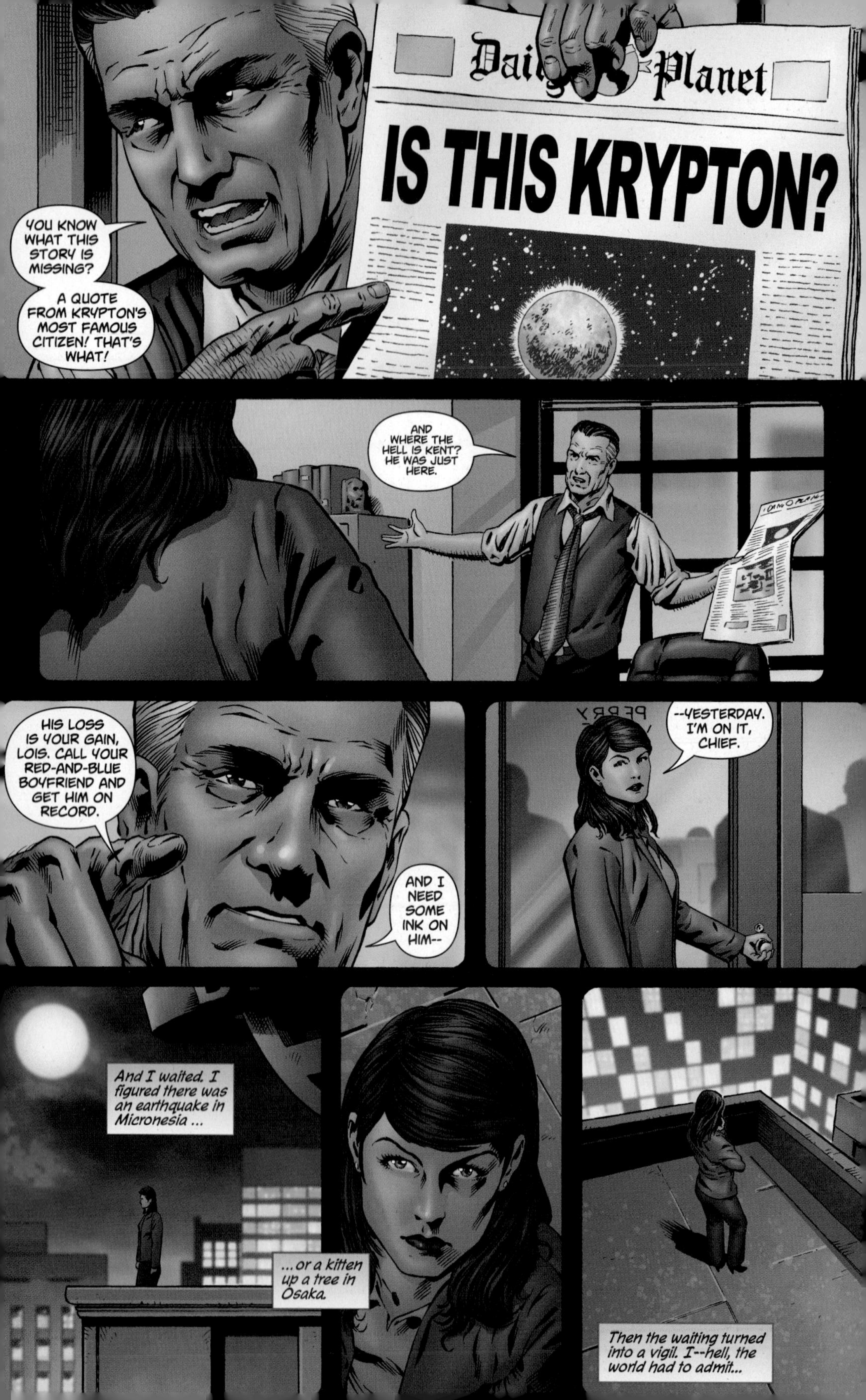

Daily Planet
IS THIS KRYPTON?
YOU KNOW WHAT THIS STORY IS MISSING?
A QUOTE FROM KRYPTON'S MOST FAMOUS CITIZEN! THAT'S WHAT!
AND WHERE THE HELL IS KENT? HE WAS JUST HERE.
HIS LOSS IS YOUR GAIN, LOIS. CALL YOUR RED-AND-BLUE BOYFRIEND AND GET HIM ON RECORD.
AND I NEED SOME INK ON HIM--
PERRY
--YESTERDAY. I'M ON IT, CHIEF.
And I waited. I figured there was an earthquake in Micronesia ...
...or a kitten up a tree in Osaka.
Then the waiting turned into a vigil. I--hell, the world had to admit...

SUPERMAN DISAPPEARS!

NOT SEEN SINCE KRYPTON DISCOVERY

| LOIS LANE ON SUPERMAN'S DISAPPEARANCE pg 3 | FULL COVERAGE ON MISSING-PERSON CASE OF THE CENTURY INSIDE! |

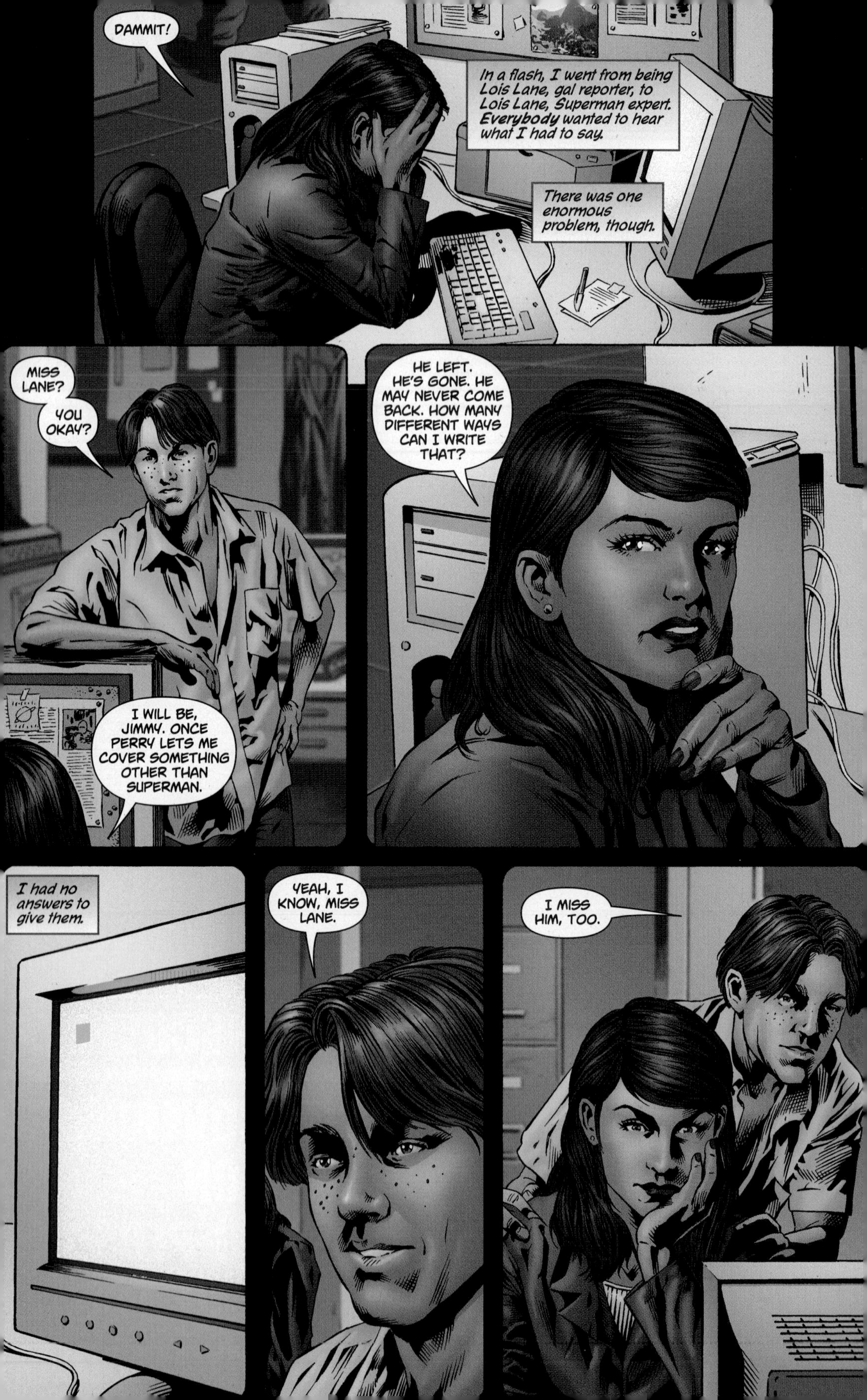
DAMMIT!
In a flash, I went from being Lois Lane, gal reporter, to Lois Lane, Superman expert. Everybody wanted to hear what I had to say.
There was one enormous problem, though.
MISS LANE?
YOU OKAY?
HE LEFT. HE'S GONE. HE MAY NEVER COME BACK. HOW MANY DIFFERENT WAYS CAN I WRITE THAT?
I WILL BE, JIMMY. ONCE PERRY LETS ME COVER SOMETHING OTHER THAN SUPERMAN.
I had no answers to give them.
YEAH, I KNOW, MISS LANE.
I MISS HIM, TOO.

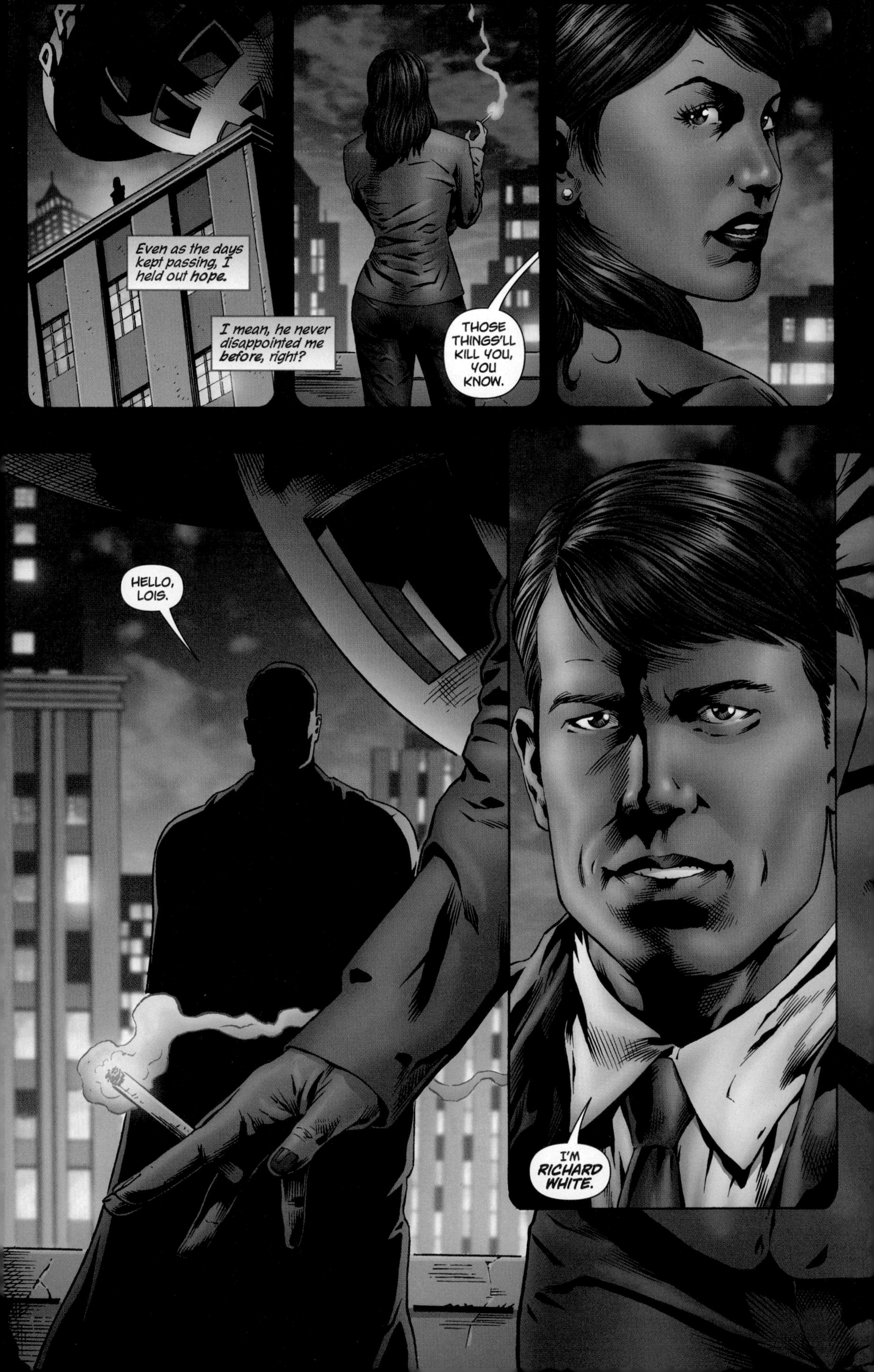
Even as the days kept passing, I held out hope.
I mean, he never disappointed me before, right?
THOSE THINGS'LL KILL YOU, YOU KNOW.
HELLO, LOIS.
I'M RICHARD WHITE.

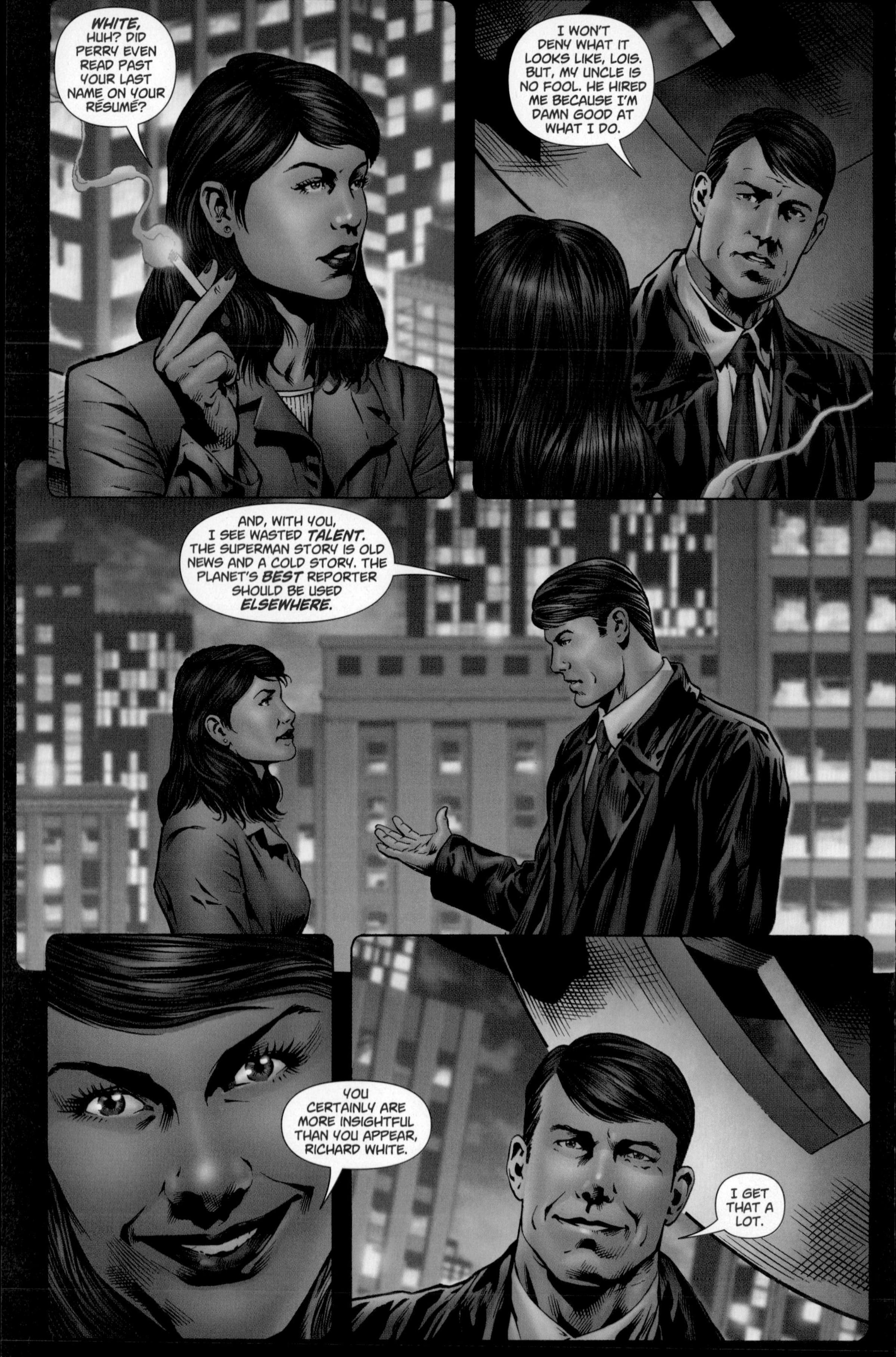
WHITE, HUH? DID PERRY EVEN READ PAST YOUR LAST NAME ON YOUR RÉSUMÉ?
I WON'T DENY WHAT IT LOOKS LIKE, LOIS. BUT, MY UNCLE IS NO FOOL. HE HIRED ME BECAUSE I'M DAMN GOOD AT WHAT I DO.
AND, WITH YOU, I SEE WASTED TALENT. THE SUPERMAN STORY IS OLD NEWS AND A COLD STORY. THE PLANET'S BEST REPORTER SHOULD BE USED ELSEWHERE.
YOU CERTAINLY ARE MORE INSIGHTFUL THAN YOU APPEAR, RICHARD WHITE.
I GET THAT A LOT.

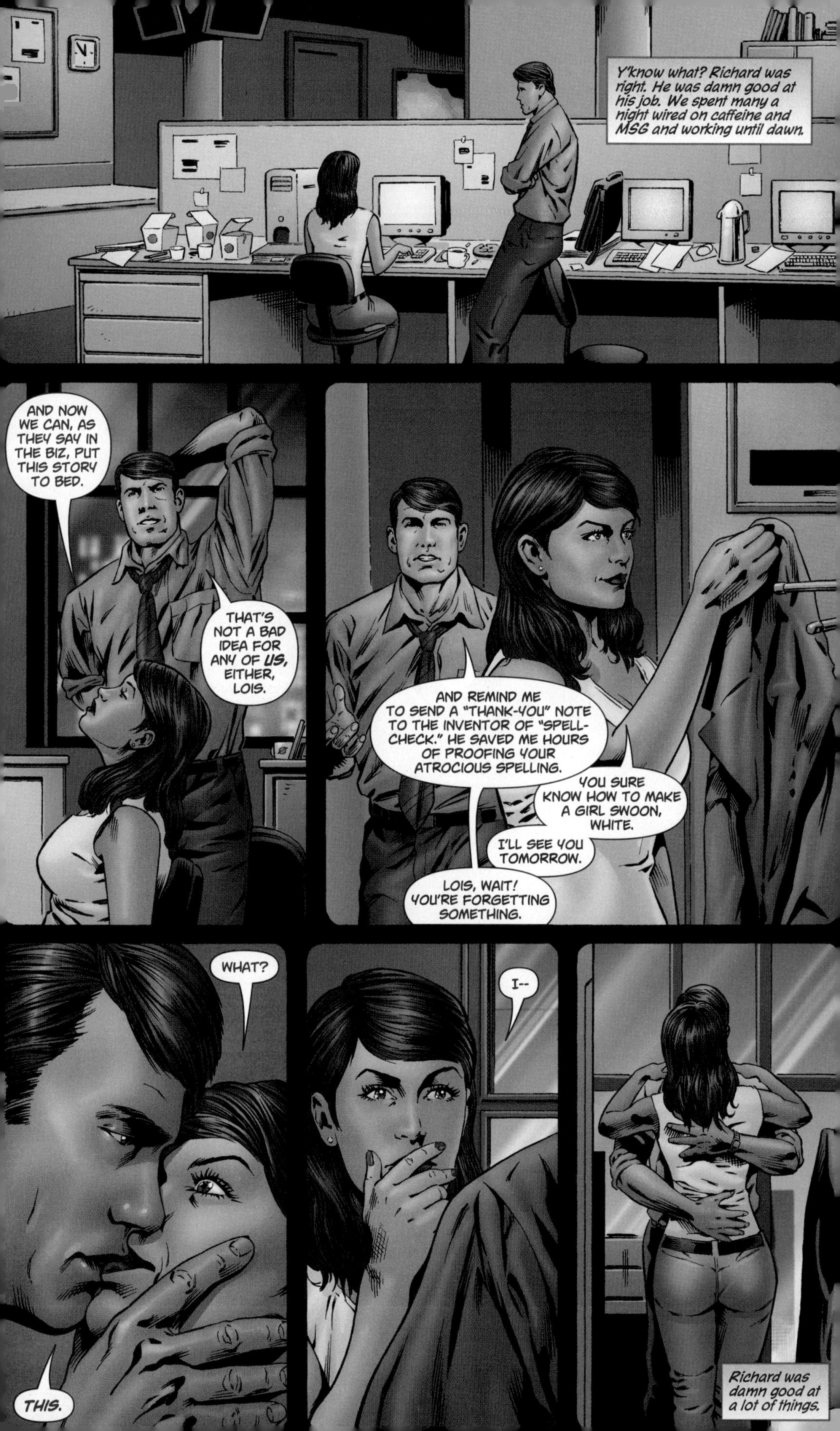
Y'know what? Richard was right. He was damn good at his job. We spent many a night wired on caffeine and MSG and working until dawn.
AND NOW WE CAN, AS THEY SAY IN THE BIZ, PUT THIS STORY TO BED.
THAT'S NOT A BAD IDEA FOR ANY OF US, EITHER, LOIS.
AND REMIND ME TO SEND A "THANK-YOU" NOTE TO THE INVENTOR OF "SPELL-CHECK." HE SAVED ME HOURS OF PROOFING YOUR ATROCIOUS SPELLING.
YOU SURE KNOW HOW TO MAKE A GIRL SWOON, WHITE.
I'LL SEE YOU TOMORROW.
LOIS, WAIT! YOU'RE FORGETTING SOMETHING.
WHAT?
THIS.
I--
Richard was damn good at a lot of things.

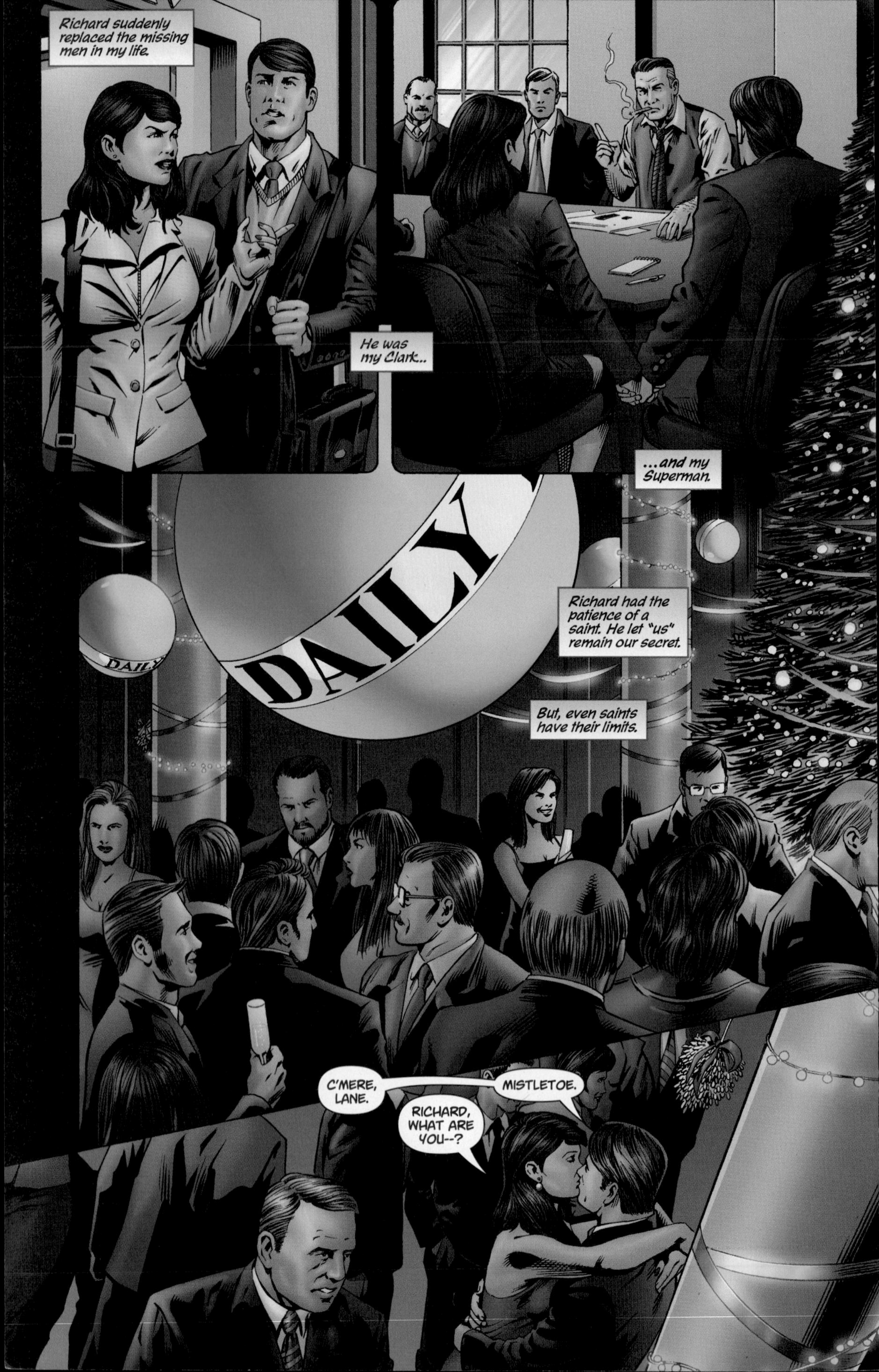
Richard suddenly replaced the missing men in my life.
He was my Clark...
...and my Superman.
DAILY
DAILY
Richard had the patience of a saint. He let "us" remain our secret.
But, even saints have their limits.
C'MERE, LANE.
MISTLETOE.
RICHARD, WHAT ARE YOU--?

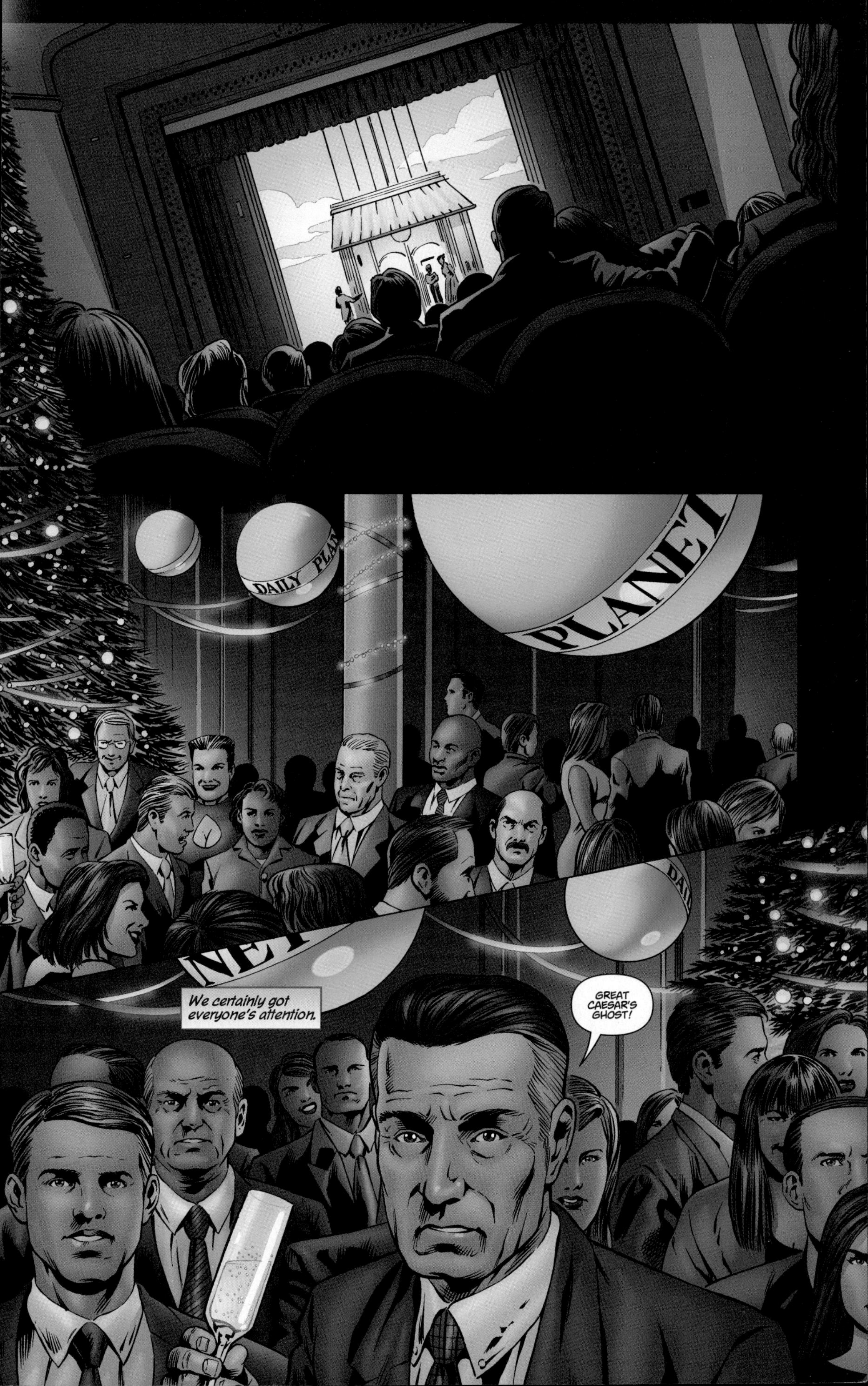
DAILY PLAN
PLANET
NET
We certainly got everyone's attention.
GREAT CAESAR'S GHOST!

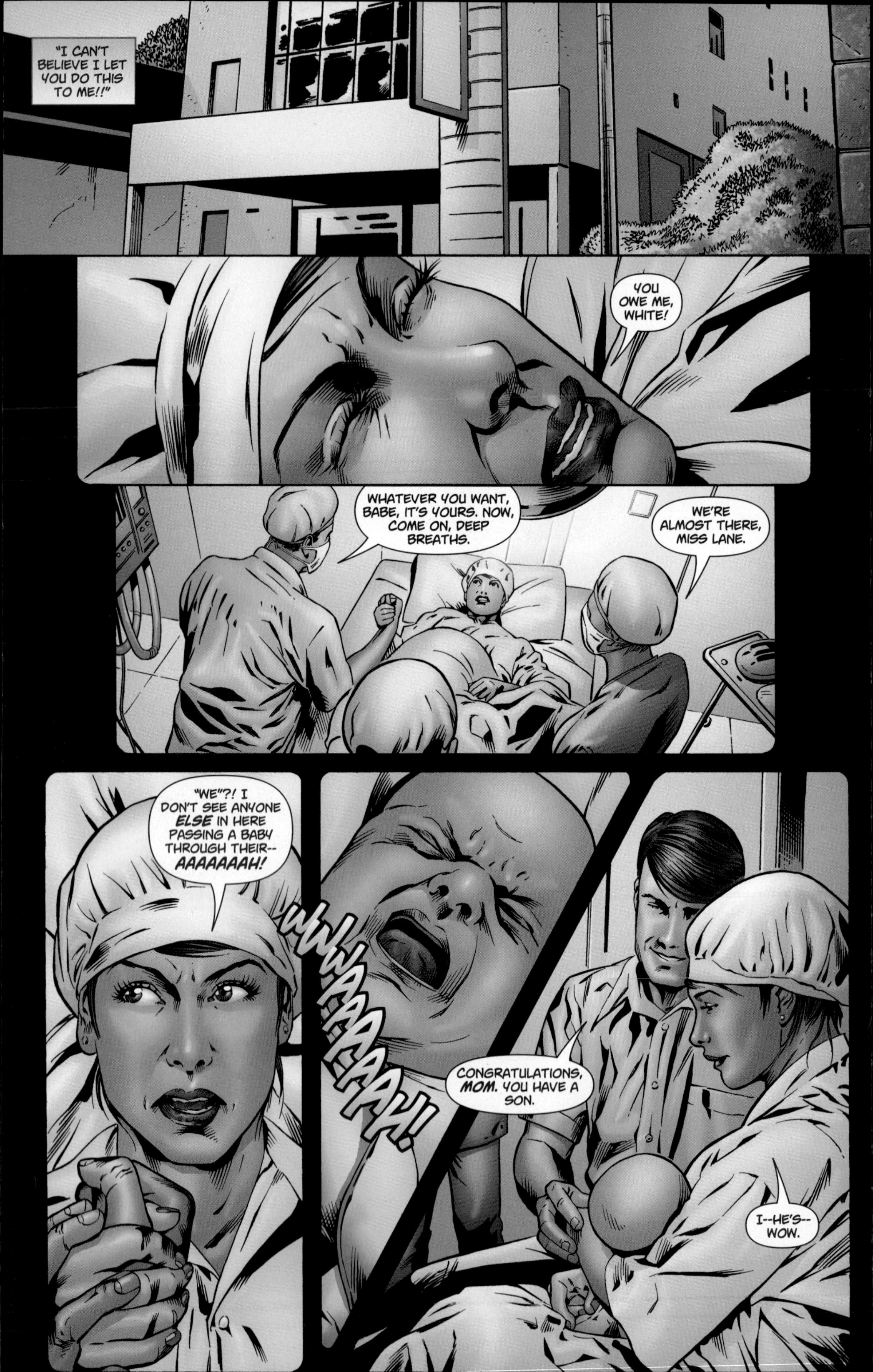
"I CAN'T BELIEVE I LET YOU DO THIS TO ME!!"
YOU OWE ME, WHITE!
WHATEVER YOU WANT, BABE, IT'S YOURS. NOW, COME ON, DEEP BREATHS.
WE'RE ALMOST THERE, MISS LANE.
"WE"?! I DON'T SEE ANYONE ELSE IN HERE PASSING A BABY THROUGH THEIR-- AAAAAAAH!
WWWAAAAAAH!
CONGRATULATIONS, MOM. YOU HAVE A SON.
I--HE'S-- WOW.

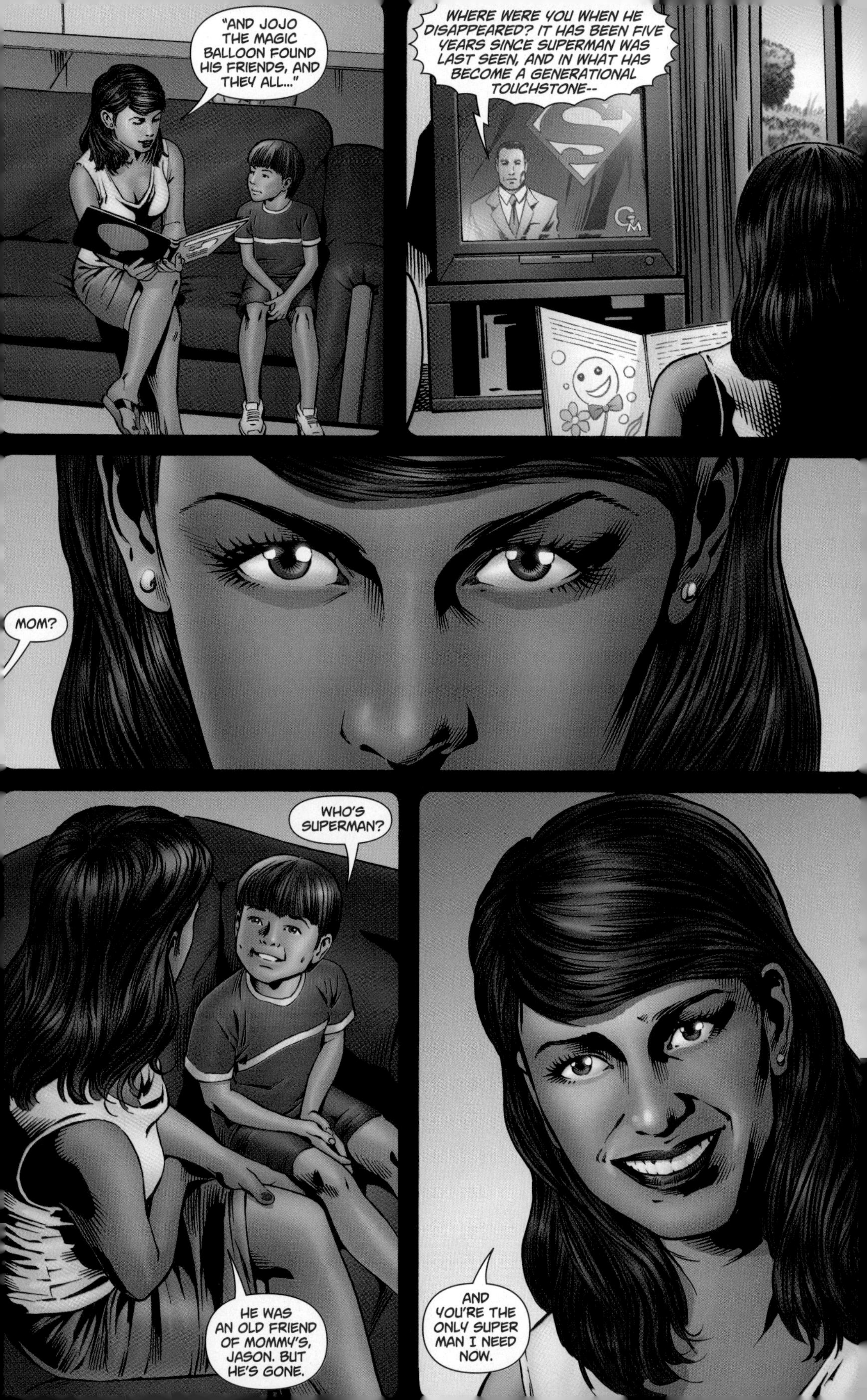
"AND JOJO THE MAGIC BALLOON FOUND HIS FRIENDS, AND THEY ALL..."
WHERE WERE YOU WHEN HE DISAPPEARED? IT HAS BEEN FIVE YEARS SINCE SUPERMAN WAS LAST SEEN, AND IN WHAT HAS BECOME A GENERATIONAL TOUCHSTONE--
MOM?
WHO'S SUPERMAN?
HE WAS AN OLD FRIEND OF MOMMY'S, JASON. BUT HE'S GONE.
AND YOU'RE THE ONLY SUPER MAN I NEED NOW.

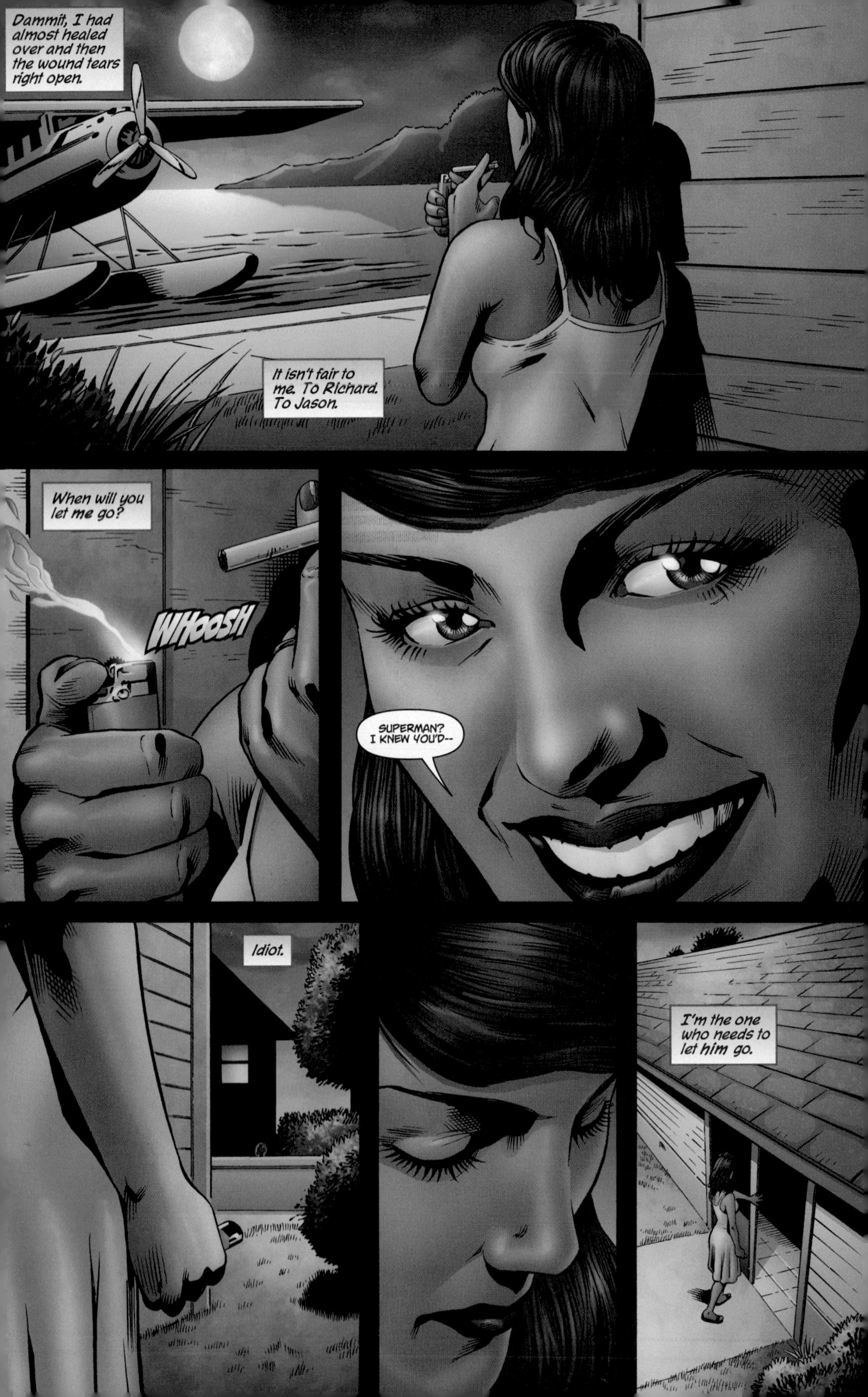
Dammit, I had almost healed over and then the wound tears right open.
It isn't fair to me. To Richard. To Jason.
When will you let me go?
WHOOSH
SUPERMAN? I KNEW YOU'D--
Idiot.
I'm the one who needs to let him go.

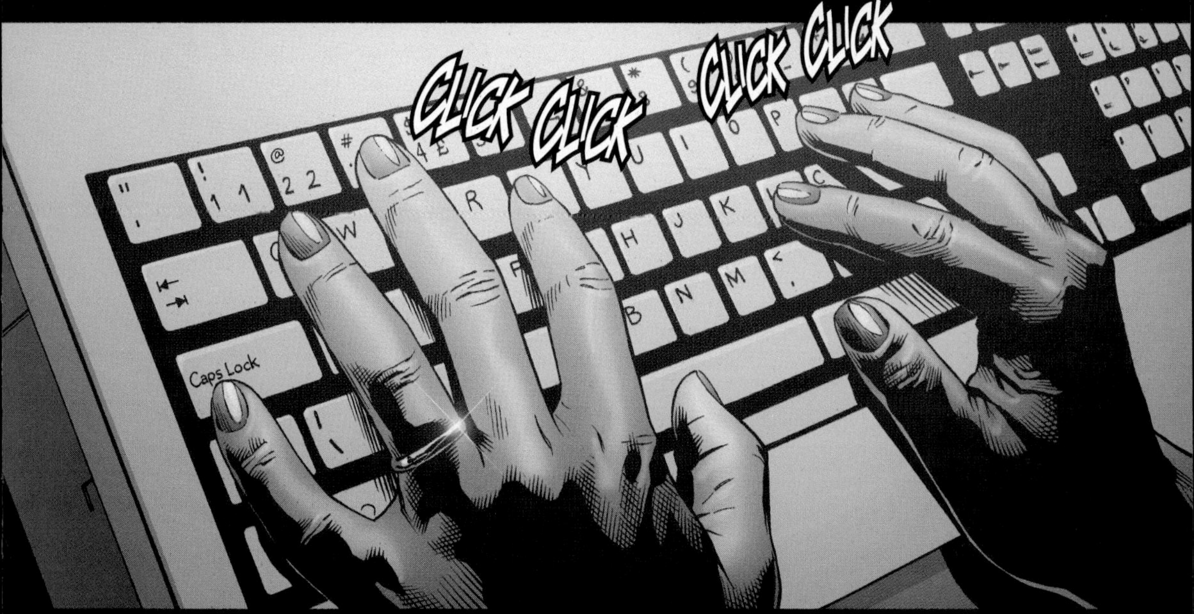
CLICK CLICK
CLICK CLICK

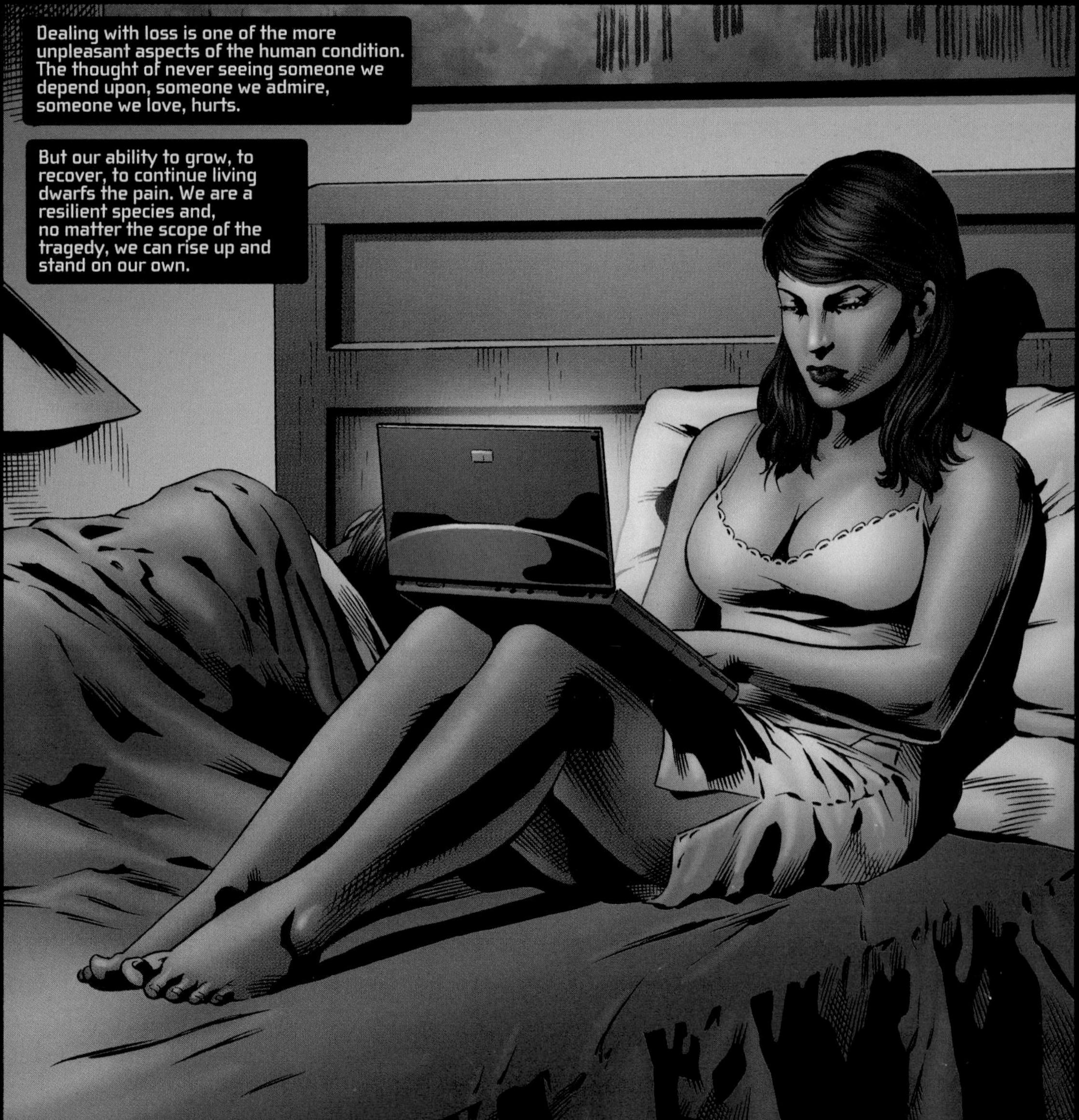
Dealing with loss is one of the more unpleasant aspects of the human condition. The thought of never seeing someone we depend upon, someone we admire, someone we love, hurts.
But our ability to grow, to recover, to continue living dwarfs the pain. We are a resilient species and, no matter the scope of the tragedy, we can rise up and stand on our own.

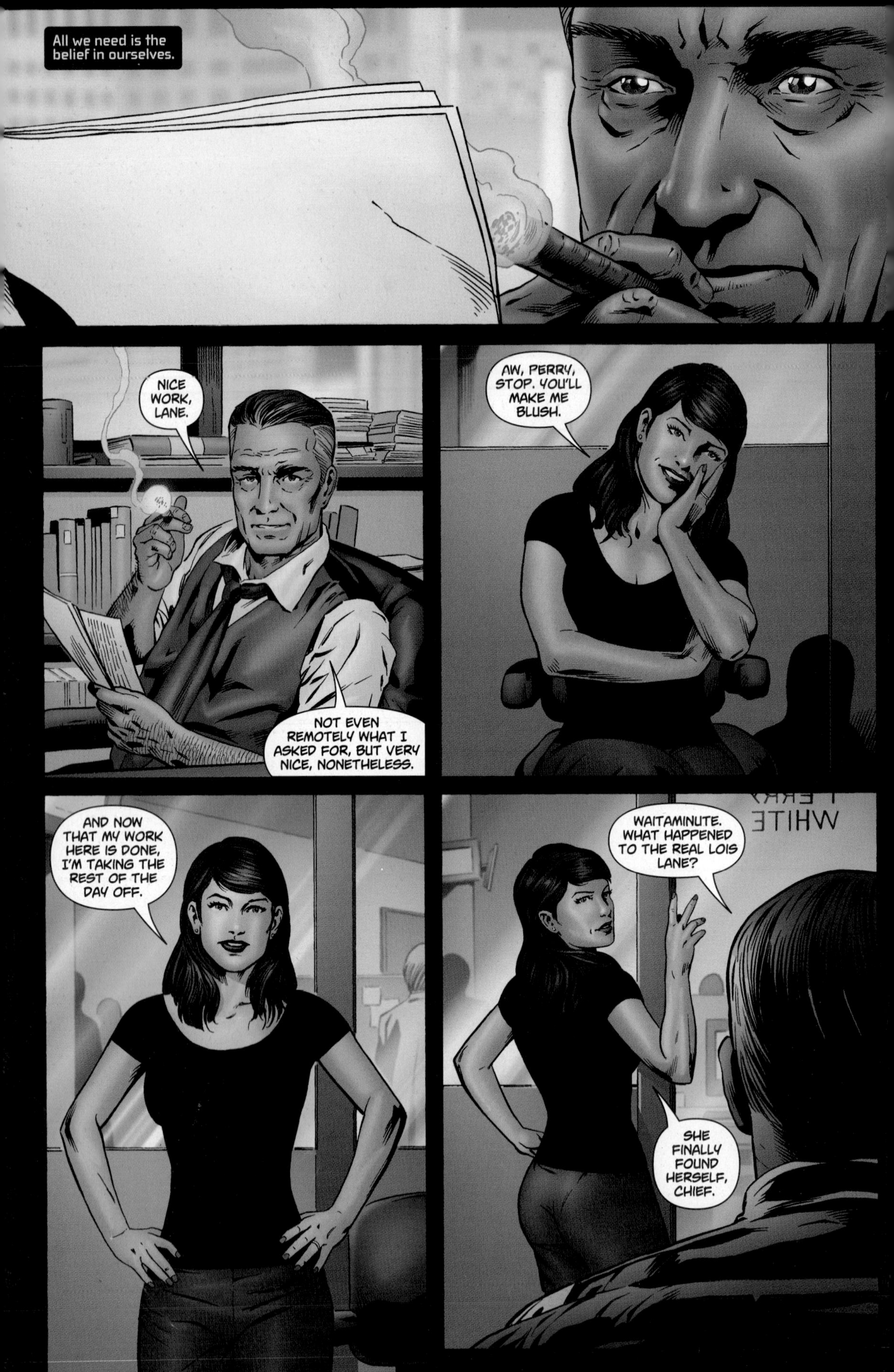
All we need is the belief in ourselves.
NICE WORK, LANE.
NOT EVEN REMOTELY WHAT I ASKED FOR, BUT VERY NICE, NONETHELESS.
AW, PERRY, STOP. YOU'LL MAKE ME BLUSH.
AND NOW THAT MY WORK HERE IS DONE, I'M TAKING THE REST OF THE DAY OFF.
WAITAMINUTE. WHAT HAPPENED TO THE REAL LOIS LANE?
SHE FINALLY FOUND HERSELF, CHIEF.

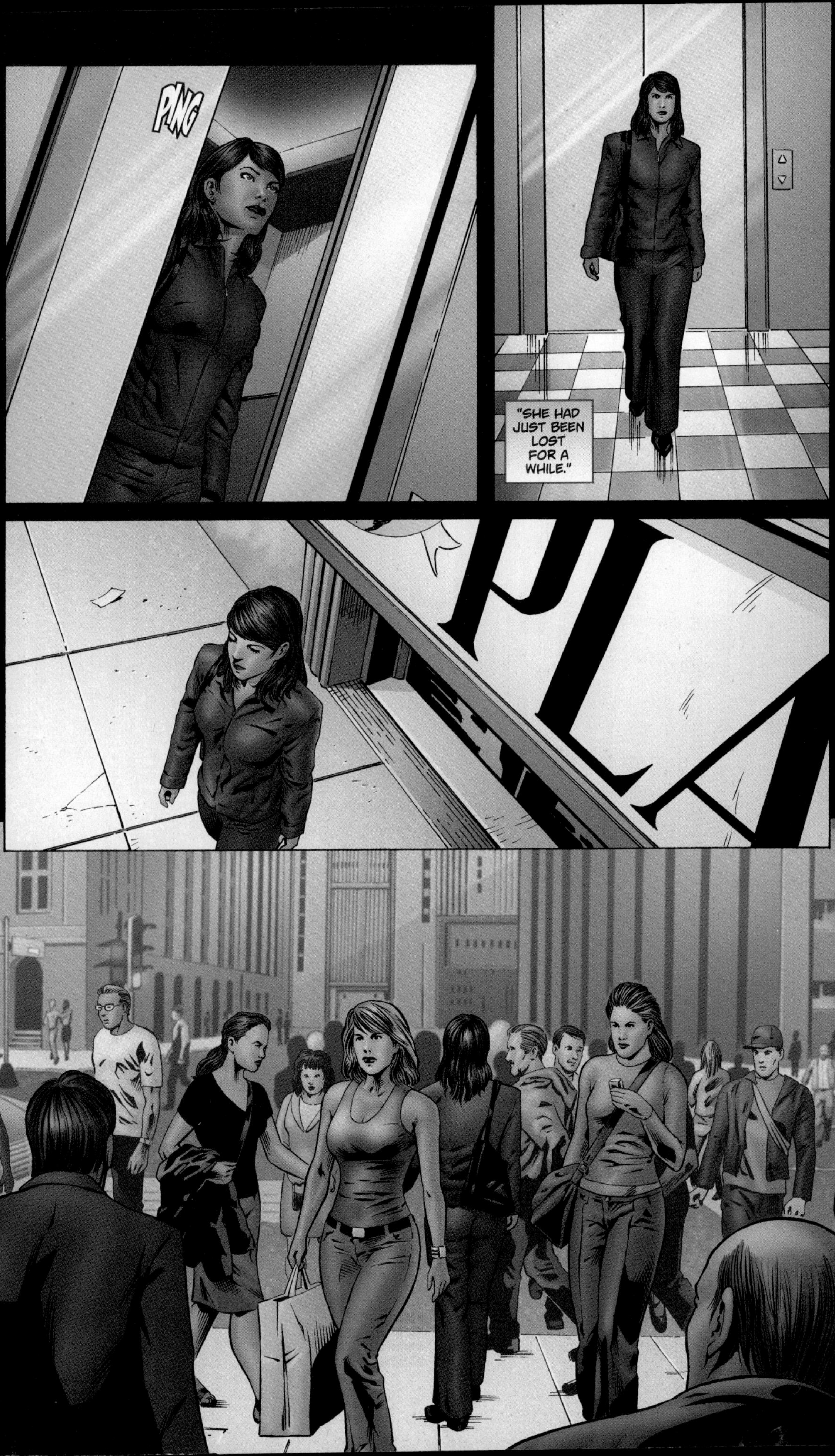
PING
"SHE HAD JUST BEEN LOST FOR A WHILE."

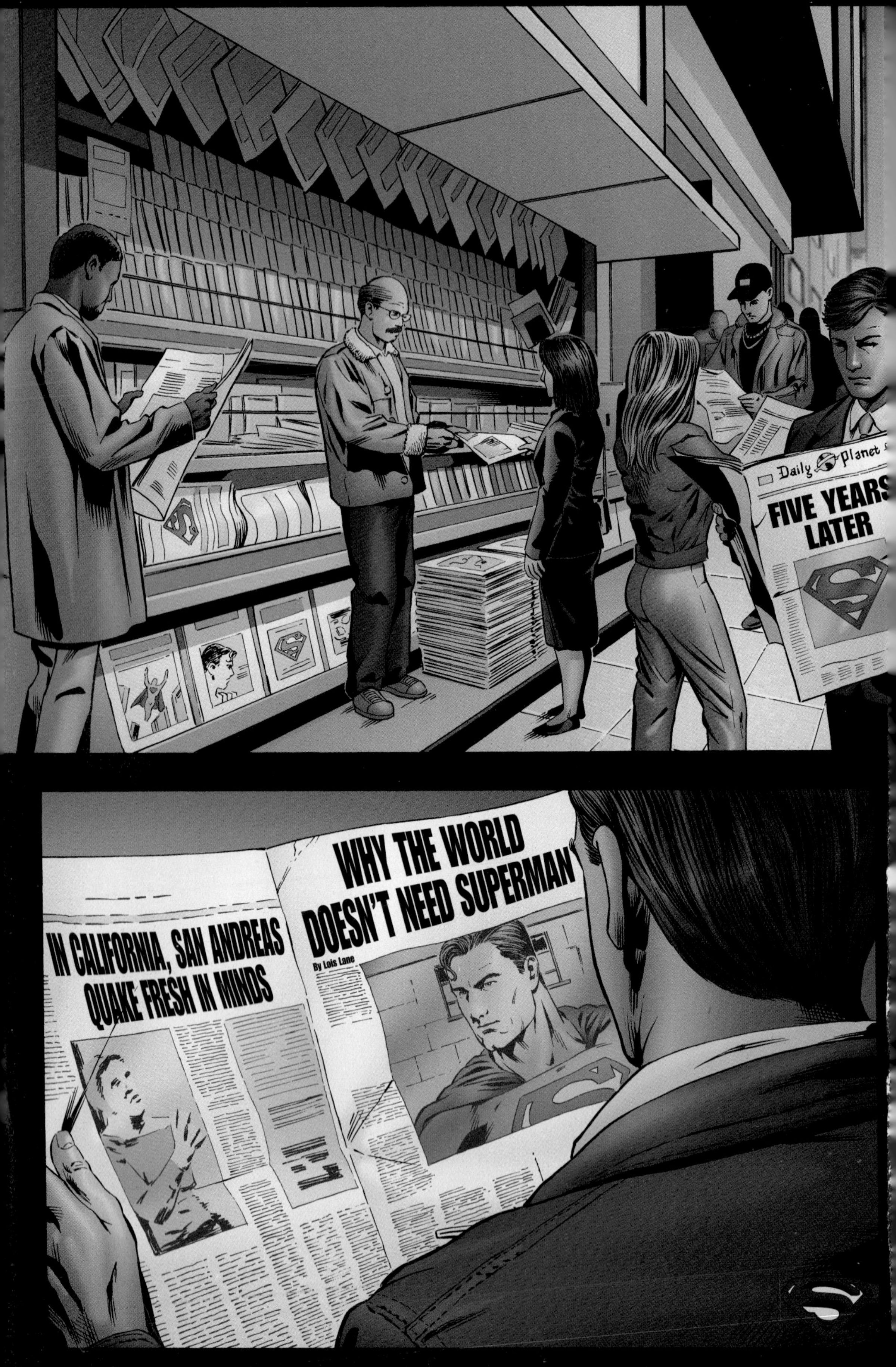
Daily Planet
FIVE YEARS LATER
WHY THE WORLD DOESN'T NEED SUPERMAN
By Lois Lane
IN CALIFORNIA, SAN ANDREAS QUAKE FRESH IN MINDS